RENEWALS 458-4574
DATE DUE

WITHDRAWN
UTSA LIBRARIES

The First Sudanese Civil War

The First Sudanese Civil War

Africans, Arabs, and Israelis in the Southern Sudan, 1955–1972

Scopas S. Poggo

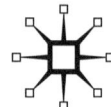

THE FIRST SUDANESE CIVIL WAR
Copyright © Scopas S. Poggo, 2009.

All rights reserved.

First published in 2009 by PALGRAVE MACMILLAN® in the Unites States—a division of St. Martin's Press LLC, 175 Fifth Avenue, New York, NY 10010.

Where this book is distributed in the UK, Europe and the rest of the world, this is by Palgrave Macmillan, a division of Macmillan Publishers Limited, registered in England, company number 785998, of Houndmills, Basingstoke, Hampshire RG21 6XS.

Palgrave Macmillan is the global academic imprint of the above companies and has companies and representatives throughout the world.

Palgrave® and Macmillan® are registered trademarks in the United States, the United Kingdom, Europe and other countries.

ISBN-13: 978-0-230-60796-5
ISBN-10: 0-230-60796-9

Library of Congress Cataloging-in-Publication Data is available from the Library of Congress.

A catalogue record of the book is available from the British Library.

Design by Scribe Inc.

First edition: February 2009

10 9 8 7 6 5 4 3 2 1

Printed in the United States of America.

Chapter 5 is a revision of "General Ibrahim Abboud's Military Administration in the Sudan, 1958–1964: Implementation of the Programs of Islamization and Arabization in the Southern Sudan," *Northeast African Studies Journal*, 9, no. 1 (April 2007): 67–101, reprinted with permission of the editor of the journal.

Chapter 8 contains revised material from "The Politics of Liberation in the Southern Sudan 1967–1972: The Role of Israel, African Heads of State and Foreign Mercenaries," *The Uganda Journal* 47 (November 2001): 34–48, reprinted with permission of the editor of the journal.

Map credit: Sudan as of 2006: Permission of the UN Cartographic Section.

Library
University of Texas
at San Antonio

*In Memory of My Beloved Father
Daniel Poggo Waran-Wunyang*

Contents

List of Maps	ix
Preface	xi
Acknowledgments	xv
Introduction	1
1 Ethnicity and Race in Modern Sudan	9
2 The Torit Mutiny of 1955: Its Causes and Failure	21
3 Legacy of the Failed Mutiny: Government Repression and Rise of the Resistance Movement	49
4 Government Counterinsurgency Methods, 1955–72	73
5 General Abboud's Response: Repression, Islamization, and Arabization, 1958–64	91
6 Emergence of Southern Sudanese Political Movements, 1960–72	113
7 Reorganization and Consolidation of the Guerrilla Movement, 1963–71	131
8 External Political and Military Involvement in Sudan's Civil War, 1960–72	145
9 The Road to Peace, 1969–72	169
Conclusion	193
Notes	197
Bibliography	229
Index	241

MAPS

Egypt under British Protection and the Anglo-Egyptian Sudan — xviii
The Provinces of Sudan from 1948 to 1973 — xix
The States of Sudan as of 2006 — xx

Preface

I am one of the five children of Daniel Poggo Waran-Wunyang (now deceased) and Anna Poni Wani-Buluk. I was born in the village of Dajur in Kajo-Kaji County in Southern Sudan in the early 1960s. My father was a farmer who also managed a grocery store for Mr. Habib, a Syrian merchant who owned the business. When I was still a little boy, my parents and I fled from Kajo-Kaji to Moyo, a town in the Madi District of Uganda, for refuge. The Sudanese government security forces wanted to arrest my father and several other Kuku businessmen for allegedly providing moral and financial support to the Anya-Nya guerrilla forces (the Southern Sudanese resistance movement) that were waging a war of liberation against the Sudan government. Indeed, many Kuku men had joined the Anya-Nya movement in Southern Sudan by the mid-1960s. But the vast majority of Kuku people fled to Uganda and became refugees in the Northern, West Nile, Central, and Western regions of that country. My parents and I settled in Gulu, a town in Northern Uganda, and were later joined by my sister and one older brother. Not until 1969 did I meet our oldest brother, who had taken refuge in Nairobi, Kenya, after the civil war in Sudan intensified in the mid-1960s. Our youngest brother was born in Gulu.

Refugee life in Gulu was a difficult matter for my family and other Southern Sudanese families (Kuku, Latuko, Madi, Bari, Lakoya, Moru, Azande, and Acholi of Southern Sudan). We had to start everything over from scratch in a new environment whose inhabitants often labeled us *loring ayela*, an Acholi expression literally meaning those who run away from a problem. To be sure, it was the civil strife in the Sudan that had caused us to flee into Northern Uganda. Our parents were hardworking and resilient—they made sure we had enough food to eat every day, had sufficient clothes, and above all, had adequate health care.

Although my parents did not have the opportunity to attend school, they envisioned sending all their children to school. While they bought us school uniforms and other educational supplies, the United Nations High

Commissioner for Refugees (UNHCR) and the Roman Catholic Church in Uganda paid our fees and tuition. Uganda provided us with the quality education we would otherwise not have obtained had my parents not sought sanctuary in that country. Mrs. Atey, a Ugandan Madi teacher in Primary One at Obiya Catholic Church School in Gulu, encouraged me to work hard and master the local Acholi language and culture. I also learned English, Swahili, and Kinubi, a heavily convoluted Arabic dialect still is spoken in Uganda today. As I grew up in Northern Uganda, I interacted with people from various ethnic and linguistic backgrounds, and this gave me a sense of appreciation of and respect for the people, culture, and languages from other parts of Southern Sudan and Uganda.

My intent to write about the history of the first civil war in Sudan is based on two events that had a profound impact on me as a refugee. First, a local Kuku clergyman named Eli, who preached the Sunday sermons in our church, one day abandoned his pastoral duty and joined the Anya-Nya movement in Southern Sudan. This remarkable decision was an expression of the frustration of most Southern Sudanese people, as well as a reflection of the magnitude of tension and conflict between the Northern and Southern regions of the country. Second, in 1966 through 1967, the Ugandan government under President Milton Obote cracked down on the Southern Sudanese refugees in Uganda who were allegedly raising money to support the Anya-Nya movement inside Southern Sudan. My mother was secretary of finance for the local Anya-Nya chapter in Gulu. Three Kuku men, who belonged to the same chapter and who also raised money, were arrested by Uganda General Service Unit personnel, tortured, and jailed for a short period. My mother was spared.

My decision to major in history at the University of Juba in the 1980s (1982 through 1986) was based on my keen interest in studying the history of Sudan, but above all in understanding the nature of the relationship between the South and the North. I particularly wanted to learn the root causes of Sudan's first civil war. In my course of study, I also realized that the history of Southern Sudan had largely been written by foreign and Northern Sudanese scholars/historians. I also learned that very few Southern Sudanese historians had attained postgraduate qualifications, in contrast to Northern intellectuals. A case in point was the employment of three Southern Sudanese lecturers in the history department at the University of Juba. This was the first generation of Southerners who had majored in history at the University of Khartoum. My ambition was to pursue postgraduate studies to the Ph.D. level and subsequently make my own contribution to the historiography on Sudan in general, and on Southern Sudan in particular. I realized one of these ambitions when I wrote my master's thesis, *The Pattern of Azande Resistance to the British Rule in the Southern Sudan, 1898–1914*, in the history department at the University of Memphis, Tennessee, in 1992.

My six-year experience (1983 through 1989) of the second civil war in Sudan had far-reaching effects. Surviving the mortar and artillery and rocket bombardment of the city of Juba, the capital of Southern Sudan where I lived, strengthened my resolve to investigate the root causes of Sudan's first civil war and write about it. I realized this dream when I completed my doctoral dissertation, *War and Conflict in the Southern Sudan, 1955–1972*, in the history department at the University of California, Santa Barbara, in 1999.

I was initially motivated to write about the first civil war in Sudan when Professor Robert O. Collins of UCSB gave me permission to access his huge collections of primary material on Sudan. Fellowships and grants from the University of California at Santa Barbara and San Diego enabled me to travel and conduct research at the Hoover Institution at Stanford University (1997), the Sudan Archive at Durham University (United Kingdom, 1997), and the Missionary Comboniani Archive in Rome and Verona (1998). These research trips also afforded me the opportunity to interview Southern Sudanese politicians and combatants who were directly linked with the first civil war. Among these important personalities were General Joseph Lagu Yakobo, Colonel Stephen B. Madut, Gordon Muortat Mayen, and Lawrence Modi Tombe in the United Kingdom; Father Vantini in Verona, Italy; and Brigadier General John Ukech Lueth, Professor Robert O. Collins, and Dr. Douglas Johnson in the United States.

The combination of information gleaned from primary material (written text) and elicited from interviews makes my book unique in the historiography on the first civil war in Sudan. This study attempts to provide an in-depth investigation and analysis of the political, economic, social, cultural, and religious problems that led to the outbreak of the first civil war in 1955. It discusses the involvement of foreign missionaries and Sudanese clergy, Arab countries, African countries, the former Soviet Union, and the Israeli government in the civil war. Foreign interference in the domestic affairs of Sudan shaped the magnitude and trend of the war and its sustenance for seventeen years. The atrocities committed by the Sudanese security forces against the Southern rebels and people are examined in the context of the North-South conflict. My holistic treatment of the first civil war is intended to assist in a full understanding the root causes of the second civil war in the Sudan, which lasted another twenty-two years from 1983 to 2005.

My book is also designed to contribute to the literature on intra-regional and inter-regional wars and conflicts that have plagued much of the African continent in the twentieth and twenty-first centuries. In addition, it sheds light on the tensions and conflicts that have risen around the world as a result of the struggle for supremacy by two of the great religions of the world, Islam and Christianity. The first civil war is also a classic example of conflicts that were fueled by the United States and the former Soviet Union as they struggled to extend their influences over the African continent during the Cold War period.

It is my hope that this book will be of value and service to the many people and institutions that would benefit from a greater knowledge and understanding of the two Sudanese civil wars. Whether individual scholars and politicians, Africans south of the Sahara, the Arabs of North Africa and the Middle East, the Israeli government, university study courses, peace and conflict resolution centers, or, and especially, Sudanese from all walks of life, all may profit from learning more about what transpired in Sudan in the second half of the twentieth century.

Acknowledgments

I am deeply indebted to Dr. Douglas H. Johnson, a historian on the Sudan who read my book manuscript in its early stages of preparation for publication. His constructive criticisms, advice, and words of encouragement helped shape my thoughts, analysis, and discussion throughout the work resulting in this book. I am also very grateful to Dr. C. Magbaily Fyle, my colleague and professor of African History in the Department of African American and African Studies at The Ohio State University, who read the book manuscript during the revision phase and gave me valuable suggestions and advice.

I would like to register my profound thanks to Dr. Raymond Dominick, professor emeritus of history at The Ohio State University, Mansfield, who read the manuscript at its earliest stage of writing and provided me with valuable insights on its various themes.

I owe a debt of gratitude to Dr. Jan Ryder, who read the manuscript in the final stages of preparation for publication and provided me with valuable editorial comments and advice.

This book would not have been completed without the financial support I received from the Center for Black Studies, the Graduate Division, the Interdisciplinary Humanities Center, and the Academic Senate at the University of California, Santa Barbara. The Institute on Global Conflict and Cooperation at the University of California, San Diego, also provided me with research and travel funds. To them, I express my deep gratitude.

A research project of this kind would not have reached its conclusion without the support I received from many individuals. I would like to express my special thanks to the following individuals in Sudan, Kenya, and Uganda who, realizing that it was important to have an oral history of the first Sudanese civil war committed to writing, agreed to be interviewed: Mr. Barnaba Dumo Wani (Khartoum, Sudan), the late Mr. Clement Mboro (Nairobi, Kenya), Mr. Eliaba James Surur (Kampala, Uganda), Mr. Daniel Jumi Tongun (Yei, Southern Sudan), Lt. General James Wani Igga

(Yei, Southern Sudan), Wojia Masiri and Enoka Digga Amen (Kajo-Kaji, Southern Sudan), my mother, Mama Anna Poni Wani-Buluk (Nairobi, Kenya), and my father, the late Baba Daniel Poggo Waran-Wunyang (Moyo, Uganda). I am very thankful to Mr. Evans Sokiri Kijore, Mr. Benjamin Lou Poggo, Mr. James Duku Janak, and Mr. Nathan Wojia Pitia, who sacrificed their time and effort to locate and interview these individuals on my behalf.

In the United Kingdom, I interviewed the following Southern Sudanese combatants and politicians who were associated with the first and second civil wars in the Sudan: Colonel Stephen Baak Madut (London), the late Mr. Gordon Muortat Mayen (London), Mr. Lawrence Modi Tombe (London), and Lt. General Joseph Yakobo Lagu (London). My interviews with these personalities would not have been possible without the assistance of Dr. Cosmas Wani Lo-Wolli. By introducing me to these individuals, sacrificing his time and energy, and providing me with food and accommodation in his house in London in the spring of 1997, he ensured that my research trip in London was a success. I owe him many thanks.

In the United States, I was fortunate to interview Southern Sudanese combatants, politicians, and academics who were directly or indirectly linked with the first civil war, as well as those who served in the regional government of Southern Sudan in the period 1972 through 1983. My special thanks go to Dr. Pacifico Lado Lolik (Dallas, Texas), Dr. Dominick Mohammed Akec (Miami, Florida), Mr. Oliver Batali Albino (Cambridge, Massachusetts), and Brigadier General John Ukech Lueth (Santa Barbara, California). I would also like to express my deep appreciation to Dr. Laura Nyantung Beny, who interviewed Mr. Albino on my behalf. I am grateful as well to the late Professor Emeritus Robert O. Collins and Dr. Douglas H. Johnson, historians and authors on the Southern Sudan, who granted me interviews and provided me with valuable foreign perspectives on the first Sudanese civil war.

The complexities pertaining to investigating Sudan's first civil war and its aftermath required the acquisition of material from a variety of sources scattered across the world. Within the United States, I obtained valuable documents from Professor Collins' private collection, now in the possession of the Sudan Archive at Durham University (UK) and Bergen University (Norway); the Hoover Institution at Stanford University; and the private archives of Mr. Sabit Alley in New Jersey and of General Lueth in Des Moines, Iowa.

In the United Kingdom, I also acquired substantial material from the Sudan Archive at Durham University. My research there was facilitated by Mrs. Jane R. Hogan, Miss Lesley Forbes, and Ms. Margaret G., all of whom are keepers of the Sudan Archive. Mr. Gordon Muortat Mayen and Mr. Lawrence Modi Tombe donated their personal papers to me. I owe them a treasure of thanks.

The scholarly assistance given to me by the archivists and librarians of the Missionari Comboniani in Rome and Verona will remain a lasting, positive impression in my academic life. I would like to express my sincere thanks and deep appreciation to their archivists and administrators: Fathers Pietro Ravasio, Mario Cisternino, and Torquato (Rome), and Fathers Gino Barsella and Bruno Novelli (Verona).

This book would not have been conceived if my beloved parents Mama Anna Poni Wani-Buluk and Baba Daniel Poggo Waran-Wunyang had not had a vision for their children's education. This book is dedicated to them. Academic role models are important in life, and I must indeed acknowledge Mr. James Duku Janka and Mr. Zamba Duku for their inspiration when I was a young refugee in primary school in Uganda in the early 1970s. I owe them a debt of gratitude. My brothers John Gwolo Kamanga Poggo, Benjamin Lou Poggo, Wilson Duku Poggo, Robert Ramba, Anthony Kenyi Awani, the late Robert Doru Lo-Kojo, and George Maring Longa, my sister Josephine Kajo Poggo and my sister-in-law Alice Keji Kamanga continuously supported me in my research and writing through advice, encouragement, and prayer. They deserve my deepest gratitude!

My special thanks also go to my former lecturers in the Department of History at the University of Juba (Southern Sudan) who inspired me to study African and Middle Eastern history: Dr. Kenneth Okeny, Dr. Lazarus Lek Mawut, the late Dr. Damazo Dut Majak, and the late Mr. Ogweta Opoka. This book is also dedicated to the University of Juba, the first institution of higher learning in Southern Sudan (1977).

I am also deeply indebted to Dr. Evelyn B. Freeman, dean and director, Dr. Ted Dahlstrand, associate dean at The Ohio State University, Mansfield, and Professor Kenneth W. Goings, department chairman of African American and African Studies at The Ohio State University, Columbus, for their academic, financial, and moral support. Their professional advice and words of encouragement will never be forgotten. Mrs. Cathy Stimpert in the Office of Human Resources and Dr. Barbara McGovern, associate professor of English, Dr. Christopher B. Phelps, associate professor of history, Dr. Heather J. Tanner, associate professor of history and Dr. Glenn Hartz, professor of philosophy at The Ohio State University, Mansfield, gave me much moral and spiritual support during my period of writing. I owe them special thanks. I am most grateful to Dr. Harold A. Ballitch, my ophthalmologist, for his continued medical treatment and moral support.

Last but not least, I would like to thank my research assistant, Mr. Adam Reno, who typed most of the new research material that I included into the manuscript.

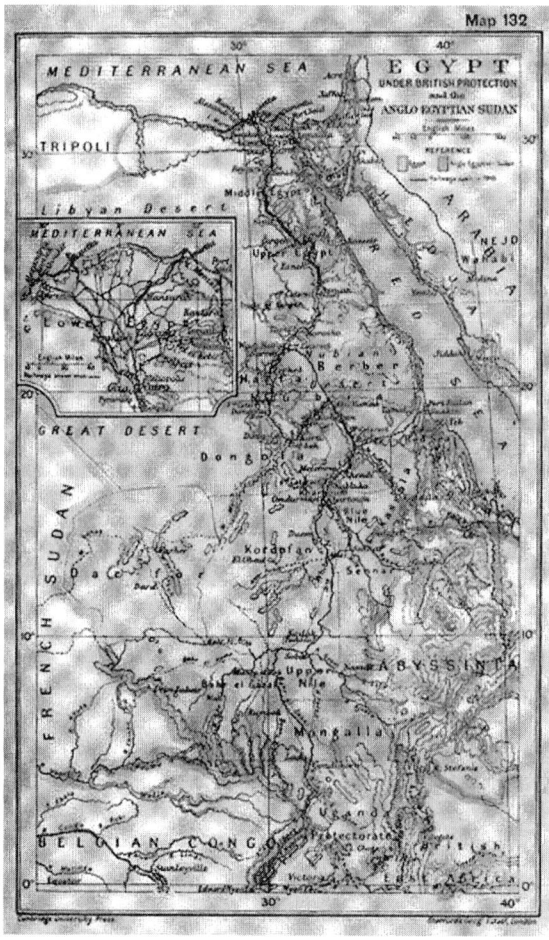

Egypt under British Protection and the Anglo-Egyptian Sudan (*Cambridge Modern History Atlas*, 1912. Courtesy of University of Texas Libraries).

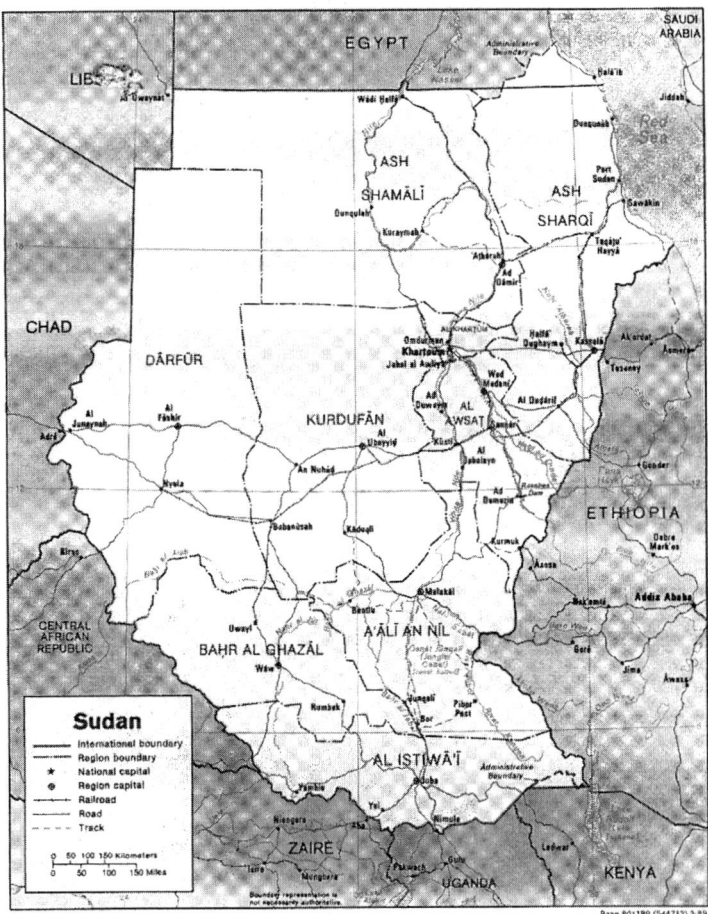

The provinces of Sudan from 1948 to1973, showing the three Southern provinces of Bahr al-Ghazal, Upper Nile, and Equatoria (U.S. Central Intelligence Agency, Courtesy of University of Texas Libraries).

The states of Sudan as of 2006, showing the modern division of the former Upper Nile, Bahr al-Ghazal, and Equatoria provinces (Courtesy of the UN Publication Board).

Introduction

THIS BOOK PROVIDES AN IN-DEPTH DISCUSSION AND analysis of the origins and development of the first civil war in Sudan, which occurred between 1955 and 1972. This was one of the longest and most devastating wars in Africa during the twentieth century. It was the culmination of ethnic, racial, cultural, religious, political, and economic problems that had faced Sudan since the Turco-Egyptian conquest of the country in 1821. The hostilities between the Northern and Southern regions of Sudan also involved foreign powers that had their own political, economic, religious, and military interests in the region. The first Sudanese civil war is therefore a classic example of the inter- and intra-regional conflicts that have plagued much of the African continent from 1950 to the present.

The period between 1955 and 1972 marked a new phase in North-South relations. It was not simply a confrontation between the well-enlightened, highly politicized, and sophisticated North and the predominantly illiterate, less-sophisticated, and generally underdeveloped South. Rather, it was a relationship marked with armed struggle between the more organized, well-trained, and well-equipped Northern Sudanese military and the poorly organized, inadequately trained, and poorly equipped Southern Sudanese rebel forces. At the national level it was a contest between the predominantly "Arab" and African Muslim North and the African Christian/traditional South. And at the international level, it was a test of Northern Sudan's racial and religious affiliations with the Middle Eastern and North African countries and Southern Sudan's racial and religious affiliations with African countries south of the Sahara.

This period also reflected the internationalization of the civil war, when foreigners became involved in Sudan's internal crisis between 1960 and 1972. During this period, the Arab countries, the Soviet Union, East Germany, Yugoslavia, Britain, and China all supplied the government of Sudan with sophisticated weapons and aircraft, with the primary aim of crushing the Southern Sudanese rebel forces. Politically, General Jaafar Mohammed Numayri acquired some elements of the Soviet Union's communist ideology and tailored them to Arab socialism, which became the aspiration of his regime. Meanwhile, the Israeli government and the Israeli Defense Forces played an important role in the consolidation of the Southern Sudanese rebel movement, the Anya-Nya, and its administrative apparatus, especially between 1967 and 1972. Israeli support for the Anya-Nya was based on geopolitical and strategic calculations, with the aim of stabbing the Arabs from the back. To that end the Israeli government diverted to the Anya-Nya forces large quantities of weapons that the Israeli Defense Forces had captured from the Arabs during the Six-Day War of 1967. Thus, the first civil war in Sudan was funded by stable governments whose goals and objectives were diametrically opposed to one another.

While this first Sudanese civil war is often viewed as a North-South conflict, conflicts also existed among the various Southern Sudanese ethnic groups, not only as neighbors in their territorial spaces, but also within the liberation movements that they formed, divided, and consolidated during the civil war. These problems were compounded by personality clashes and personal ambitions within the leadership of the Southern Sudanese rebel forces, as well as in their political organizations. All these forces worked together to frustrate the efforts of the Southern Sudanese people, and consequently led to the loss of hundreds of thousands of Southern lives in the face of powerful and ruthless repression by the Sudan government. Many other hundreds of thousands of Southern Sudanese were displaced from their homeland and sought refuge in Uganda, Zaire, Kenya, Ethiopia, or the Central African Republic.

As a historian who was born and raised during the first civil war, I have endeavored to investigate every available source pertaining to the war. My intent has been to obtain as much information as possible in order to present as objective a discussion and analysis of the events of that war as I am able. Integrating information gleaned from the printed word with that elicited from interviews with Southern Sudanese who were directly or indirectly linked to the war has been the only feasible way to attempt a balanced discussion. In my research, I have consulted the private archive (materials now available in the Sudan archive at Durham University, United Kingdom, and the University of Bergen, Norway) of Professor Emeritus Robert O. Collins in the Department of History, University of California, Santa Barbara; records at the Hoover Institution at Stanford University; the Public Record Office in London; as well as the Missionari Comboniani archives in Rome and Verona. In addition, I have received documents and personal papers donated to me by Sudanese and non-Sudanese individuals living in Africa, Britain, and the United States. I have also consulted newspaper articles on microfilm, journal articles, and private papers written about the first civil war. However, realizing that the printed word is not always absolute, I have attempted as well to solicit information from Southern Sudanese intellectuals, politicians, and combatants through oral interviews. My interviews have been confined primarily to Southern Sudanese living in the diaspora (Uganda, Kenya, Sudan, Britain, Italy, and the United States), whom I sought out for two reasons. First, they were willing to be interviewed about the war and conflict in Sudan, and I wanted to hear a Southern perspective on the first civil war, since much of this viewpoint is lacking in the books written about Sudan's civil wars. And second, much of the political, economic, and social history of Southern Sudan remains unwritten. It is the Southern personalities who participated in, experienced, and witnessed events during the civil war who are in a position to provide accurate information about the war in the South.

In March 1997 in London, I interviewed Gordon Muortat-Mayen, a Dinka and former president of the Nile Provisional Government in Southern Sudan from 1969 to 1970. I also had the opportunity to interview General Joseph Yakobo Lagu, a Madi and the former commander in chief of the Anya-Nya armed forces and the Southern Sudan Liberation Movement (SSLM) who played a major role in the rise and consolidation of the Anya-Nya movement. An example of personal ambition for political power and the need to build a cohesive population for an armed struggle, Lagu overthrew the Nile Provisional Government of Muortat in April 1970. In their interviews, these two Southern leaders were pragmatic and impartial in their judgments about the various issues that shaped the development of the civil war and its conclusion. They were concerned about presenting the facts and the truth about the war—both wanted the world at large, and the Sudanese in particular, to fully understand that the first civil war was not simply a national conflict, but one that became internationalized to serve the interests of foreign powers.

Within the United Kingdom, I was also able to interview Colonel Stephen Baak Madut, a Dinka and officer in the Anya-Nya movement; at the time of our meeting, he was the representative of the Sudan People's Liberation Army/Movement in the UK. As a former student of Rumbek Secondary School who witnessed the student strikes in the 1960s, Madut was able to provide me with first-hand information about the Southern students' experiences and the role they played in the liberation struggle. Also in the UK I interviewed Lawrence Modi Tombe, a Bari, a former student at Makerere University, a politician, and a former Sudanese ambassador to Romania in the 1990s, whose insights into the civilian and military governments in Khartoum were most valuable.

In April 1997, I also interviewed Brigadier General John Ukech Lueth, a Lwo-speaker from Bahr al-Ghazal province, a former Anya-Nya officer, and later a senior officer in the Sudanese Army. Laura N. Beny interviewed Oliver Batali Albino (on my behalf), a Makaraka who graduated from Khartoum University and served in the Anya-Nya movement as a political agent. He is also author of *The Sudan: A Southern Viewpoint* (London, 1971). In addition, I interviewed Dr. Dominic Akec Mohammed, a Dinka from Northern Bahr al-Ghazal who represented the interests of the Anya-Nya in the United States.

In 2005, I interviewed Dr. Pacifico Lado Lolik, a Lakoya from Eastern Equatoria, a medical doctor, and former minister of health in the regional government of Southern Sudan in the period 1973 through 1983. He was the architect of the decentralization program that resulted in redividing the South into the three regional governments of Bahr al-Ghazal, Upper Nile, and Equatoria. I also extended my interviews to former representatives and combatants of the Anya-Nya who now live in Uganda and Southern Sudan. For example, my own mother, Anna Poni Wani-Buluk, a Kuku from Central Equatoria who was financial secretary of the Anya-Nya in exile during the civil war, provided me with valuable information. Former Anya-Nya officers and NCOs now living in Southern Sudan also gave me detailed accounts about their combat missions against the Sudanese army in different parts of the region.

In addition, in 2004 to 2005, I had the rare opportunity to contact veteran Southern politicians in Uganda, Kenya, and Sudan who experienced both civil wars and served under successive Khartoum civilian and military regimes, as well as the Southern regional governments in the period 1972 to 1983. I was able to reach them through relatives and friends who know them well. My impartially designed questionnaire enabled me to elicit rare and valuable information from a number of leading Southern personalities.

Clement Mboro, an Ndogo from Western Bahr al-Ghazal who participated in the Juba Conference of 1947, served as assistant district commissioner and district commissioner in various districts of Southern Sudan, as minister of the interior in the caretaker government of Sirr al-Khattim, and as speaker of the Southern Regional Assembly. He is now deceased. Eliaba James Surur, a Pojulu from Central Equatoria, was a teacher, founder, and former leader of the People's Progressive Party in Equatoria, a member of the National Assembly in Khartoum, and is currently legal adviser to

President Salva Kiir Mayardit of the Government of Southern Sudan. As a survivor of the Juba massacre of July 8–9, 1965, Surur was able to provide an eyewitness account of the atrocities committed against the Southern Sudanese by Arab soldiers from Northern Sudan. This information is crucial to understanding the magnitude of death and suffering in Southern Sudan during the first civil war.

Barnaba Dumo Wani, a Kuku, a civil engineer, former minister of housing and education in the regional government of Southern Sudan in the period 1973 to 1980, and former governor of Equatoria, was interviewed in Khartoum. He provided me with valuable insights into North-South politics prior to and during post-independent Southern Sudan. I also obtained valuable information from him about the Torit mutiny, General Ibrahim Abboud's program of ethnic cleansing in the South, and the ethnic conflicts during the period of local autonomy in Southern Sudan.

Daniel Jumi Tongun, a Bari from Central Equatoria, was interviewed in 2004 in Yei District of Central Equatoria. He is the oldest of all my interviewees (aged 90 at the time), and has an amazingly bright memory of all the important political events in Southern Sudan that could be traced to the Juba Conference of 1947. He was trained as a catechist and bookkeeper, but became deeply involved in North-South politics. He, together with Marko Rume, a Kuku bookkeeper for the Equatoria Corps in Torit, were the masterminds of the 1955 Torit mutiny. They planned the mutiny together with the officers and NCOs of the Equatoria Corps. He provided me with detailed information about the mutiny and its consequences, the administrations of Ismail el-Azhari, General Abboud, Mohammed Ahmed Mahgoub, and General Numayri, as well as Abel Alier's regional government in Southern Sudan. He also gave me eyewitness accounts of the Juba massacre.

The first Sudanese civil war has been the subject of much discussion and analysis by Sudanese (Northern and Southern) and non-Sudanese scholars alike. Mohamed Omer Beshir, Oliver Batali Albino, Dunstan M. Wai, Deng D. Akol Ruay, Cecil Eprile, Edgar O'Ballance, and Douglas H. Johnson have all discussed and analyzed the political, economic, and social issues pertinent to the war.[1] The depth of research, the kinds of sources consulted, and the treatment of various themes have varied from one scholar to another.

Little attention has been paid to the immediate causes of the mutiny of the Southern soldiers of the Equatoria Corps in the town of Torit in Eastern Equatoria in August 1955. While Wai and O'Ballance have discussed the actual outbreak of the mutiny, they have not thoroughly considered the consequences of its failure. Thus far, the *Report of the Commission of Enquiry into the Disturbances in the Southern Sudan during August 1955*, a government document, remains the most comprehensive treatment anywhere of the mutiny's outbreak.[2]

Unlike these previous works, I have focused my attention on British colonial policies, the Southern reaction to these policies, and the immediate causes of the Torit mutiny. I have endeavored to present a thorough discussion and analysis of the factors leading to the mutiny and the actual planning, coordination, and subsequent execution of the plan. I have also explained why the mutiny failed as well as its far-reaching consequences for the South. New information from my interview with Daniel Jumi Tongun, one of the key planners of the mutiny, has shed additional light on many issues that had hitherto been unclear. In addition, Sudanese government documents, primary documents from Southern Sudanese politicians and rebels, as well as information gleaned from interviews with actual participants and witnesses to the mutiny and its aftermath have enabled me to present a new interpretation of its legacy. Personal papers, Southern rebel documents, and my interviews with Joseph Lagu and Southern politicians like Gordon Muortat Mayen and others who worked closely with the Southern insurgency have also yielded new and detailed information about the early resistance movements.

In addition to Wai, Lilian Passmore Sanderson and Neville Sanderson have written extensively on the military administration of Ibrahim Abboud.[3] I have, however, presented a new interpretation of his government policies toward the South, using new information obtained from the archives of the Missionari Comboniani in Rome and Verona in Italy, Catholic newspapers in the United States published during Abboud's regime, and information obtained from interviews with key Southern Sudanese politicians.

Wai was the first scholar to write about Israeli military assistance to the Anya-Nya forces during the first civil war. Like the former Soviet Union, Israel, a key ally of the United States in the Middle East, had geopolitical interests in Southern Sudan, but the discussion of Israeli military involvement there has been insufficient. In light of this, I have endeavored to investigate and write about the sources of weapons particularly for the Anya-Nya. Archival materials and interviews with Lagu, Lueth, Madut, and Dr. Dominick Akec Mohammed have yielded much information. Clement Mboro, a former minister of the interior in the Sudan government, provided valuable information on the role of the Southern Front inside Sudan. I have thus presented new and substantial information on the sources of arms supplies for the Anya-Nya movement as well as for the Sudanese military forces themselves.

Archival materials, Catholic missionary documents, and interview information have yielded valuable information on the harsh treatment of Southern Sudanese civilians by Northern security forces. The reign of terror in Southern Sudan led not only to the loss of lives, but also to internal displacement and the flight of refugees into neighboring countries. I have thus made the first attempt to shed light on the atrocities committed by the Northern Sudanese security forces against the people of Southern Sudan.

Eprile, Wai, Johnson, and Abel Alier[4] have all dealt with the Addis Ababa Agreement that ended the war, signed in February 1972 between the government of Sudan and the Southern Sudan Liberation Movement. They have all presented interesting and intriguing perspectives on the start of the peace process, the negotiations, the signing of the agreement, and its subsequent ratification by Numayri's government and the Sudanese Socialist Union. My interviews with Southern Sudanese critics and supporters of the agreement like Lagu, Muortat, Albino, Madut, Tombe, Mohammed, Lueth, and Tongun have above all shed new light on the peace process and the hasty negotiation and subsequent signing of the accord. I have also been fortunate to interview former cabinet ministers in the High Executive Council of the autonomous regional governments of Alier and Lagu in the period 1972 through 1982: Clement Mboro as speaker and minister of public service and manpower in Alier's administration; Barnaba Dumo Wani, minister of housing and public utilities and later minister of education in Alier's administration; Dr. Pacifico Lado Lolik, minister of health in Lagu's administration; and Eliaba James Surur, director general in the Ministry of Education in Alier's and Lagu's administrations. All these politicians have provided me with valuable new information about the start of the peace process between Lagu's SSLM and Numayri's administration, the phase of the peace negotiations, and the subsequent signing of the peace agreement. All of them have presented new and rare information that does not exist in previous works on the Addis Ababa accord; this is thus a significant contribution to the literature on peace talks and peace agreements in the Sudan.

This study has thus attempted to make an original contribution to the literature on war and conflict not only in Sudan, but also in the developing world at large. I have focused my discussion and analysis on important, and yet less-investigated, topics of the first civil war. These topics deserve an in-depth investigation and a holistic analysis to fully understand the causes of that long civil war, which was so devastating to the population, the infrastructure, and the environment of Southern Sudan.

* * *

Finally, a word needs to be said about the difficulties of writing an objective historical account, especially about something involving recent events where passions still run high. As noted, the Southern viewpoint about the first Sudanese civil war has been missing in the historical literature—much of the discussion has been presented either by Northern Sudanese or non-Sudanese scholars. Not surprisingly, some of the works are a reflection of Sudanese government policy, which has consistently denied any oppression of the people in Southern Sudan or any atrocities committed against them. Indeed, many Northerners themselves remain unaware of these conditions and events.

Yet at the same time, it is a challenge for me as a Southern Sudanese to be entirely objective myself as I lived under a powerful and oppressive regime, and I am also a part of the historical events described. I have interviewed Southern Sudanese politicians and combatants because this generation is dying out, and the information they have to provide is so valuable, but I also recognize that while providing us with a Southern perspective, they necessarily have their own biases, so their information is not going to be entirely accurate. I have thus sought to corroborate this information with that gleaned from archival or primary material. My primary aim has been to present the Southern viewpoint, thereby helping to fill in a large gap in the existing literature and make a significant contribution to the historiography on war and conflict in Sudan; to the best of my ability, I have presented the material and analysis as objectively as I am able. In the end, readers must take into account the biases on both sides when judging events for themselves. It is my hope that my book will provide answers to, or shed light on, several key issues and questions that many people in the Sudan, in particular, and the world at large, have pondered for the past fifty-two years.

CHAPTER 1

ETHNICITY AND RACE IN MODERN SUDAN

THE LAND OF SUDAN

MEDIEVAL ARAB TRAVELERS CALLED THE TERRITORY immediately below the Sahara desert that extends from the Atlantic Ocean to the Red Sea *Bilad al-Sudan*, literally meaning the land of the blacks. The modern Republic of Sudan, which lies between latitudes four degrees south and twenty-two degrees north of the equator, derives its name from that Arabic phrase. Covering 967,499 square miles, it is the largest country in Africa, stretching nearly 1,400 miles from its Northern boundary with Egypt to its Southern border with East Africa and extending 1,200 miles east to west.[1] It is surrounded by nine countries: Egypt to the north, Libya and Chad to the northwest, the Central African Republic and the Democratic Republic of the Congo to the west, Uganda and Kenya to the south, and Ethiopia and Eritrea to the east. The Red Sea forms the Eastern boundary of Sudan, separating it from the Arabian Peninsula.

Sudan is broadly divided into four regions, characterized by differences in terrain, climate, soil, and vegetation. The Northern region, between latitudes eighteen and twenty-two degrees north, is characterized by vast sand, sand dunes, and rock. It is part of the Sahara Desert, with extreme temperatures in winter and summer. Most people in this region have close racial, cultural, and religious ties with their neighbors in Arabia to the east and Egypt to the north. The people survive mainly by irrigated agriculture along the banks of the Nile, though in past decades many have moved farther south to big cities like Khartoum and Omdurman and to the

Gezira Scheme, a large irrigation project in a rich agricultural area, in search of employment opportunities and better living conditions.[2] The Central region of Sudan extends from latitudes ten to eighteen degrees north. This region is characterized by desert, semidesert, and semitropical conditions. Weather conditions here are not as harsh as those north of the eighteenth parallel. This region is watered by the White and Blue Niles, which converge at Khartoum. The Gezira Scheme is located in the confluence of the two Niles. This area is also thickly populated. Three important cities developed around the confluence of the White and Blue Niles: Khartoum, the capital city of Sudan is located at the junction of the two rivers. Khartoum North lies on the right bank of the Blue Nile and is adjoined to Khartoum city by a bridge. Omdurman, a historic and commercial city, is the largest of the three cities and lies on the west bank of the White Nile, just where this river meets the Blue Nile.[3]

The Central region also includes the area of the Southern Blue Nile, which is fed by tropical rains in the summer and experiences a dry winter season. Savannah woodland and grassland exist here, and farming and livestock grazing are important activities. The Ingessena Hills stand out distinctly in this relatively flat plain.

The Eastern region of Sudan, inhabited by the various Beja ethnic groups, is characterized by the Red Sea Hills and flat plains.[4] Desert, semidesert, and tropical conditions prevail in this region. It receives a fair amount of rainfall that allows sedentary agriculture.

Prior to the military takeover by General Omar Hassan al-Bashir on June 30, 1989, the Western region of Sudan comprised the areas of Kordofan and Darfur. Today these regions have been subdivided into states. Thus Kordofan has been divided into Northern and Southern states. The topography in the Northern part is generally flat and is characterized by desert and semidesert conditions with almost no rainfall during the year. Arab camel nomads coexist with their neighbors, the Nuba people. In the south, the terrain rises to form the massive Nuba mountains—a significant landmark in this region that has shaped the political, economic, and social institutions of the Nuba. Agriculture is the most important economic activity.[5]

Darfur lies in the Western region of Sudan and has been subdivided into Northern, Southern, and Western states. The Northern state is generally flat, and has characteristics similar to those of the Sahara Desert. The Meidab Arabs, a small minority group, keep camels. They coexist with their non-Arab neighbors, the Zaghawa, who are African people who have embraced Islam. The Western state is characterized by flat plains dissected by the massive *Jabal Marra* (Mount Marra), which rises three thousand feet above sea level. The state has a semitropical climate and vegetation. Meanwhile, the Southern state is generally flat with semidesert climatic conditions and vegetation.[6]

THE LAND OF SOUTHERN SUDAN

The region we now call Southern Sudan was not historically a part of *Bilad al-Sudan*. A number of factors prevented medieval Arab travelers from penetrating it. The vast bogs and swamps called the Sudd in the flat plains of the hot, humid climate and numerous diseases all posed major obstacles to foreign intrusion.[7]

The British administration in the Sudan from 1898 to 1956 demarcated the Southern from the Northern region at the tenth parallel for political and administrative reasons. The region south of this parallel covers an area of about 250,000 square miles. Although today it is divided into ten states under a federal system of government, the British originally divided the region into three distinct provinces—Bahr al-Ghazal, Equatoria, and Upper Nile—in the first decade of the twentieth century.[8]

The name Bahr al-Ghazal is derived from the Arabic name *Bahr el-Ghazal*, which literally means the river of the gazelles. Today, it has been subdivided into four federal states. Watered by the Bahr el-Ghazal river and its tributaries, it is generally an ironstone plateau characterized by savannah woodland and grassland. The flat plains of this region are seasonally flooded by rainwater or rivers, forming vast swamps. Cattle herding and cultivation are main economic activities. The Dinka, the largest ethnic group, and their neighbors, the Lwo-speaking Jur, the Bor Balanda, the Bongo-Sere, and the Fertit, Njangugule, and Kreish occupy this vast expanse of land.[9] Wau is the political capital and the financial district of the region.

The Upper Nile region of Southern Sudan lies to the east of Bahr al-Ghazal and north of Equatoria. Much of the region is flat plain with both thick fertile clay soil and sandy soil (especially in the north). The southwestern part is a watershed characterized by valleys and permanent streams. The vast permanent swamplands or *sudd* are found where the Sobat River and the White Nile converge. Some areas of Upper Nile are characterized by rolling plains and isolated rocky hills. The region receives a sufficient amount of rainfall and seasonal flooding to support both animal grazing and farming. The vegetation is savannah woodland and grassland except in the permanent swampy areas.[10]

The political capital and commercial city of Upper Nile is Malakal, which lies in Shilluk country. This region is predominantly occupied by Western Nilotic and Lwo-speaking people comprising the Dinka, Nuer,

Shilluk, Burun, and Anuak. Their primary occupation is cattle herding, but they also practice subsistence agriculture.[11]

Equatoria is uniquely located in the extreme Southern part of Sudan. Today it has been divided into three federal states: Eastern, Central, and Western. The topography is characterized by flat, rolling, and undulating plains with hills and mountains scattered here and there. The region is crisscrossed by rivers and streams, the most prominent being the White Nile, which cuts through the heartland of the region.

The vegetation of much of Eastern and Central Equatoria is savannah woodland and grassland. Western Equatoria is characterized by thick bushes and gallery forest, an extension of the equatorial rain forest of the Congo Basin. Though rainfall throughout Equatoria varies considerably depending on the topography, it is generally sufficient to support subsistence agriculture, which is the most important economic activity in the region. Juba has historically been the seat of government and the financial district of Southern Sudan.

THE PEOPLE OF SOUTHERN SUDAN

The Southern region of Sudan is inhabited by African peoples with diverse traditional values, norms, customs, and belief systems. Throughout much of the twentieth century, scholars referred to the people of the region as "primitive" or "pagan." C. G. Seligman, a British anthropologist, embarked on the first ambitious research project to document the various ethnic groups and their cultures. His research was published in his monumental work, *The Pagan Tribes of the Nilotic Sudan* (1932). This book helped British administrators in the South to understand the origins, ethnic composition, cultures, and languages of the people in this region.[12]

Scholars who have written about Southern Sudan have presented a variety of views about its people. Mandour El-Mahdi, Francis M. Deng, and Mohamed O. Beshir have described them as "aborignial" and "Negroid."[13] These terms are loaded with negative connotations and have no place in modern historical accounts. Dustan M. Wai and Deng D. Akol Ruay have presented a fairly detailed discussion of the people of the South that sheds more light on the ethnic composition of the region than the works of El-Mahdi, Deng, and Beshir.[14]

However, Edgar O'Ballance is the first author on Sudan to place the people of the Southern Sudan into the three major linguistic groups of the Sudanic, Western Nilotes, and Eastern Nilotes.[15] This is the most honest and accurate way of describing the people of the South. Although these groups have distinct historical origins and patterns of migration, they are also characterized by varying degrees of intermingling or cultural borrowings, whether through peaceful contacts or warfare, with the victor most likely absorbing the vanquished ethnically or culturally.

The Sudanic people of Southern Sudan are divided into the Moru-Madi and the Azande. The Moru-Madi were the first inhabitants of Southern Sudan. Migrating from the vicinity of the Congo Basin, they are thought to have firmly established themselves in the territory by AD 1000.[16] Ethnic groups today include the Moru, Madi, Logo, Kaliko, Avukaya, Lulubo, and Lugbara.[17] The Azande occupy a vast area in the heart of Africa. They are found in Western Equatoria in the Congo-Nile watershed as well as in parts of the Central African Republic and the Democratic Republic of the Congo.[18]

Linguistically, the term "Nilotes" or "Nilotic" (in reference to the Nile) is used to denote people other than the Bantu, Sudanic, Afro-Asiatic, or Khoi-san who speak closely related languages and are believed to have descended from a common ancestor.[19] They are distributed over a large area of northeast Africa and Southern Sudan.[20] They are divided into three broad groups, the Eastern, the Western, and the Southern. The last group is found in parts of Kenya and Tanzania.

Linguistically, the Western Nilotes are divided into two distinct groups: the Dinka-Nuer and the Lwo-speaking.[21] They are the largest ethnic group in Sudan, occupying the vast flat plains of the Bahr al-Ghazal and Upper Nile regions. Subgroups include the Agar, Aliab, Ciec, Malual, Atuot, and Bor. They keep large numbers of cattle and lead a typical nomadic lifestyle, though some engage in subsistence farming during the rainy season.[22] Many have played important political and military roles in Southern Sudan in particular, and the Republic of Sudan in general.

Physically, culturally, and linguistically related to the Dinka are the Nuer, and they may have had a common ancestor. The two peoples have maintained contact with each other, either peacefully or through warfare, over the centuries,[23] and there has been a great deal of "miscegenation and cultural borrowing" between the two.[24] Like the Dinka, the Nuer are divided into subgroups, including the Lau, Lek, Gaawar,[25] Atwot, and Jikany.[26] The Nuer are pastoralists and inhabit the swampy areas and savannah grasslands of the Upper Nile region, occupying both banks of the White Nile.[27]

Other Western Nilotic groups include: 1) the Shilluk, who occupy the most northerly part of Southern Sudan in the flat plains on the east and west banks of the White Nile, where they farm and raise livestock;[28] 2) the Anuak, who occupy the flat plains and the banks of the Baro, Grila, Akobo, and Sobat rivers;[29] and 3) the Acholi, a Lwo-speaking people who today occupy Northern Uganda and part of Eastern Equatoria.

Among the Eastern Nilotes are found the Bari-speaking groups of the Bari proper, the Pojulu, Kuku, Kakwa, and many others. They are linguistically and culturally related and claim a common ancestor.[30] The Bari were the earliest of the Eastern Nilotic groups to penetrate the region of Equatoria[31] and today inhabit a vast territory in Central Equatoria. The Pojulu also occupy territory in Central Equatoria, bordering the Bariland in the east, the Kakwaland in the west, and the Kukuland to the south. The intermixing of various Bari, Madi, Pojulu, and Kakwa clans and Lugbara families and individuals resulted in the formation of a unique cultural and linguistic group of people today called the Kuku. The Kuku comprise over one hundred clans whose backgrounds can be traced to the various immigrant groups in the Kukuland.[32] Today they occupy the territory now called Kajo-Kaji. The Kakwa occupy three countries—Sudan, Uganda, and the Democratic Republic of the Congo.

Other Eastern Nilotic groups include the Lakoya, Latuko, and Taposa of Eastern Equatoria. The Lakoya inhabit the East Bank of the Nile— their settlements are east of the Bari and north of the Acholi.[33] The Latuko occupy a vast territory east of the Nile in Eastern Equatoria. The Taposa people currently inhabit the extreme southeastern part of Eastern Equatoria and were "the latest arrivals" in the region.[34]

The boundaries separating Southern Sudan from its neighbors are artificial, as they were the product of colonial administration. Thus, some ethnic groups such as the Azande have settlements in the Democratic Republic of the Congo and the Central African Republic; the Acholi, the Madi, and the Kakwa spill into the Northern and West Nile regions of Uganda, though the Kakwa also inhabit northwestern Democratic Republic of the Congo; while the Nuer and the Anuak occupy parts of Western Ethiopia. Meanwhile, within Sudan the northernmost Dinka people in the Bahr al-Ghazal region and the Shilluk of the Upper Nile region can be found in the territory immediately north of the tenth parallel.[35]

RACE AND ETHNICITY NORTH OF THE TENTH PARALLEL

Understanding the ethnic composition and cultural diversity of the people who live north of the tenth parallel can help to shed light on the root causes of the racial, ethnic, cultural, and religious conflicts among the diverse groups throughout the country. The people who live south of the tenth parallel have for many decades collectively referred to those living north of the parallel as "Arabs."[36] This is a faulty interpretation or representation of the people of that area. According to the 1956 population census in the Sudan conducted by the British administration, 39 percent of the population claimed Arab ancestry while 55 percent were people of African descent. Of the 55 percent, 30 percent lived in the Southern region while 25 percent coexisted with their Arab neighbors in the Darfur, Kordofan, and Eastern regions of Sudan.[37] As the late John Garang de Mabior, former vice president of Sudan, pointed out, the Northern region has more people of African ancestry than the Southern region.[38] Because the two civil wars in Sudan (1955 through 1972, 1983 through 2005) have made conducting a comprehensive and accurate census of the country's population extremely difficult, any population figures between 1956 and 2005 are suspect.

The term "Nuba" today refers to the more than fifty African ethnic groups that occupy the Nuba Mountains in the Southern Kordofan state of Central Sudan.[39] They constitute the largest of the "non-Arab" groups living north of the tenth parallel. The Nuba people are believed to have descended from the Kingdom of Kush in the eighth century BC. For several thousand years they inhabited the entire territory of Kordofan. In the sixteenth century, the first wave of Arab invaders into this region forced the various Nuba ethnic groups to retreat to the Nuba Mountains, where they settled permanently. Nuba culture, traditional values, norms, belief systems, customs, and languages are rich and diverse,[40] but one-fourth of the population in Southern Kordofan also comprises Arab nomads, traders, and merchants, as well as government employees. The Fellata, who are descendants of West African immigrants primarily from Mali, Niger, and Nigeria, are scattered across the length and breadth of the region. It is difficult to estimate the population of the Nuba people, as many obstacles stand in the way: insecurity, war, drought, famine, deaths, decline in births, and massive intra- and interregional migrations (large numbers of Nuba have migrated to Khartoum in search of sanctuary or employment opportunities).[41]

Large and diverse ethnic groups also occupy the Darfur region in the west. Nearly the size of France, Darfur has been divided into three distinct zones reflecting its ethnic composition: Northern, Western, and Southern. Northern Darfur is inhabited largely by non-Arab groups called Zaghawa and a small group of Arabs called Meidab.[42] Indigenous black Africans, including the Fur, Massalit, Daju, and Berti, occupy much of the territory on both sides of the Jabel Marra in Western Darfur. Southern Darfur is home to the Baggara people, who are the product of intermingling and intermarriages between Arab immigrants and their African neighbors in the eighteenth century. They claim Arab descent, embrace Arab culture, and speak Arabic. Although the African and "Arab" people of Darfur are overwhelmingly Muslim, some African ethnic groups in Darfur have retained some of their cultural traits, customs, belief systems, and languages.[43]

In previous discussions pertaining to the North-South conflict, the people of the Kordofan and Darfur regions have been collectively referred to as "Northerners." This description was based primarily on the fact that the people who inhabit these regions have embraced the Islamic faith as well as the Arab and Islamic cultures. Large numbers of them speak Arabic in addition to their own indigenous languages. However, the representation of these people as "Northern" is misleading. It is true that Arab ethnic groups also occupy Northern Kordofan and Northern Darfur, but African peoples like the Nuba inhabit Southern Kordofan, the Zaghawa occupy the Northern region, while the Fur and Massalit inhabit the Western region of Darfur. The Fellata people have occupied parts of the Darfur region, the Gezira in the confluence of the Blue and White Niles, and parts of the Bahr al-Ghazal region.

The Nubians are indigenous African people who occupy the extreme Northern part of Sudan and the Southern frontier of Upper Egypt.[44] Construction of the Aswan High Dam in the 1960s resulted in the flooding of a vast portion of lower Nubia, necessitating the resettlement of 90,000 people elsewhere. As a result, many Nubians now inhabit territory near the Ethiopian border.[45] The Arab Muslim conquest of Egypt in 640 threw open the door for Arab immigration into the land of Nubia. Between the seventh and fourteenth centuries, several Arab Muslim families, motivated by the desire to spread Islam, gradually infiltrated into Nubian territory.[46] The Arab immigrants intermixed and intermarried with the Nubians, leading to their Arabization and Islamization. Some branches of the Nubians who became Arabized and today practice farming along the banks of the main Nile are the Barabra and the Ja'ali. The Barabra lived in Lower Nubia, but their descendants in the Republic of Sudan are the Sukkut and Mahas, who still speak related Nubian languages. The Ja'ali group occupying the region south of the Sukkut and Mahas peoples comprises a number of ethnic groups in Old Nubia. This group of Nubians is thoroughly Arabized, and their descendants claim Arab descent.[47]

The Beja are indigenous non-Arab people who iinhabit the Red Sea Hills in the Eastern region of Sudan.[48] Over the centuries, large numbers have embraced Islam and some traits of the Arab and Islamic culture. They speak Arabic in addition to their local languages. Because of intermarriage between the Beja and the Arabs, it is not surprising that the Ababda, a branch of the Beja, who occupy the extreme Northern part of the Beja territory, are Arabic-speaking.[49]

In the pre-Islamic era, the indigenous people of the Red Sea Hills, notably the Beja and the northernmost Nubians, had contact with Arabs from the Arabian Peninsula. Small groups of Arabic ethnic groups arrived on the west coast of the Red Sea as traders and settlers.[50] The earliest record of Arab immigration into the Eastern, Central, and Western part of the Sudan was two centuries prior to the birth of Christ, but several waves of Arab immigration into the Sudan had little impact on the indigenous peoples and cultures of the country because they came in small groups. The vast majority was confined to the Eastern region and their influence was restricted. These immigrants did not bring to the Sudan a unique culture and religion, as occurred with the advent of Islam in the seventh century.

The entry of the Arabs into the Northern Sudan during the Islamic era is of great historical significance. Following the defeat of the Byzantine forces in Egypt by the Arab Muslim forces in 640, large numbers of Arab nomads traveled to Egypt and subsequently headed south in search of grazing land. The conquest of Egypt also paved the way for the penetration of the Arab Muslim armies into the region south of Egypt, and waves of Arab invasion brought them to the Sudan.[51]

At the advent of the fourteenth century, various Arab ethnic groups settled in the Northern and Central regions of the Sudan. Generally speaking, two large groups of Arabs—the Qantani (southerners) and the Adnani (northerners)—penetrated the Sudan. They came to inhabit the Butana and the Blue Nile watershed[52] and the valleys of the Nile.[53] Meanwhile, the Baggara, the Kababish, and the Hamar, who had acquired camels and cattle, journeyed westward in search of grazing land for their animals and subsequently settled in the Kordofan and Darfur regions. The Kababish and Hamar in particular were amalgams of several ethnic groups in the eighteenth and nineteenth centuries.[54]

The various Arab ethnic groups in the Sudan, whether nomads or farmers, intermixed and intermarried with the indigenous African peoples, including the Nubians, the Beja, and the Nilotes. The racial, social, and cultural associations between these diverse ethnic groups started in the seventh and continued until the sixteenth century. The Arab ethnic groups in particular "received an infusion" of the blood of the Nilotic peoples of the Southern Sudan. In modern times, certain branches of the Sudanese population have acknowledged that the people or ethnic groups that have settled in the Central, Eastern, and Western regions of the country cannot claim "pure Arab origin." The peoples in these regions have various degrees of mixed African, Arab, Beja, or Nubian blood.[55] As Ruay notes, "There is no clear-cut pigmentational dichotomy among the various ethnic groups in the Sudan. The complexion ranges from brown to black."[56] Stephen Wondu, a former Sudan People's Liberation Movement representative in the United States, sees ambiguity in the definition of the Sudanese "Arab" identity on the basis of skin pigmentation, "The line between Africans and Arabs is very blurred . . . we talk about Arabs in terms of the individual's own decision to identify himself or herself as an Arab . . . it is self-definition—self identity."[57]

Francis M. Deng identifies African ethnic groups in other parts of East and West Africa that intermingled and intermarried with the Arabs in the seventh century when Islam was being aggressively propagated. He cites a "racial characteristics look" in Sudan similar to that of the African peoples in Ethiopia, Eritrea, Somalia, Chad, Niger, Mali, Mauritania, and Senegal.[58] Certainly the ethnic groups in these countries that have an infusion of Arab blood comfortably regard themselves as Africans. According to Deng, the people of Northern Sudan have an "identity crisis." He argues that identity in the Sudanese context is "a function of how individuals and groups identify themselves and are identified by others on the basis of race, ethnicity, religion, language, culture, or region."[59] Although they clearly acknowledge the presence of African blood in their veins, the Northern Sudanese prefer to be called "Arab."[60] Wondu argues that the Northern Sudanese "would like to look eastwards or northwards in search of superior culture."[61] While Deng concurs with Wondu, he emphasizes that Northern Sudanese "Arabs" do not want "non-Arabs" to associate Sudan with sub-Saharan Africa (black).[62]

Al-Baqir Al-Afif Mukhtar for his part asserts that in reality, most Northern Sudanese exhibit African facial or bodily features, for example, dark skin, broad noses, and hair texture.[63] He also notes that although the Northern Sudanese view themselves as "Arabs" in the country, the Arab people, especially in the Gulf countries, have a negative perception of them. The Arabs in the Middle East do not regard the Northern Sudanese as "Arab," and they clearly demonstrate this by calling them *abid* (meaning "slave" in Arabic). The Arabs of the Arabian Peninsula and those in the Fertile Crescent (Iraq) consider themselves the "real Arabs." They are the focal point of Arab identity, while the Northern Sudanese stand on the periphery of Arab identity.[64] Some Northerners attempt to enhance their "Arab" physical features by marrying women with much lighter skin. Some men straighten their hair to resemble "real" Arab hair. Both acts are undertaken primarily to promote an Arab image and the legitimacy of belonging to the race of the Muslim prophet or to Arab ancestry.[65] In addition, as Ruay notes, the Sudanese Arab must speak Arabic fluently to legitimize his social position in "Arab" society.[66]

Given this identity crisis among the Northern Sudanese, Deng essentially categorizes the Northern population into three groups. The uneducated or less sophisticated people who lead a nomadic lifestyle in the countryside are frequently referred to as "Arab" as a sarcastic way of describing their social condition. The urban elite often look down upon them. Meanwhile, some Northern Sudanese fiercely defend their Arab identity by tracing their genealogy to the Prophet Muhammad, who founded the Islamic faith in the Arabian Peninsula.[67] At the same time, some Northern Sudanese intellectuals who are politically astute and have embraced the Islamic faith and culture prefer to identify themselves with Arabism. In this particular context, race or skin color is not a critical issue in gaining socioeconomic or political status in society. Thus, many Northerners call themselves "Arab" out of religious, political, and economic motives—essentially they present themselves as an integral part of the Arab nation while also promoting Arab interests. They want to partake in the "shaping and sharing [of] power, wealth, and other national values."[68] Thus, the word "Arab" is loosely used in this context.

In short, the Arab Muslim armies as well as the various Arab ethnic groups that entered the Sudan at the advent of Islam in the seventh century introduced a new race, a new culture, and a new belief system to the indigenous peoples of the country. The Arabs brought their Arab and Islamic cultures, the Islamic faith, and the Arabic language. These new elements increased the country's racial, ethnic, cultural, linguistic, and religious diversity.[69] Today Sudan is a unique country in Africa endowed with all these diverse elements that have made it the crossroads between black Africa and Arab North Africa or the Middle East. It was John Garang's contention that the people of Sudan should have capitalized on this rich diversity and created "a unique renaissance or civilization on the Nile," because the indigenous African people and the Sudanese who claim Arab descent contributed their own cultures, languages, and religions. Wondering why the leadership in Khartoum since Sudan's independence (January 1, 1956) has consistently labeled Sudan an "Arab and Islamic" country, Garang strongly urged the "Arab" ethnic groups in Northern Sudan "to liberate themselves psychologically" and proudly call themselves "Sudanese." While he recognized Sudan to be a macrocosm of Arab and Islamic as well as African cultures, he was critical of its national and international identity as Arab and Islamic.[70]

Perhaps if the people of Sudan had used the uniqueness of their country to create a Nile Valley civilization reflective of African and Arab civilizations, this would have provided a foundation for establishing a strong, stable, and prosperous nation. Instead, race, class, and religion have been the defining elements in establishing government institutions, designing economic policies, shaping foreign policies, and establishing diplomatic relations with countries in North Africa, the Middle East, and sub-Saharan Africa. The result is that the Sudanese economy, private and public institutions, and foreign affairs are dominated by people from the North, while the vast majority of the black African people have been marginalized in the public and private domains. This situation has fomented tension and conflict between the "marginalized" peoples (in Southern Sudan, Southern Blue Nile, Darfur, Kordofan, and the Beja Red Sea Hills) and the political and economic elite in Northern Sudan. A case in point is the protracted civil wars Southern Sudan witnessed in the periods of 1955 through 1972 and 1983 through 2005. Thus, the multiplicity of races, ethnicities, cultures, languages, and religions have proved more of a "curse" to the Sudanese people than a "blessing" to the country.

CHAPTER 2

THE TORIT MUTINY OF 1955

ITS CAUSES AND FAILURE

TURCO-EGYPTIAN PENETRATION OF THE SOUTHERN SUDAN

ANY ATTEMPT TO INVESTIGATE THE FUNDAMENTAL ISSUES that brought about the outbreak of the first civil war in Southern Sudan in 1955 requires an understanding not only of the marked differences between the North and the South, but also of the broader historical backdrop against which events would play out. The stage began to be set as far back as the 1820s, when Turco-Egyptian forces first established control over the Northern Sudan as they sought natural resources and economic expansion. The Southern Sudan remained isolated, as it had for many centuries, by the upper Nile swamplands known as the Sudd and the forests and mountains farther south and east. In 1841, however, this isolation was broken when Turco-Egyptian steamers penetrated the interior of the South, and exploitation of the animal and human resources of the region began. The Turco-Egyptians and Northern Sudanese Arabs first scoured the region for ivory but soon resorted to slaving, which provided them with great profits.

Continued Turco-Egyptian exploitation and economic turmoil in the Sudan created conditions favorable to the rise of a Muslim holy man and zealot named Muhammed Ahmed Ibn Abdalla, who in 1881 announced himself to be the Mahdi, an Islamic messianic figure whom Islamic tradition holds will arise before judgment day to restore the true religion of Islam over the world. Believing he had been divinely chosen to rid the Sudan of its Egyptian rulers, he gathered an army and by 1885 had driven the Egyptians and British (who had taken control of Egypt three years earlier) from most of the Sudanese territory they had occupied. In that year, his forces captured Khartoum, and al-Mahdi established a theocratic Mahdist state.

British Administration of the Southern Sudan

The theocratic Mahdist government lasted until 1898, when it was defeated by Anglo-Egyptian forces that invaded the Sudan. The victory over the Mahdist movement paved the way for establishing an Anglo-Egyptian administration in Khartoum, known as the Anglo-Egyptian Condominium. Although Egyptian rule was restored over the Sudan, it was part of a joint exercise of authority by the British and Egyptians. The Mahdist defeat also paved the way for subsequent British penetration into the South. In 1902, when British forces began making inroads into the flat plains of the Southern Sudan, the people in this region became highly suspicious. The British therefore adopted an administrative program aimed at treating the Northern and Southern Sudan separately as distinct entities.[1] To this end, in 1906, it laid down the Closed Districts Ordinance, which prevented Northern administrators, soldiers, police, or merchants and traders from penetrating the South; to enter the region, Northerners had to obtain permits from the central government in Khartoum.

Before the Southern Sudan could be completely secured under British control, the Anglo-Egyptian administration had to deal with what Lord Cromer, the consul general in Cairo and architect of British policy in the Sudan, called "the savages who inhabit this region."[2] While British administration in the Sudan relied heavily on the Egyptian treasury to execute its programs in the North, it could not afford funds for construction works in the South. The only available funds went for maintaining British officials in the South and suppressing occasional uprisings by Southern peoples. Thus, to minimize financial expenditures on administering the South, Lord Cromer proposed introducing an administration based on the powers of the local chiefs of the various Southern peoples.[3]

In practice, British administrators chose to bypass the chiefs and deal directly with the local inhabitants. This meant they had to shoulder both executive and judicial responsibilities. British district commissioners became so preoccupied with such duties that they had little time to attend to administrative matters. They had little knowledge of local laws and customs, and in most cases had limited experience dealing with diverse ethnic issues.[4]

The British failure to administer the Southern Sudan directly necessitated formulating a new strategy. Thus, under a new doctrine of Native Administration, followed from 1910 to 1930, the British emphasized devolution of power to the chiefs as a means of decentralizing the administration. To ensure that British officials worked hand in hand with the local chiefs, it was clearly spelled out that "administration is to be left, as far as possible, in the hands of the native authorities. . . . Native chiefs are to be encouraged to administer their own tribes in accordance with native customs, in so far as these customs are not entirely repugnant to ideas of justice and humanity."[5] As one official put it, "I take it that it is now clearly recognized that the policy of the Government is to get the administration of affairs which are purely native back onto a tribal basis and that the function of the Government is to supervise, guide, and mould tribal organization, rather than to destroy such systems of customary law, discipline, and culture as the natives already possess."[6]

The British expanded the powers of the chiefs' courts by giving the chiefs the opportunity to exercise judicial as well as administrative duties. Chiefs were required for the first time to keep records of activities in their courts, but some chiefs did not come from societies with a centralized system of administration, and such responsibility was not only new, but overwhelming. Nevertheless, "the Sudan government set out to make the South safe for Africanization."[7] In fact, the policy of Native Administration implemented in the Southern Sudan helped to prevent further political "disintegration caused by nearly a century of incomers."[8]

Although the Native Administration seemed the most ideal system for maintaining law and order, collecting taxes, and keeping the peace among the various ethnic groups in the Southern Sudan, it did not effectively resolve the region's political, economic, social, and security problems in the first three decades of the century. The British administration recognized the military threat posed by the truculent pastoral and agricultural Nilotic and Sudanic peoples of the South such as the Dinka, Nuer, Latuko, and Azande. To contain the threat, the Foreign Office in Cairo appointed British military officers as governors, deputy-governors, district commissioners, and assistant district commissioners in the Southern provinces of Bahr al-Ghazal, Upper Nile, and Equatoria.[9] These officials had discretionary powers to wage war against hostile ethnic groups or administer justice in accordance with government policy. Many served in particular administrative areas for twelve to fifteen years before they could be transferred to other administrative units. Meanwhile, they were expected to learn the customs and languages of the inhabitants they administered. Because the Southern Sudan was considered a hardship post, these British officials were given three months vacation every year. In fact, over a fifty-year period, no more than thirty officials served in the vast Southern region. As a result, the absence of British officials in their administrative units for long periods of time adversely affected both administration and economic and social development.[10]

British administration in the Southern Sudan did not make any significant effort to train a cadre of Southern administrators to assist them in their day-to-day work or to assume their positions while they were away from their districts or regions for three months leave. Thus, Southern chiefs, on whom the British primarily relied to assist them, were never sufficiently politicized to clearly understand the government machinery. The vast majority of Southerners continued their traditional lifestyles, which traced back to ancient times. As described by Clement Mboro, who would serve in many different capacities in future Southern Sudanese governments, "The British kept us [Southerners] like animals in the cage."[11]

Barnaba Dumo Wani, a Kuku civil engineer and politician, stated that prior to 1948, the British administration in the Sudan made no attempt to recruit Southern Sudanese into the school of public administration or the police, prisons, and military colleges. Not until the election of the first Southern members to the Legislative Assembly in 1948 in Khartoum did these politicians take the first initiative to pressure the colonial administration into recruiting and training Southerners in the various professions so they could become an integral part of the government machinery. Thus, it was only in 1949 that, for the first time, five Southern Sudanese who had been trained as clerks and bookkeepers were selected and admitted into the public administration school of Gordon Memorial College in Khartoum, among them Clement Mboro.[12] Gordon Muortat Mayen, a Dinka Gar from Bahr al-Ghazal, and Elia Lupe, a Kakwa from Central Equatoria, were admitted into the police officers school, where they trained for two years and then graduated.[13]

According to Mboro, he and his fellow Southerners who were admitted into the public administration school were trained for two years and immediately after graduation were given the title of *Sub-Mamur* (district officials);[14] they were then to rise to the rank of *mamur* and assistant district commissioners in the administrative hierarchy. However, not until 1953 was another batch of recruits, drawn primarily from Rumbek Secondary School in Bahr al-Ghazal, sent to the public administration school in Khartoum. To increase the number of Southern administrative officials, teachers, bookkeepers, and clerks were also recruited and trained,[15] but these would graduate too late to fill the posts the British would begin evacuating and filling with native Sudanese the following year.

Economic Underdevelopment of the South

Economically, Northern Sudan, in marked contrast with the South, had made significant advances "in every field, local Government, irrigation schemes, higher education, [and] industrial development."[16] The Anglo-Egyptian administration in Khartoum was only too happy to concentrate its efforts in the North and simply pay lip service to development in the South. The maintenance of law and order required British attention but did not call for massive expenditure of funds or deployment of large numbers of soldiers.[17]

In essence, the South was not deemed to be "real estate" worth developing for the benefit of the Southern Sudanese in particular or for the general welfare of the Sudan. Communications in the three Southern provinces remained poor, not to mention the rudimentary transportation system that existed between North and South. Much of the flood plain in the east and north of the Southern region consisted of swamps, which created enormous transportation difficulties.[18]

Moreover, the British administration in Khartoum, fully aware of the exploitation of human and animal resources in the South by the Turco-Egyptians, their Northern Arab middlemen, and the Mahdists during the nineteenth century, also had concerns about preserving the traditional ways of life of the people in the region. Thus, it was ambivalent about promoting "material progress" in the South that might open the region to foreign intruders with economic interests. Although British officials seemed to care about the people of Southern Sudan, none of the five civil secretaries who served in Khartoum between 1921 and 1953 ever visited the three Southern provinces.[19]

For the first three decades of the century, the British administration was preoccupied with pacifying the various ethnic groups of the South. Not until 1929 was Nuer resistance finally broken, and not until 1930 was the entire South pacified.[20] Thus, despite the agricultural and livestock potential, there was no economic development in the Southern Sudan in the first four decades of the century. Insecurity, politics, and geography were critical factors preventing economic development.

Nevertheless, the Southern governors of the provinces of Bahr al-Ghazal, Upper Nile, and Equatoria began seriously discussing the question of Southern economic development in the 1920s. In the mid-1930s, Governor General Sir Stewart Symes began espousing new ideas about economic development in the Southern Sudan, but the Great Depression of the 1930s also severely hurt the economy of the Sudan. Faced with a tight budget, the British administration did not seriously consider Southern economic development until 1944, when the governor general presented "a major initiative in economic development" in the South. Thus, in 1946, a five-year plan that spelled out a total budget of E£14 million for the whole Sudan channeled E£1,272,200 into the South. E£1 million of this was earmarked for the Zande Scheme at Nzara in Western Equatoria, which was established to produce cotton in order to generate revenue for the Southern Sudan in particular.[21]

This lack of economic development in the Southern Sudan prior to the end of the Second World War adversely affected the region politically, economically, and socially. The lack of infrastructure (roads, railways, telegraphs, radio transmitters) severely affected the mobility of British officials and the Southern peoples as well as communication from one region to another. According to Douglas H. Johnson, the British administration built railway lines only to areas with valuable economic resources or strategic considerations.[22]

Thus, the Southern Sudan remained underdeveloped in every way. This uneven development between North and South that became apparent in the decades preceding Sudanese independence inevitably widened the gap between them. This, in turn, increased Southerner's suspicions and fears for their future in the event the Sudan was granted independence as a unitary state.[23] Southern intellectuals and politicians remained highly suspicious of joint British and Northern Sudanese plans for the region being developed at this time. These fears would later become a reality as events leading to Sudan's independence began to unfold.[24] This lack of development would also have profound consequences for the Torit mutiny, which would find itself badly hampered by the lack of infrastructure.

EDUCATIONAL DEVELOPMENTS IN THE SOUTH

When the Anglo-Egyptian administration was imposed on the Sudan following the defeat of the Mahdist state in 1898, the mold was set for unequal political, economic, social and educational developments between the North and South. This was most clearly visible in the area of education. The Anglo-Egyptian administration pursued two separate educational policies, one applying to the Arab and Muslim North, the other to the South.[25]

In the North, between 1902 and 1947, the Anglo-Egyptian government opened elementary, intermediate, and secondary schools, Gordon Memorial College, and vocational and technical schools. Professional and technical training were emphasized with the primary aim of providing a cadre to fill "low-paid, subordinate posts in government departments."[26] At the same time, the government was cautious about providing the kind of "literary" education that might enlighten the Northern Sudanese and cause them to agitate for freedom from foreign domination.[27]

Still, a few Sudanese were sent abroad for post-secondary education in Beirut and Egypt. Within the country itself, Sudanese had no opportunities for higher education.[28] Nonetheless, the foundation of education laid down in Northern Sudan yielded fruit over the years: Northern political consciousness increased, and Northerners became increasingly sophisticated in their political organizations.[29]

Meanwhile, during the first two decades of the century, educational trends in the South differed greatly. Preoccupied with security problems and having limited financial resources, the Anglo-Egyptian administration struggled to control the various Southern ethnic groups, which resisted all forms of alien domination.[30] Although administration required the involvement of local chiefs in running day-to-day affairs in their territories, there was no demand for literate Southerners. A small number of clerks were needed to assist British administrators, but this task could be entirely carried out by Christian missionaries, who were "anxious to teach English in order to facilitate the spread of the Word of God."[31]

Thus, Southern education was not taken seriously by the top educational and administrative officials in Khartoum. The security and financial problems that haunted Sir Reginald Wingate, governor general in the Sudan from 1899 to 1916, further strengthened his belief that the South was better left in the hands of Christian missionaries. The involvement of missionaries in Southern education would mean the building of schools, recruitment of teachers, and the provision of teaching materials, all without financial burden on the government.[32] Thus, the handing over of all educational matters to the Christian missionaries in the South was based on financial and administrative considerations.

The British thereby encouraged Christian missionaries from England, Europe, and the United States to go to Southern Sudan. Religious "spheres" were created to prevent the various sects from clashing with one another. Left on their own from 1902 to 1920, the Christian missionaries opened poorly financed schools with lower educational standards than in the North. The mission schools were not primarily meant to produce well-educated and politically conscious Southerners, but rather to teach the latter how to read, write, and in some cases recite the Christian scriptures.[33]

The main motive of missionary education was not only to save souls, but also to save the Southern Sudanese peoples from deprivation by Arab slave traders and bring them a sense of civilization. To the Southern Sudanese, however, missionary education itself appeared to threaten their traditional values, beliefs, and customs. Chiefs sought to protect the status quo and resisted attempts to spread the Christian faith, while others were openly hostile. Thus, the only adherents the Christian missionaries won were refugees from disturbances in French Equatorial Africa, peoples dislocated by Mahdist activities in the South, and orphans and others who had been abandoned.[34] Although the missionaries welcomed people from varied backgrounds into their schools, the education they provided was rudimentary. The British administration did not provide trained teachers, but was happy if the missionaries taught the children in English, the language of administration in the Southern Sudan. The boys were taught handcrafts, carpentry, bricklaying, and simple clerical work. Girls were given lessons in needlework and music in addition to English. The objective of the Catholic missionaries was "civilization through learning and work, meant to prepare the way to the Christian religion."[35]

After the various Christian missionaries had languished in the Southern Sudan for two decades with limited funds, in 1922 the British administration for the first time showed interest in Southern education. There had been no significant social, economic, or educational development in the region; technical training was seriously lacking; and not only was the general education of Southern students discouragingly low in quality, but the number of "half-educated" students turned out was extremely small.[36]

In 1924, the British administration began to emphasize education in the South in line with the doctrine of Native Administration. At the same time, its increasing activities in the region necessitated creating a better-trained cadre to assist the district commissioners in their day-to-day responsibilities. This meant recruiting local men with the skills to work in a government bureaucracy.[37]

In 1924, the British administration decided to allocate funds to support missionary educational activities in the South. In his Annual Report of 1925, the governor general indicated that increased "economic and administrative development in the Southern Sudan demands additional educational facilities." Thus, the "happy combination of missionary enterprise and experience on the one hand, and of government aid, on the other, should afford sure ground and opportunity for the development of the negroid and pagan peoples."[38] In 1926, the administration finally appointed an inspector of Southern education, who was to be resident in the South and whose responsibilities included investigating and recommending the most suitable kind of educational system for the people of the Southern Sudan.[39]

The chief inspector of schools, E. R. J. Hussey, visited Bahr al-Ghazal and Upper Nile to assess the condition of Southern schools.[40] He was also dispatched to Uganda to study the educational system there in the hope it could be adapted to the educational needs of the Southern Sudanese, who had many things in common with their neighbors farther south. This visit was significant because it later led to the creation of two levels of education in the Southern Sudan: elementary schools run in the local vernacular language and tailored to the interests of the people, and intermediate schools taught in English that were established primarily to produce teachers, clerks, and other junior officials.[41] Not until 1948 would Rumbek Secondary School be opened as the first secondary school in the Southern Sudan.

However, fifty years of British colonial rule and Christian missionary presence in the Southern Sudan ultimately had little impact on the education of its inhabitants. Thus, by the time Sudan attained its independence in 1956, the South had only one secondary school (at Rumbek in Bahr al-Ghazal), a few secondary school graduates, one intermediate school (at Atar in Upper Nile), five university graduates who had received their degrees in the North, and a handful of junior administrative officials. The South lacked engineers, doctors, and agriculturalists. In economic terms, the South lacked industrial development.[42] This lack of an educated class would also prove momentous for the outcome of the Torit mutiny.

The Equatoria Corps Is Established

The period 1912 to 1919 is best remembered in the history of the Southern Sudan for the beginning of serious discussions by British officials about a policy of separating the South from the North. C. H. Stigand, governor of Mongalla Province (later named Equatoria Province), aggressively pursued this "Southern policy." His original plan was based on a desire to develop the South economically, which could be done only by detaching it from the North, "An administrative change which is sorely needed, and which must take place before any great advance can be made, is the complete separation of the Negro provinces of the Sudan from the Arab provinces."[43] Stigand based his argument on the fact that any set of rules, laws, or regulations pertaining only to the Northern provinces could not be applied to the South. Noting the differences in customs and local conditions in both parts of the country, he argued it would be unfair to generate revenue in the South for developing the North. Thus, Stigand put forward a plan in which "the Negro provinces should be put in a class by themselves, under a vice-governor-general if necessary, and given what can be spared in the way of revenue, and allowed to work out their own salvation, under the laws and regulations which may be considered best suitable to the people and local conditions."[44] V. R. Woodland, who succeeded Stigand in Mongalla, followed in his footsteps. In 1920, he sent a memorandum to the civil secretary indicating his determination to pursue the policy of developing the Southern Sudan separately, "My own opinion is that the time has come either to cut off this province from the rest of the Sudan or to institute a more incisive policy as regards its administration."[45]

It was in this context of preventing Northern Sudanese political, religious, and cultural influences from infiltrating the South that a Southern army was established. The British administration clearly recognized that the security of the Southern Sudan could only be guaranteed if the soldiers came from that region. As early as 1910, Governor General Wingate conceived the idea of establishing a purely Southern Sudanese battalion whose recruits would be drawn from Southern ethnic groups under the command of British officers. The language of command was to be English, and the Southern soldiery was to observe the Christian faith.[46]

To free the South from Arab and Muslim domination, Northern soldiers, who had formed the bulk of the army in the South, were gradually eliminated from the Southern provinces. The last Northern troops left the South in 1917, and in that year, the people of the Southern provinces took control of their own army. For a number of reasons, the British colonial administration was enthusiastic in establishing the Equatoria Corps, especially in Equatoria province. First, the people in this province were "cooperative and adaptable." Second, the province of Equatoria shared borders with Uganda, Kenya, Ethiopia, and the Congo. It was therefore in the interests of the British administration to secure the Southern borders.[47]

The British administration selected Torit in Latukoland in Eastern Equatoria as the headquarters of the Equatoria Corps for both geopolitical and strategic reasons. East Africa was easily accessible from Torit.[48] Also, the Latuko were known for their military prowess. In the first decade of British colonial administration in Eastern Equatoria, the Latuko had fiercely resisted this alien power, even raiding those villages that cooperated with British authorities. The enormous difficulties that the British faced in pacifying the Latuko prompted the British inspector to describe them as "pig-headed" and "exceedingly stubborn."[49] Ethnographic studies conducted among the people of Eastern Equatoria following the pacification of the Latuko indicated that the Latuko were brave warriors and were also enthusiastic in serving in the colonial army. According to Pacifico Lado Lolik, "Getting them into the army was one way to get them controlled, and at the same time their bravery would make the Equatoria [Corps] a very strong army."[50] Thus, the British liked recruiting the Latuko into the Equatoria Corps because they were not only brave but disciplined.

The Equatoria Corps in Torit was composed of Nos. 1, 2, and 5 Companies. Small ethnic groups such as the Lango, Immotong, Pwoni (Lafon), Acholi, and Ohoriok (Lakoya) of Eastern Equatoria, the Pojulu and Kuku of Central Equatoria, and the Moru, Baka, Mundu, and Avukaya of Western Equatoria largely constituted the No. 1 Company and a portion of No. 2 Company. The Latuko constituted the largest group in No. 2 Company, though they never formed the majority in the rank and file of the Equatoria Corps.[51]

According to Barnaba Wani, the Latuko soldiers formed the majority in the No. 2 Company of the Equatoria Corps because this was an "elite force" that patrolled "the cattle-rustling border areas with Kenya, Uganda, and Ethiopia."[52] Meanwhile, in Bahr al-Ghazal, most soldiers in No. 3 Company of the Equatoria Corps in Wau were composed of Dinka. In Malakal, Upper Nile province, the Dinka, Nuer, and Shilluk constituted the No. 4 Company of the Equatoria Corps.[53]

Robert Collins has further summed up the responsibilities of the Equatoria Corps in Southern Sudan thus: to assist the colonial British administration in maintaining law and order; to control the smuggling of guns across the borders; to prevent conflicts between the "truculent" and "hostile" nomads and farmers who were struggling for control of grazing lands, cultivable land, and water resources; and to provide protection for the wild game, especially elephants that were hunted for their ivory.[54]

INCREASED SOUTHERN POLITICAL ACTIVISM AND THE PROLIFERATION OF POLITICAL PARTIES

The end of World War II marked a new phase in British colonial history in its vast empire around the world. The subjects of the British Empire were agitating for self-determination and complete independence from their colonial masters. Some formed political parties and presented their demands to the colonial rulers through their political leaders. Others sent petitions to the monarchy in Britain demanding self-rule, while still others took up arms and waged guerrilla warfare to liberate themselves from their colonial masters. In the Sudanese context, the Northern intellectuals chose a peaceful approach to political and economic independence, rather than use of force. Thus, Northern political parties like the National Unionist Party (NUP) and the Umma Party spearheaded the demand for independence from British colonial rule. The members of both parties were well educated and well organized, and they worked consistently together to achieve their goals, but these Northern political elites also undermined the Southern viewpoint concerning Sudan's independence.

Meanwhile, a few Southerners in Northern Sudan had begun exercising their political rights. A group of educated Southerners in Khartoum and Omdurman had already formed a political party known as the Black Block. Its aims were "to promote the interests of the dark-skinned and largely non-Arab peoples of the south and to help raise the area out of its state of backwardness and ignorance."[55] The party made alliances with groups whose objectives and living conditions were similar to theirs. Although they advocated independence for the South, the depth of that commitment was revealed when they made an alliance with the Umma Party of the North.[56] The Black Block was viewed unfavorably by the NUP because the latter feared it would emphasize the racial element in the Sudan and consequently jeopardize the NUP's objective of "unity of the Nile Valley" (union between Egypt and the Sudan). Some Southerners also opposed the Black Block on similar grounds.[57]

The period 1949 through 1951 witnessed a further proliferation of Southern political parties, and in 1951, Southern politicians Buth Diu Thung, Stanilaus Paysama, and Abdel-Rahman Sule founded the Liberal Party. Missionary-educated Southerners began to run for office either individually or loosely affiliated with the Liberal Party. The South elected and sent thirteen members to the Legislative Assembly in Khartoum, which officially opened on December 16, 1948.[58] The assembly provided its members the opportunity to discuss political, economic, and social issues in a democratic atmosphere and "represented a major change in the Sudan Government's policy."[59]

Southern politicians in the assembly encountered an unfavorable political climate, as their outlook and aspirations differed from their Northern counterparts. These differences became even clearer when on March 26, 1951, the Constitution Amendment Commission, comprising Northerners and a single Southerner, Buth Diu Thung of the Liberal Party, was formed "to advise the Governor General on what steps were to be taken towards self-government."[60] Although Southern members of the Legislative Assembly were hardly a force to be reckoned with, Thung demanded federal status for the South and a federal system for Sudan as a whole. When he found himself ignored, he walked out of the assembly and subsequently withdrew from the commission, protesting that "Northern members proved to be intransigent in not accepting either of his proposals for separation or unity with constitutional guarantees for the South."[61] Although such guarantees were included in the draft constitution and subsequently passed by the Legislative Assembly in April 1953, they were later deleted at the conference in Cairo in June 1953 where the future of Sudan was discussed.[62]

Northern Sudanese Political Parties and British Administration Discuss Sudan's Independence

The year 1953 marked the beginning of the Sudan's bid for independence from Anglo-Egyptian rule. Discussions between the Sudanese political parties and the British administration were aimed at paving the way for self-determination of the Sudanese people. Each of the main Sudanese parties had its own agenda.[63]

The two dominant Northern parties were the NUP and the Umma (Nation) Party. Since its founding during World War II, the NUP, led by Ismail el-Azhari, had "fully supported Egyptian efforts to realize Nile Valley unity."[64] The NUP's primary agenda was to unite the Sudan with Egypt politically to form a single, sovereign nation under the umbrella of the Nile Valley, but the Umma Party, directly linked to the Mahdist movement under the leadership of the Mahdi's son, Sayyid Abdel Rahman el-Mahdi, favored independence from both Egypt and Britain. In a speech at an Umma Party rally, Rahman stated, "We will never accept unity of the Nile Valley. No one but the Sudanese can decide the future of this country."[65]

The Liberal Party for its part advocated complete independence of the Sudan from the British, but wanted the South to have federal status under a Sudanese government. Although the party represented the views of Southern Sudanese, it was not consulted in the discussions about the Sudan's self-determination in Cairo in 1953.[66] According to Clement Mboro, Southern Sudanese were deliberately excluded from the Cairo talks because to the Northern political parties the Southern voice did not matter insofar as decisions pertaining to the future of Sudan were concerned. Indeed, when the Southern members of the assembly inquired as to why they were entirely excluded from the Cairo meeting, the NUP and the Umma Party simply told them they had no political party.[67]

Mboro stated that he, as a member of the electoral college, together with other Southern members of the Legislative Assembly, met with the leadership of the NUP and the Umma Party in Khartoum in 1950 "to discuss the acceleration of the pace of self-government." In that meeting, the Southerners and the Umma Party politicians expressed concerns about Sudan's road to self-government and subsequent independence since they were not yet ready for self-government. Their strong opposition was reflected in the parliamentary vote—self-government for Sudan narrowly passed by one vote. The NUP favored hastening the pace for self-rule. El-Azhari wanted Egyptian help so that in the event Sudan achieved independence, the NUP would become the ruling political party.[68]

Nevertheless, the British vowed to protect Southern interests. They tried to include in the discussions safeguards for the South, but these were rejected by the Northern political parties and by Egypt. The Southern demand for federation was also rejected. Although the British had veto powers at the time and could have turned the tide in the South's favor, they chose to ignore Southern demands because they had already committed themselves to self-determination for the Sudan.[69]

Nevertheless, Britain wanted to maintain its influence in the Nile Valley and its control of the Suez Canal. This struggle for control of the Sudan by the British and Egyptians drew the attention of Northern political parties from the Southern Sudan. Entangled in interparty rivalry, Northern political parties totally ignored the South in a meeting held January 10, 1953, in Khartoum "to discuss the basis for an agreement by the Condominium [Egypt and Britain] powers on Sudan's independence." The Liberal Party was left out of this meeting.[70]

On February 12, the British ambassador to Egypt, Sir Ralph Stevenson, and the Egyptian prime minister, General Muhammed Neguib, signed what became known as the Cairo Agreement on behalf of their governments.[71] This granted the Sudan sovereign status and its people the right to exercise self-determination. A committee comprising representatives from Britain, Egypt, and the Sudan were to work together with the governor general of the Sudan as he exercised his authority over the country. This basically ratified an agreement already signed by the Northern political parties in Khartoum in January. Again, the Southern Liberal Party was excluded from the Cairo Agreement.[72]

DEMOCRATIC ELECTIONS IN THE SUDAN AND THE BEGINNING OF SUDANIZATION

The Cairo Agreement led to the Sudan Self-Government Statute of 1953 and paved the way for elections to the first Sudanese parliament in Khartoum that same year. In this parliament the South was allotted only twenty-two seats, while the Northern parties elected seventy-five members for a total of ninety-seven. Because Southerners were a minority, they were always outvoted in parliamentary debates. Thus, the Southern influence in the parliament was almost negligible as far as crucial issues pertaining to the South in particular and Sudan in general were concerned.[73]

The NUP won most of the seats in the new House of Representatives and its leader, Ismail el-Azhari, became prime minister. The news of this "striking success" was warmly received in Egypt. General Neguib believed that "unity of the Nile Valley" was close to being achieved.[74]

El-Azhari's accession generated fears among Southern politicians in Khartoum because of his advocacy of Nile Valley unity. In January 1954, Buth Diu Thung, a Southern member of parliament, asked El-Azhari about a rumored press release regarding his government's determination to pursue this policy. To allay Southern fears and frustration, the new prime minister made a declaration, "My Government cannot carry out such [an] agreement, which demands a free and neutral atmosphere for self-determination. The government will complete Sudanization, effect evacuation [of] foreign troops and dismiss all factors which may influence the people's choice."[75]

According to Clement Mboro, when El-Azhari toured the Darfur and Kordofan provinces in the later part of 1955, he was very well received by a large number of people on horseback and camelback carrying slogans that read "Sudan for Sudanese." The Umma Party had overwhelming support from the people of Darfur and Kordofan, and their expressions of the desire to become independent from foreign domination apparently convinced the prime minister that his political base, and the survival of his political party, should not depend primarily on those Northern Sudanese and the Egyptian politicians who supported the unity of the Nile Valley. Thus, El-Azhari realized that it was politically expedient for him to reverse his previous firm support for Egypt to that of self-government and independence.[76] Certainly his party victory in any election would depend primarily on support from the Sudanese people, and not from the Egyptian politicians and people.

As the Sudanese began to exercise their rights to self-determination and independence, the different political parties sought to gain control of the administrative machinery. The British stated their readiness to leave Sudan, but not in a state of "administrative chaos." A committee to study and recommend replacement of British civil servants and technical experts with Sudanese was needed to ensure a successful transition. On February 20, 1954, a Sudanization Committee was appointed and ended up recommending some 80 to 90 percent of posts for Sudanization "at an early date."[77] Again, the South was not represented on this crucial committee. It was therefore obvious to Southerners from the start that they would be cheated by Sudanization.[78]

In response, on August 27, a meeting of the Liberal Party was organized at Malakal by Abdel Rahman Sule (president) and Buth Diu Thung (general secretary). More than three hundred Southern supporters demanded that Southern officials be promoted to higher positions. An NUP member who hoped to secure a Southern political alliance with an eye to future political elections sent a memorandum to El-Azhari listing positions that should be given to Southerners. He warned that without such promotions, "there can be no other alternative to solve the Southern problem except more chaos and more intrigues by the opposition and communists." However, the Sudanization Committee promoted only four Southerners to the position of assistant district commissioner and two to *mamur*.[79] Thus, Southerners received only six positions out of eight hundred held by Britons and recommended for Sudanization.[80] Northern Sudanese, on the other hand, were delighted to be filling the posts being vacated by their long-time masters.

Georgia Denk Kir, a Southern businessman in Gogrial, summed up the grievances of the Southerners following the announcement of the results of the Sudanization Committee, "It means our fellow Northerners want to colonize us for another hundred years."[81] Certainly, Southerners were "openly cheated."[82] According to Wani, Sudanization was essentially a replacement of British and Egyptian officials, technical experts, and organized forces (police, prisons, and army) by Northern Sudanese,[83] while according to Mboro, Southerners "felt cheated." They were obviously disgruntled with the El-Azhari administration, which "accelerated the pace of violence in Torit,"[84] referring to the mutiny to come.

Years later, Joseph Lagu, commander-in-chief of the Anya-Nya, expressed similar frustration:

> As the British started leaving the South, their administrative posts and business firms were taken up by Northern Sudanese who previously had not been allowed to work or settle in the South. The Southerners began to feel more and more strongly that their country was being colonized by Arabs and that their great expectations from independence boiled down to the replacement of one master by another. The Northern officials looked down upon the Southerners, openly discriminating against them and on the whole treated them as subject people. . . . They kept on insulting and abusing us, often using the word *abeed* (slaves) when referring to Southerners.[85]

In June and July of 1955, as Sudanization continued, new Northern Sudanese managers arrived at Nzara (in Zandeland in Western Equatoria) to replace British administrators and technical staff. The new management hastily dismissed three hundred workers at the industrial complex en masse "without regard for economic and political repercussions." On July 26, when Elia Kuze, an Azande and Liberal Party member, visited Yambio to demonstrate his support for the workers, he was arrested, tried by the district commissioner, and sentenced to seven years imprisonment for civil disobedience and attempts to rally his people against El-Azhari's government.[86] In a show of sympathy for Kuze, workers at Nzara demonstrated, and the Northern administrators in the town ordered the army and police to shoot them. Northern merchants also fired their guns at the mob. Eight people died at the scene.[87]

During the Sudanization Program, the soldiers of the Equatoria Corps and their counterparts in Bahr al-Ghazal and Upper Nile were also openly cheated. Northern "Arab" officers replaced the British and Egyptian officers. Thus, the Southern soldiers constituted the rank and file, with only a few NCOs. The highest rank Southerners held was second lieutenant, and only a few held this rank before the Torit mutiny (others were promoted to it after the mutiny to solicit their help in tracking down the mutineers who had escaped).[88]

In view of Southern bitterness and hostility toward the North in general, and him in particular, El-Azhari hastened the promotion of Southern Sudanese to district commissioners. The irony in these promotions was that these district commissioners were assigned to Juba District or to rural administrative units within "an important District." A case in point was the first appointment of Clement Mboro in Yirol subdistrict. He was later transferred to Juba District in his capacity as district commissioner, but in reality he was responsible only for the administration of Terekeka, a rural area north of Juba that did not even have the status of a subdistrict.[89] Certainly Southerners were deeply disappointed when Sudanization ended in 1955.[90]

SOUTHERNERS DEMAND A FEDERAL SYSTEM

Relations between Northerners and Southerners continued to deteriorate. Southern politicians increasingly and vigorously demanded federation. In October 1954, leading members of the Liberal Party and others organized a conference in Juba to solicit the support of Southerners for their agenda: federal status for the South within a united Sudan. The organizers announced on October 26 that the "southern people stand firmly for full Sudan independence and are opposed to unity with Egypt: and that Sudan shall become a free democratic republic with a Sudanese head, chosen for a specific period. . . . that south and north Sudan should remain one country on federal lines."[91]

Southern politicians felt that only a federal system could provide safeguards for them in an independent Sudan. As an observer remarked, "The demand for federation had . . . spread widely beyond the small educated elite to the chiefs, village headmen and their followers since it reflected a general Southern-Black African fear of the Arab Northern domination."[92]

Southern agitation was this time taken seriously by the NUP and El-Azhari. In 1954, El-Azhari began a tour of the Southern region in an effort to rally the Southern Sudan behind his new government, but wherever he and his entourage went, they were "ridiculed by Southerners."[93] While in Malakal, El-Azhari narrowly escaped assassination by a Southern official. The official, who held a knife, was arrested before he could reach the prime minister.[94] Nonetheless, during his tour El-Azhari promised to raise local salaries to match those in the Northern Sudan.[95]

The prime minister also visited Juba in Equatoria Province to explain his new vision for the Sudan at large, and the Southern Sudan in particular. While there, he witnessed two paradoxical incidents. Daniel Jumi Tongun, a Bari catechist, bookkeeper, political activist, and veteran politician, had mobilized the Juba population to accord the prime minister a warm reception, but as chairman of the mobilization committee, Tongun told the crowd that he would listen carefully to El-Azhari's speech, and that if he determined the prime minister's message to be detrimental to the political aspirations of the people of Southern Sudan, he would rise up and quietly walk out of the hall in protest, and he expected the crowd to follow suit.[96]

Indeed, while in Juba, El-Azhari was given a warm welcome. He met with the provincial chief administrators, civil servants, members of the organized forces (the army, police and prisons), and merchants. When he finally addressed the large number of people gathered in Juba Hall, he emphasized the unity of the Nile Valley, something to which Southerners were completely opposed. Tongun, dismayed and disappointed with El-Azhari's speech, walked out of the hall in protest and the crowd followed. The prime minister and his accompanying delegation were embarrassed and disappointed, while Tongun was labeled a political agitator and traitor.[97]

To the people of Juba, the incident clearly indicated that El-Azhari was an enemy of the people of Southern Sudan; the civilians and members of the organized forces believed that he did not have the interests of Southerners at heart. They thought that the prime minister's goals and objectives reflected only the interests and aspirations of the people of the North. Meanwhile, El-Azhari and his delegation acknowledged that a rift still existed between the peoples of the South and North. To them, the walkout was an expression of the Southern contempt for and hostility toward them in particular, and the North at large. Southerners were seen as agitators and rebels who deserved to be handled with "an iron hand."[98] Indeed, during his term in office, El-Azhari often used harsh statements to describe his policies toward Southern Sudan.

When federal status for the South was finally approved in the parliament in Khartoum, "federation" meant two different things for Northerners and Southerners. For Southerners it meant "an arrangement by which [the] South attains a status of equality with the North." The government in Khartoum interpreted federal status to mean separation from the North. A typical example of efforts to persuade Southerners to drop the idea of federal status for the South occurred when the district and assistant district commissioners of Yambio "toured the District to obtain from the Chiefs signatures supporting the Government. All forms of pressure were used to obtain their consent, trickery not excluded."[99]

The government's efforts to sway Southerners from their demand for federation did not stop them. Finally, on December 19, 1955, the Constituent Assembly passed a resolution stating that "federation for the three Southern provinces will be given full consideration by the Constituent Assembly."[100] As Bona Malwal M. Ring described Southern concerns, "The Southerners believe that if a man has the right to choose unity, he has with it the right to choose what sort of unity. Not only that, but he has also the right to decide against unity if it does not benefit him. How violently the north opposed this choice is well known to every living Sudanese."[101]

Relations between North and South Continue to Deteriorate

Political developments in the South were each day fomenting hostility among Southerners. In May 1955, the two Southern members of the NUP who held ministerial positions tendered their resignations over El-Azhari's policy toward the South. These two members joined the Liberal Party and urged Southerners to join in forming a Southern bloc. A meeting was scheduled for June, which the government tried to foil.[102]

That same month, in a speech to Southern members of parliament El-Azhari conveyed a message of coercion, "The Government must use all its force and strength . . . the Government shall not be lenient . . . it has army, its police and all its might."[103]

Southern frustration and hostility grew each day. Barnaba Wani, in his third year at Rumbek Secondary School, witnessed the arrogant behavior of the Northern administrators, officials, and military officers toward Southerners during and after the period of Sudanization. The "Arab" merchants from the North who controlled the economy throughout the South exhibited similar arrogance. To the Southerners, this group "represented the most hated influence of Northern Sudanese."[104]

As the state of insecurity continued to deteriorate in the South, rumors spread among the public and the organized forces about the Sudan government's plans to dissolve the Equatoria Corps. This purely Southern battalion was a symbol of power and prestige for the people of Southern Sudan. They had fought alongside the British forces against the Germans and Italians in Africa during World War II.[105]

Tensions were heightened further with the appearance of a telegram purportedly coming from Prime Minister El-Azhari and describing his intentions for the South: "To all my administrators in the three Southern provinces; I have just signed a document for self-determination. Do not listen to the selfish complaints of Southerners. . . . Treat them according to my orders. Any administrator who fails to comply with my orders will be liable to prosecution. In three months' time all of you will come round and enjoy the work you have done."[106]

The contents of the telegram were certainly forged, and its source remains obscure, though the subsequent Commission of Enquiry into the Southern Disturbances presumed that it was a Southern clerk at Juba. This false message was circulated far and wide in Equatoria: Yambio, Meridi, Nzara, Yei, and Torit all received copies. Meanwhile, a Lieutenant Saturlino further distorted its contents before circulating it among the Equatoria Corps. The government took no steps to investigate the source of this forged document.[107] The policemen (Southern and Northern) at Torit simply claimed preoccupation with the "arrow incident" of August 7, 1955, in which a Southern soldier had shot an arrow and narrowly missed a Northern officer. Also, while some administrators at Torit heard about the telegram, others learned of it only after the mutiny.[108]

Events Leading to the 1955 Torit Mutiny by the Equatoria Corps

The failure of the government to investigate the fake telegram further encouraged Saturlino, who was arrested for allegedly conspiring to murder the Northern officers at Torit. When on August 14 the Khartoum government ordered evacuation of the "wives and children" of these officers, Southern troops construed this as a prelude to implementing a government plan to exterminate the Southern soldiers there.[109]

Northern officers in the Torit garrison took extra precautionary measures, "All officers [were to] be armed by day and night, and . . . they were to walk or sleep in twos."[110] On August 14, the No. 2 Company of the Equatoria Corps was ordered "to proceed to Khartoum to take part, as representatives of the Southern Corps in a march past to celebrate the evacuation of foreign troops from the Sudan." This was followed by a written order from the commanding officer of the Southern Corps on August 16. The arrest of a Lieutenant M. T. Taffeng deepened the fears of Southern officers and men. Taffeng claimed that the transfer to Khartoum was "a trap in order that the Northern troops might have a free hand to do what they like with your wives and children, and you will be killed in Khartoum yourselves."[111] The government in Khartoum was indeed disguising its motives in transferring Southern soldiers to the North for their participation in celebrating Sudan's independence on January 1, 1956. The reality was that it wanted the soldiers removed from the South in order to permanently deploy them in the North to prevent the possibility of a Southern armed rebellion that might lead to secession.[112]

While the political and military situation in the South grew more serious, life in Khartoum continued normally. In fact, on August 16 the Sudanese government "voted unanimously in favor of the evacuation of foreign troops to start the process of self-determination—which in the present frame of mind of the Sudanese people means nothing less than complete independence and full sovereignty." To a crowd of about thirty thousand gathered outside the parliament, El-Azhari asserted that "the Sudan [has] asked for its liberty and it [has] been granted." Proudly he noted, "Never before [has] a nation obtained freedom so easily."[113]

The plans of the Sudan government to evacuate the children and wives of Northern Sudanese soldiers in the South further contributed to the hostile political and military situation there. According to Wani, who was returning from a scout camp in Britain, a Sudan Airways airplane was chartered by the Sudan army to transport Northern troops from Khartoum to Juba on August 16. He was fortunate to board a mail truck to Rumbek on August 17 since the mutiny began the following day.[114] Certainly, the El-Azhari government was flexing its military muscle in the South in the event of a political or military crisis.

At the same time, members of the Equatoria Corps at Torit were preparing to take action. The Southern public and members of the organized forces were becoming increasingly suspicious and hostile toward any Northern political or military designs. As early as October 1954, following El-Azhari's ill-fated visit to Juba, Daniel Tongun and Marko Rume, a Kuku politician, began holding discussions in meetings and by correspondence about the possibility of organizing a widespread rebellion in the South. According to Tongun, there was a general consensus among the soldiers in the Southern garrisons of Equatoria, Bahr al-Ghazal, and Upper Nile that if the Southern region was marginalized in discussions pertaining to their future aspirations, they would refuse to be transferred to the North.[115] The Southern politicians and soldiers of the Equatoria

Corps were realizing that the only option left for them was the use of force.[116]

Meanwhile at Torit, four Southern NCOs—Lance Corporals Mutek, Akeo, and Lubega, and Corporal Matiang—held a series of meetings.[117] Their original plan was to provoke widespread disturbances in all the major garrison towns of Sudan with the aim of getting rid of the Northern troops and Arab merchants and asserting independence for the South.[118] They hatched an even more grandiose plan as well to enlist the help of British troops in Kenya. Because good cooperation had existed between the Torit garrison and the King's African Rifle (KAR) of East Africa in the early years of the Anglo-Egyptian Condominium,[119] the plotters thought the British troops would readily come to their assistance in the event of a mutiny against the Sudanese army in Southern Sudan.[120]

According to Tongun, the two master plans for the mutiny were handed to Rume, who at the time was a bookkeeper and cashier for the Equatoria Corps garrison in Torit. He subsequently delivered them to Tongun. In Tongun's view, the plans for the mutiny were well-conceived, though they required wider coordination efforts. For that reason he cautioned the soldiers at Torit against their premature execution. In a letter to the Equatoria Corps NCOs who had masterminded the plan, he advised them to wait for the return of key Southern members of parliament, like Benjamin Lwoki and Buth Dui Thung (who were in Khartoum at the time), to brief them about the political situation in the country before staging the rebellion.[121]

The Mutiny Unfolds

Events ran ahead of the politicians. On August 18, when the Southern troops in Torit were told to embark on trucks destined for Juba, subsequently to be transported to Khartoum by steamer, they rejected all orders. They then attacked the Northern officers and broke into the armory to secure arms and ammunition. The Southern soldiers shot and killed the Northern officers, burned their houses, and looted their property.[122] On the same day, about 190 Southern troops mutinied at the Southern towns of Juba, Yei, Yambio, and Meridi. In the first wave of disturbances in the three Southern provinces, seventy-five Southerners and 361 Northerners lost their lives.[123]

Messages were now exchanged between Torit and Nairobi in Kenya. The first garbled message of the mutineers wired by Corporal Martirio Lokita of No. 3 Signals stated: "I have to report to you that troops Torit is now break down. Repeat. Troops is now badly break down. We need your most urgent help. We are lack of weapons and ammunitions. Please they got their troops Haggana have now taken Juba and no transport for Istiwa Torit to go to attack them conditions fair in Torit. Juba conditions bad."[124]

This telegram did not receive a prompt reply. In desperate need of heavy weapons and ammunition, and amid the deteriorating situation in Torit, the mutineers sent four more telegrams to Nairobi. British surprise and concern about the military situation at Torit were finally expressed in a telegram to the mutineers:

> References your messages to Likitaung. It is now understood from reports received in Khartoum that you have mutinied. This is most serious crime, which British consider, is very wrong and you can expect no repeat no help from the British. They are very sorry to hear you have done this and they advise you to stop your mutiny. They advise you to warn all other troops to stop also. You should get in touch with the Sudanese Government by any possible means. British are sure that a fair and full enquiry will be made. From British troops Sudan. Please acknowledge this signal. Nairobi.[125]

On August 19, the office of the governor general in Khartoum sent an emergency confidential telegraph to the Foreign Office in Cairo, explaining the deterioration of the security situation in Western Equatoria, especially in Yei, Yambio, and Meridi, where communications had been cut. It indicated that Southern soldiers in Meridi had mutinied and that civilians were being assaulted, and asserted that the governors of Wau and Malakal urgently needed troops from Southern Sudan to assist them. The message noted there were six companies of Northern troops that could be deployed in the South, but Sudan Airways alone could not rapidly transport them there. The commanding officer of the Royal Air Force was urged to secure the help of the Middle East Air Force to provide seven airplanes, while the Foreign Office in Cairo was requested to exert much effort to acquire these aircraft. The telegraph concluded that four more companies needed to be flown to Juba to protect the lives of British officials, other foreigners, and Northern Sudanese who lived outside Juba.[126]

On August 20 and August 21, a Southern officers' plan was put to troops of the Equatoria Corps to attack Northern troops at Juba and Mongalla with military assistance from the KAR in Uganda. This military plan was separate from that of Torit. Lieutenant Albino Tongun was ordered to command two companies to Ngangala (twenty miles from Juba), where a contingent of the KAR from Nimule (on the Sudan-Uganda border) was based. The failure of this plan caused more panic and despair.[127] The mutineers had engaged in wishful thinking.

The situation was a matter of grave concern to Prime Minister El-Azhari, who immediately dispatched a telegram to the troops at Torit:

> By your mutiny you have made a very serious crime. But I want to make it clear to you all and to give you my personal guarantee and word of honor that if you put down your arms now and surrender to the Sudanese a full and fair investigation will be made about the causes of the mutiny and each one of you will be given full opportunity to explain reasons for his actions. If you are ready to do this I will arrange for two or three representatives of the Sudanese Government to meet two or three representatives of you at the place on Juba Torit road which will be explained to you in a further message. The representatives of each side will move to the meeting place under white flags. When they meet they will discuss the arrangements of your surrender. Please acknowledge the receipt of this message immediately and then send your full reply within twenty-four hours.[128]

This message was rejected outright by the mutineers. Instead of surrendering, they demanded that the government order the evacuation of the Northern troops from Juba to the North. An exchange of telegrams between the prime minister and the Southern troops at Juba and Torit yielded nothing. Suspicious of Northern treachery, the mutineers suggested involvement of the United Nations.[129]

The British governor general, Sir Alexander Knox Helm, still head of state and commander in chief, now ordered the Royal Air Force to airlift Northern troops to Juba, while sending T. W. H. Luce, a former deputy governor of Equatoria, with a message to the Southern troops asking for their surrender and promising that "justice would take its course."[130]

Royal Air Force planes now transported eight thousand Northern troops to the South to crush the revolt and restore security.[131] Although the mandate of the Anglo-Egyptian forces in Sudan had expired, this military assistance was based on three considerations: "To reaffirm British consistency with the Anglo-Egyptian Agreement of 1953, and to safeguard British interests in the Suez Canal. . . . To ensure a lasting British influence on an independent Sudan. To avoid the emergence, at the time, of an independent African State in the South adjoining the British East African Territories, hence, avoiding the dangers of her influence on them."[132]

The large number of Northern troops in Juba was instrumental in enforcing the terms of surrender. The governor general also sent the mutineers a message similar to the prime minister's, "I give you my guarantee that if you surrender peacefully, the Northern troops will do you no, repeat no, harm when they take you under arrest." The governor general's message carried more weight than the prime minister's, for it made clear that the mutineers could expect no British assistance. And so on August 27, the rebels surrendered to Northern troops at Torit.[133] The following day near the Nile ferry, representatives of the government troops and the Equatoria Corps in Mongalla also concluded an agreement for surrender. On August 31, Northern troops entered Torit to find that those mutineers who had refused to surrender had fled. Two policemen, some medical personnel, and some surviving Northern soldiers were all the Northern relief force encountered.

The surrender agreement of August 30 was received with mixed feelings by the mutineers. Some took the governor general's orders seriously and laid down their arms, while others refused. In essence, the Southern troops split up. Those who surrendered believed they would be forgiven for their actions, but contrary to their expectations, they were arrested. Three hundred were hurriedly tried and sentenced to death by firing squad. Their summary execution brought the total of Southern dead to 355. Meanwhile, those who disobeyed the order fled to the hills on the Uganda-Sudan border where, with their meager arms and ammunition, they became insurgents.[134]

Causes of the Torit Mutiny and Reasons for Its Failure

The 1955 disturbances were the result of the accumulated frustration and fears of a very long period. In the words of Bona Malwal, "The northerners' attitude toward the south and the inferior treatment given to the south made the social distance between the two sections grow so great."[135]

According to Joseph Lagu, Sudanization as pursued by Prime Minister El-Azhari (while the British governor general was still in the Sudan) was one immediate cause of the Torit mutiny. During the period between self-government and independence, the "Southerners saw floods of Northern Sudanese coming to the South to take the positions generally held by the British. . . . Southerners saw this as neo-colonialism, not independence."[136]

Another factor was the conflict between El-Azhari and the Egyptians. El-Azhari had won election with the help of Egyptian money, but instead of conforming to the "unity of the Nile Valley," he opted for independence. According to Lagu, this enraged the Egyptians, who "fanned the trouble among Southern MPs . . . which led to the mutiny of 1955. . . . Agitation from Egypt and disappointment from the Southern Sudanese is the cause of the 1955 mutiny in Torit!"[137] Clement Mboro confirms Lagu's statement that Egyptian officials in the South campaigned against El-Azhari's government, which was leaning heavily toward self-government and independence for Sudan. According to Mboro, when he was district commissioner in Tonj in Bahr al-Ghazal prior to Sudan's independence, Egyptian officials had encouraged Southerners to kill the Northerners in their territory.[138]

The failure of the mutiny also had its roots in several other factors. Chief among them was the slowness of the British in developing the South. If Southern Sudan had a well-developed infrastructure, the planning, coordination, timing, and outcome of the Torit mutiny might have been different. When the mutiny broke out, the soldiers of the Equatoria Corps were unable to effectively and efficiently communicate with their counterparts in the Equatoria Corps garrisons in Wau, Bahr al-Ghazal, and Malakal, Upper Nile. They relied on telegram equipment unable to transmit enormous amounts of information rapidly. Telephone equipment was nonexistent in the South, let alone radios. In general, the road network throughout the South was not well developed. The flood plains in Bahr al-Ghazal and Upper Nile presented obstacles for trucks, especially during the rainy season when all seasonal roads were covered with water and bridges were damaged or washed away. Also of importance is that the soldiers of the Equatoria Corps and politicians like Tongun and Rume who planned the mutiny had to rely primarily on messages delivered by hand, which in turn depended on the departure and return of trucks between towns, from Juba to Torit and back.

The Torit mutiny was also impeded by the limited development of administration and an educated class under British rule. Planning, coordinating, and executing a rebellion against a government with its financial resources and military forces at its disposal any time also required intelligence, vision, courage, and willpower on the part of the Southern Sudanese, but all the educated Southerners were scattered throughout the three Southern provinces and so were not available at one particular time to plan the Torit mutiny together. It was clear that educated political activists like Tongun and Rume risked their lives on behalf of the Southerners to work collaboratively with the soldiers of the Equatoria Corps in Torit to organize a rebellion.[139] When the mutiny in Torit occurred, the South had fewer than ten trained administrators. This number was not only too small, but the administrators were trained too late to have any profound impact on the political mobilization of the Southern masses or the planning and coordination of the rebellion throughout the South.

Moreover, the earlier British administration had essentially divided the Southern region into administrative units at the district and provincial levels. Officials had made no attempt to encourage the movement of ethnic groups from one territorial space to another. This meant that old rivalries or hostilities between neighboring ethnic groups persisted. And so the various Southern ethnic groups, who remained largely illiterate, had no sense of a common nationalist perspective or political aspirations for an independent Southern Sudan at the start of the mutiny.

In addition, Sudanization as it applied to the military greatly hampered the revolt. Most soldiers in the Equatoria Corps belonged to the rank and file. There were only a handful of NCOs and only a few Southerners who had been promoted to the rank of lieutenant.[140] Thus Southern soldiers were not very knowledgeable about the command-and-control structures of the Sudan Defence Force—Northern Sudanese officers had a complete grip on these military structures as well as communication and transportation.

Another important factor was that in the early years of British colonial administration in the South, British officers in the KAR had been borrowed to serve in the region.[141] The cooperation that had existed between the Equatoria Corps and the KAR gave the mutineers in Torit the impression that the latter would come to their aid in the event of a rebellion against the Sudan government. This is clearly evident in the telegram that the mutineers sent to the British colonial officials in Nairobi. But this was simply an illusion.

* * *

The first Southern attempt to secure its independence from the North by the use of force had ended in failure and tragedy, but the desire for self-determination was not quenched. The mutineers who refused to surrender to Sudan's security forces fled into the bushes and mountains of Southern Sudan to organize an insurgency movement that would wage a liberation war against the Sudan government for seventeen years. For their part, the Southern members of the Constituent Assembly in Khartoum had consistently demanded federal status as the basis for attaining self-determination for the people of the Southern Sudan, and they wanted to achieve this goal peacefully instead of through use of arms.

On December 19, 1955, Prime Minister El-Azhari introduced a motion in the Constituent Assembly "calling for an immediate independence for the Sudan." The resolution that was adopted to this effect was "promptly recognized by Britain and Egypt."[142] Governor General Knox Helm was not there to witness it: shortly after ordering the airlift of Northern troops, "suddenly the Governor General asked to [go] for the holidays ... from which he never returned." He stayed in Britain.[143] On January 1, 1956, Sudan achieved its independence.

CHAPTER 3

LEGACY OF THE FAILED MUTINY

GOVERNMENT REPRESSION AND RISE OF THE RESISTANCE MOVEMENT

IMMEDIATE AFTERMATH OF THE FAILED MUTINY

THE MUTINY OF THE EQUATORIA CORPS ON AUGUST 18, 1955, against the Northern Sudanese officers and men at Torit marked the beginning of North-South hostilities. The mutiny was the culmination of frustration after many years of discrimination by Northern Sudanese officials. Southern grievances were compounded by the Sudanese government's refusal to grant federal status to the South. It was in light of these circumstances that the people of Southern Sudan took up arms to fight for self-determination.

The conspiracy to mutiny at Torit had been conceived mainly among Latuko soldiers of the Equatoria Corps. Although a few soldiers of the Nile East Bank ethnic groups participated, they were not as active as the Latuko. As a result, soldiers stationed at Wau, the capital of Bahr al-Ghazal, and Malakal, the capital of Upper Nile, were not part of the initial plan to revolt. Thus, when Northern troops suppressed the mutiny, the Latuko suffered most: many were arrested, tortured, and executed. In fact, of all the people prosecuted on the East Bank in Equatoria, 66 percent were Latuko; most Latuko had family members who were arrested and imprisoned or executed after the mutiny. This provided the impetus for organizing a guerrilla movement whose primary aim was to avenge the dead, as well as to assert independence for the people of Southern Sudan.[1]

In Equatoria, particularly at Yei and Kajo-Kaji, people received news of the mutiny at Torit with bitterness, and the Kakwa and the Kuku were motivated to take up arms—spears, bows, and arrows—against Sudanese policemen, prison guards, and particularly Arab merchants. A few Northern Sudanese policemen at Yei were killed by Southern Sudanese policemen. When the news arrived at Kajo-Kaji, panic spread throughout the community. The Kuku viewed armed rebellion by Southerners as an attempt to rid themselves of Arab political, economic, and religious subjection. A few Kuku men attacked Arab merchants in their shops. Some merchants were wounded but managed to escape to Moyo in Uganda. The enraged Kuku mob burned the Arab merchants' houses and stores.[2]

As in other parts of the South, here the Sudanese government urged the soldiers of the Equatoria Corps, Southern policemen, and prison guards to surrender, assuring them of safe haven. And so those who had mutinied at Torit, as well as the policemen and prison warders at Yei and Kajo-Kaji who had killed a few Arab merchants and policemen, surrendered. The government distributed leaflets by airplane in Kajo-Kaji granting amnesty to the Kuku, and the Kuku policemen were urged to assemble in Yei town to demonstrate their allegiance to the government.[3]

In good faith, the Kuku policemen agreed to surrender at the government police post at Yei, but when they had assembled, the Sudanese security forces fired upon them. Many died on the spot, and only a few managed to escape. Some Kuku civilians who owned a few shops at Kajo-Kaji were arrested, taken to Khartoum, and sentenced to prison terms ranging from six to eight years for not having rescued or shown sympathy to the Arab merchants when the Kuku mob raided their stores.[4]

Although news of the Torit mutiny quickly reached the soldiers of the Equatoria Corps at Wau and Malakal, they did not consider it a matter of grave concern. At first they believed the mutiny was only a "Latuko/Arab problem," but when the Northern troops who were flown to the South to suppress the rebellion harassed the Southerners, "civilians lost confidence and became alert and ripe for revolution."[5]

In Bahr al-Ghazal, news of the Torit mutiny and its subsequent suppression caused Northern authorities and security forces to panic. For example, in October Clement Mboro, assistant district commissioner of Yirol, and another Southern administrative official were arrested and transported to Wau. There Mboro was accused of conspiring to kill the Northerners in his jurisdiction; he had been brought to Wau in particular "to show the people" that he was an agitator. Mboro and his colleague were tried and found guilty of conspiracy to kill the Arabs in Yirol. Although Mboro argued that the allegations against him were unfounded as he had himself helped accommodate the families of Arab merchants who were frightened by the deteriorating security situation in Equatoria and Bahr al-Ghazal, the authorities in Wau did not consider his arguments convincing enough to judge him innocent. He was sentenced to three months and his colleague to two years. They were transferred to Kobar Prison in Khartoum to serve their jail term; there Mboro hired a defense attorney, who secured his release in February 1956.[6]

Following the surrender and subsequent arrest of the mutineers of the Equatoria Corps, an investigation by the Sudan Defense Force discovered the names of Daniel Jumi Tongun and Marko Rume in a telegram containing a complete plan of the mutiny sent to Juba, Wau, and Malakal by the soldiers in Torit. This evidence led to their arrest, as well as that of several soldiers of the Equatoria Corps.[7]

The Northern Sudanese security forces searched the houses of Tongun and Rume looking for more documents or evidence that would further implicate them in the mutiny. Although they were imprisoned in Juba, Northern Sudanese officials in Torit who had come to Juba demanded they be transported to Torit for more thorough investigation, especially since they had been identified as key conspirators of the mutiny. When news of their arrest spread in Juba, eight hundred civilians protested, expressing their grievances against the Sudan government in a mass demonstration. This was the first and biggest demonstration ever organized by the Southerners in Juba, and it caused great commotion that frightened government officials as well as the local Arab merchants.[8] The police fired tear gas at the demonstrators to disperse them, but fearing the demonstration might get out of control and the security situation in Juba deteriorate further, government officials abandoned the idea of sending Tongun and Rume to Torit.[9]

Alarmed at the military situation in the South, government security forces arrested an additional seventeen hundred Southerners, including all tailors and Southern businessmen who owned small grocery stores. These people were chained and transported to Khartoum for further interrogation. The tailors questioned the purpose of their interrogation, wondering if tailors had ever overthrown a government. Tongun and Rume were interrogated more thoroughly than the others. As he later recalled, in his testimony Tongun asserted, "We don't like you. My plan would have been to order the Southern Sudanese soldiers to capture the airstrips in Torit, Juba, Bahr al-Ghazal, and Upper Nile so that no government airplane would land. We would then capture the steamer, and then declare our intention to secede from you [Northerners]. We are not politicians nor do we know politics. . . . We do not like you at all—we cannot forget the atrocities that you committed against our ancestors. If it means death, so be it!"[10]

The interrogator in Khartoum acknowledged Tongun's frankness and honesty and urged the authorities to return him to Juba. Hassan Bashri, a Northerner who had brought Tongun, Rume, and other Southerners to Khartoum for interrogation, was informed by the judge that he should return Tongun and the other accused Southerners to Juba. When he informed the authorities in Juba of this arrangement, they refused out of fear that the civilians in Juba might organize further demonstrations in support of the accused Southerners. They wanted large numbers of Northern troops to be deployed to Juba first.[11]

Thus, Tongun, Rume, and the other accused Southerners were returned to Juba only after Northern troops had been deployed and the arrested Equatorial Corps mutineers had arrived there as well. The 1,750 Southerners who were returned to Juba were provided accommodation at Roton Camp, a few miles to the north. There Tongun and Rume were subjected to further interrogation. About ten to twenty of the accused were brought before the interrogators to testify against them, but all of them told the interrogators frankly that they did not know the two accused and were unaware of their implication in the mutiny. Owing to the lack of credible evidence against Tongun and Rume, the interrogators recommended that the governor of Equatoria Province release them. The police commander in Juba granted them permission to have access to defense lawyers, of whom one from Khartoum determined they were not guilty of conspiracy and treason. Nevertheless, they languished in prison several months before being released.[12]

CONTINUED SUPPRESSION OF THE SOUTH BY THE NORTH

The suppression of the mutiny did not end the hostility between the North and South. The Sudanese security forces continued to employ a variety of repressive measures against Southerners: "intimidation, burning, prison, public execution and arbitrary arrests . . . aimed at instilling awe of Arab power in the minds of Southerners."[13] All kinds of torture were "inflicted on prisoners daily throughout the South in an attempt to extract false evidence, and about twenty thousand Southerners were transported to the Northern prisons for hard labor, with prison terms ranging from a few years to life imprisonment."[14] This political upheaval in the South would eventually force about thirty thousand people to flee to Uganda, Kenya, the Belgian Congo, and the Central African Republic.[15]

Northern Sudanese troops traveling from Juba to Wau "mistreated and tortured the civilians" upon their arrival at Wau.[16] They set houses on fire at Kpaile, arrested and tortured the local inhabitants, destroyed crops, and confiscated animals. Such brutal measures were also adopted in Upper Nile Province.[17] At Malakal, Northern paratroopers attacked the police and prison headquarters, and fighting with Southern policemen and prison guards continued for a day. No. 4 Company of the Equatoria Corps had already been transported by steamer from Malakal without knowledge of the mutiny.[18]

Sudanese troops and administrators were determined to reestablish a firm grip on the Southern provinces. Northern Sudanese troops occupied every military garrison or post that had been previously occupied by the Equatoria Corps. By October 1955, the Equatoria Corps had been eliminated; some soldiers were imprisoned, some were executed, and others escaped into the mountains and forests. Many Southerners fled to Uganda and Ethiopia. Northern Sudanese troops, police, and prison guards, vowing to prevent any future insurrection, replaced Southern police and prison guards.[19]

This occupation of Southern Sudan by Northern Sudanese troops marked the inauguration of a reign of terror. They intimidated, tortured, and killed Southerners arbitrarily without regard for guilt or innocence. Northern Sudanese schoolteachers were given firearms, while Southerners were refused weapons. Southern officials were dismissed or imprisoned on mere suspicion or without cause. Southern Sudanese were constantly humiliated by Northern administrators, soldiers, police, and merchants who referred to them as *abid* (slaves). Northern Sudanese troops, police, and traders raped Southern women but refused to appear before traditional courts.[20]

In 1957, in the town of Yei in Equatoria, police and soldiers raided homes in a single day and burned about seven hundred houses; about ten thousand houses were set ablaze in the same year by Sudanese security forces in the South. Southern politicians lived in fear of intimidation, arrest, and possible execution.[21]

As a further demonstration to Southern Sudanese that a united and independent Sudan did not mean equality between the two peoples, African and Arab, the Southern mutineers of August 1955 were not released from prison in the general amnesty accompanying Independence Day, January 1, 1956. Conditions for amnesty were stipulated thus: "Criminals in prison for life will be let out if they have served 10 years, those in for 10 years if they have served five years, and sentences of four years or less will be reduced to as many months. . . . Those convicted under semi-political sections of the penal code—contempt of the Government, injurious falsehood, and the like—will be absolutely discharged."[22] Although these conditions were to apply to all Sudanese regardless of race, religion, gender, and ideology, Southerners considered them nothing but rhetoric. Prime Minister Ismail el-Azhari stated that the "amnesty only applied to those sentenced before August 16." Thus, all Southerners who were tried after the August 18 disturbances were excluded. This injustice further increased fears about the Northern Sudanese Arabs in the future independent Sudan.[23]

The two years following Sudan's independence witnessed no improvements in Southern social, economic, or political life. Rather, this was a period of continued hardship under an Arab-dominated government. In the 1954 Sudanization Program, Southerners had felt openly cheated in the posts left vacant by British civil servants, police, and the army. After independence, the situation did not change for the better. Southerners were "discriminated [against] in all jobs whether government or private.... The few that are employed are subjected to humiliating conditions."[24] In fact, some types of jobs were reserved for Northern Sudanese Arabs only. In the Foreign Ministry and the Employment and Selection Boards, not a single Southerner could be found. These discriminatory practices were spelled out by a "liberal Northern Arab" (who had lived in Southern Sudan) in a letter to a Sudanese newspaper published on September 11, 1957: "The legacy of the Northerners is a great enterprise and to my great sorrow, very few understand it. Here [in the South] the Northerner is either a governor or a merchant; they look for gain, a dirty gain, and drink the blood of naked bodies as if they were half English ... and the young employee is addicted to satiate his instinct to spread corruption among people who are ignorant; this is the condition of the Northerner except for a few by the mercy of God."[25]

POLITICAL AND ECONOMIC CONDITIONS BEFORE THE MILITARY TAKEOVER

As noted in the previous chapter, before and after Sudan's independence, politics were dominated by the two major Northern parties: the Umma Party and the National Unionist Party (NUP). Some background knowledge of these two parties is vital to understanding the nature of Sudanese politics and the rise and fall of successive governments in the post-independent era. The two parties "used expediency and maneuver to capture office.... Both Parties used state power and state resources in much the same way to enrich a small group of the privileged, and the religious allegiance held by each party helped to mystify the process to the masses."[26]

The Umma Party, which had favored independence from Britain and Egypt, had its foundation firmly established in the "House of the Mahdi." It was affiliated with the Ansar sect and attracted its followers largely from the Western region of Darfur as well as the "Arabs" who owned land along the White Nile. The members of the Ansar sect formed the private army of the Umma Party, providing it with political support and security. They could be quickly mobilized for warfare if the need arose. Meanwhile, the "Arab" landed proprietors along the White Nile served as the legitimate religious leaders of both the sect and the political party.[27] The party also secured a financial package from the World Bank for its land owners along the White Nile, who had become an integral part of the cotton growing schemes. These financial resources enabled them to engage in commercial investment and also to participate in the modern sector of the Sudanese economy.[28]

The NUP, which had originally favored unity with Egypt and was affiliated with the Khatmiyya sect (a Sufi religious order), drew its adherents primarily from the "Arab" communities in the Northern provinces and the Kassala region of Eastern Sudan. Prior to Sudan's independence, these people were farmers who settled in villages and subsequently became town dwellers. Many were traders, and at the advent of independence they became a privileged class. They had access to capital investment and consequently became an integral part of Sudan's modern economic sector. The NUP supported entrepreneurship among its followers, who gradually benefited from foreign investment in Sudan.[29]

Meanwhile in the South, economic development was nonexistent both before and after independence. There were no industrial or agricultural projects capable of generating revenue for the indigenous people. Southern Sudanese had no access to capital investment, let alone the acquisition of entrepreneurial skills. Thus, the entire Southern economy came to be dominated by Northern Sudanese traders who mainly belonged to the two commercial groups affiliated with the Umma Party and the NUP. Many Southerners migrated to the North to seek employment and better economic opportunities. There, their cheap labor was exploited.[30]

The Western region of Sudan was no different from the South. Douglas H. Johnson argues that the successive governments of Sudan deliberately did not develop the peripheral areas of the country so that large populations could be displaced to provide migrant workers for the large agricultural schemes in the Northern and Eastern regions of Sudan. Moreover, during British administration of the country, infrastructure had been built only in areas that had viable economic resources, such as the railway lines from Khartoum to Port Sudan along the Red Sea, and to Wau in Bahr al-Ghazal.[31]

The South Withdraws from the Government

While conditions deteriorated, Southern assembly members continued their demand for a federal system of government. The Commission of Inquiry formed after the 1955 mutiny found that "the Southern Army revolt was the final outburst after the Southern political claims had been frustrated."[32] Southerners inside and outside the assembly became increasingly vocal, threatening "to break away if their demand for federation was not accepted."[33] Although the governing NUP and virtually all Northern Sudanese political parties ostensibly agreed to the Southern demand,[34] the Northern parties were more preoccupied with important issues concerning Sudan's independence than with a federal system of government. A motion introduced by Southern assembly members obliged the Northern parties to agree that federation would "be fully considered" by the Constituent Assembly after independence. This motion seemed to reassure naïve Southern politicians, and assembly members of all political parties voted unanimously for the motion on December 19, 1955.[35]

After independence the Southern demand for federation was totally ignored by the Northern parties. In December 1956, El-Azhari formed a National Committee of forty-six members to draft the first Sudanese constitution; it included only three Southern members, who were overwhelmed by the Northerners.[36] In December 1957, after a year of political wrangling, the Southern representatives finally withdrew from the National Committee. The Northern representatives were only too happy to continue and declared: "The Sudan is a unitary Parliamentary Democratic Republic . . . Islam is the official religion of the state . . . [and] Arabic is the official language of the state."[37]

While parliamentary arguments provoked more tension, social and economic conditions did not improve. Southerners in Khartoum began to experience discrimination in public clubs, which previously had been fully shared. Northern Arab merchants flooded the South and "got [an] absolute economic monopoly."[38] Then, on January 18, 1958, the census results from 1956 were finally published and indicated that Southerners constituted about 30 percent of the country's population. In a further injustice to Southerners, the Southern political parties represented only 26 percent of the total seats in the assembly.[39]

In the 1958 elections, Southerners were determined to elect representatives capable of confronting the Northern politicians without fear of favor.[40] As Bona Malwal notes, "The 1958 Southern representatives were a group more united in their cause and more determined to achieve the southern rights."[41] This determination was frustrated when the Northern parties violated the electoral laws, with Northern administrators supporting Arab candidates in Southern constituencies.⁴² Cypriano Koryang testified to age discrimination in Kapoeta. In 1953, he had been disqualified because, at age twenty-eight, he was under the "prescribed age" of thirty: the same grounds were cited for excluding him five years later in 1958. His opponent, an Arab merchant, was elected "unopposed."⁴³

Despite these obstacles, Southerners managed to win a total of thirty-six seats. Twenty-five of the new parliamentary members proceeded to set up the Southern Bloc, while the remaining eleven "remained uncommitted or independent."⁴⁴ Father Saturnino Lohure, who had run as an independent, was nominated by the Southern Bloc to head the Liberal Party parliamentary group.

Meanwhile in the North, the Umma Party under Abdalla Khalil won sixty-three seats, the People's Democratic Party (PDP) twenty-seven, and the NUP forty-five. Because the Umma Party did not have a majority, it was obliged to form a coalition with the PDP.⁴⁵ During the election campaign, Northern politicians had demonstrated their political sophistication and arrogance in various ways. The Kapoeta incident was one such example. In another, Ali Abdel Rahman, who would later become interior minister in Khalil's government, stated, "Sudan is an integral part of the Arab world and as such must accept the leadership of the two Islamic religious leaders of the Sudan; anybody dissenting from this view must quit the country."⁴⁶

Rahman's attitude toward the South was reflected in May 1958 when the Northern politicians "troubled [sic] their unitary and Islamic Constitution for approval⁴⁷" by the new parliament. The Southern MPs, dissatisfied and disgruntled with Northern political manipulation, walked out of the parliament in protest. Although the Northerners succeeded in persuading the Southerners to return, the latter agreed only to explain the reasons for their walkout. On June 16, Father Saturnino voiced the concerns of the Southerners:

> The South has no ill-intentions whatsoever towards the North; the South simply claims to run its local affairs in a united Sudan. The South has no intentions of separating from the North, for had that been the case, nothing on earth would prevent the demand for separation. The South claims to federate with the North, a right which the South no doubt possesses as a determination which reason and democracy grant to a free people. The South will at any moment separate from the North if and when the North so desires directly or indirectly, through political, social and economic subjection of the South.⁴⁸

Father Saturnino's speech to the parliament marked the end of formal Southern participation in discussion of the nation's political, economic, and social problems. Withdrawal of the Southern MPs also had a profound impact on political activism in the Eastern and Western Sudan, where people began to demand "more say in their local affairs and less subjection to Khartoum."[49] These developments worried the Northern political parties, which now saw them as a threat to Arab control of the new Sudanese government. "The fear of a possible rally of the indigenous African populations to press for a federal status provoked much uneasiness" to the point that the "government's foundations were shaken."[50]

THE MILITARY TAKEOVER OF GENERAL ABBOUD

From September to November 1958, political developments in Northern Sudan worked against the government of Abdalla Khalil. The coalition of the Umma Party and the PDP was fragile, particularly because the Umma Party was seeking to turn Sudan into an Islamic kingdom and make its spiritual leader, Abdel Rahman el Mahdi, king. The economy was on the verge of collapse, and demonstrations broke out in Khartoum in October. Siricio Iro, a member of the Liberal Party and the only Southerner appointed to the Supreme Commission (the collective head of state), described the financial situation thus, "Most of the Government's services were being paid out of money which had originally been borrowed from foreign countries for development schemes, and neither the beginning of these schemes nor the repayment of these loans was in sight. If nothing happens to change the situation we shall not be able to pay for our services in the next month or two."[51]

The army was not oblivious to these developments. As economic conditions deteriorated, General Ibrahim Abboud, commander in chief of the army, announced that "the army . . . would not stand by to allow the country to collapse."[52] These statements were ominous to the Sudanese, "who had hitherto disassociated the army from politics."[53] Abboud had seen the country's economy declining dramatically and attributed that largely to the weakness of Khalil's administration. Above all, he was opposed to possible federal status for Southern Sudan.[54]

Prime Minister Khalil, realizing his government was in a difficult political and economic position, chose to hand power over to the military, which was composed almost entirely of Northerners with almost all Arab officers. On November 17, 1958, the army under General Abboud took power in a bloodless coup.[55]

According to Oliver Albino, the military "takeover was calculated to prevent Southerners from making the demand for federal constitution—a demand which also quickly spread in the North among indigenous non-Arab tribes."[56] For his part, Gordon Muortat Mayen did not consider the army's intervention in political issues justified, arguing that if Khalil's government had exerted more effort to solicit support from the thirty-six Southern representatives, he might have stayed in power—though with concessions to the Southerners.[57]

General Abboud now decreed a state of emergency throughout Sudan and set up a military government. He became acting prime minister, president, and commander in chief of the Sudan Armed Forces. The five-man Supreme Council that had existed in Khalil's administration was disbanded and replaced with a new Supreme Council of the Armed Forces, which comprised thirteen military officers and held legislative, executive, and judicial powers.[58] The parliament was dissolved and the 1956 interim constitution suspended indefinitely.

The military coup was well received by Northern Sudanese, who had lost their confidence in the politicians and yearned for political stability and economic prosperity. The general belief in the North was that "that the army would . . . silence the South with an iron hand."[59] Many considered the takeover as "the last bulwark against . . . Southern claims. It put an end to any negotiated settlement in the Sudan and also to the Sudan becoming a multi-racial state."[60]

Southern Sudanese, on the other hand, did not receive the military takeover well, considering it a "slap on many a Southerner face."[61] The future of the South in a united Sudan now looked bleak indeed.[62] Southerners had genuine concerns and fears under General Abboud's military rule, whose policy they saw as being:

> . . . to keep the South in a united Sudan at all costs irrespective of means used . . . Not to develop the South while their [sic] is still certainty that it may break away . . . To break the link between Southern intelligentsia with the Southern public, by keeping the former in the North and carefully watching those in the South . . . Keeping Southerners out of defense and security forces as much as possible, meanwhile no effort is spared in finding a fault with those who had joined these forces before the outbreak of the 1955 revolt and immediately thinning them out . . . Forcing the Arab culture and ways of life . . . Keeping the South out of contact with the outside world.[63]

This statement reflected Southern Sudanese fears about the new military regime of General Abboud. Indeed, Abboud appeared determined to implement his new policy in the South by all means necessary to achieve his goals. Southerners now had to figure out ways and means to contain the general's arrogance and military might in the South. They had only one of two alternatives left before them, "to resort to violence in order to force a solution, or . . . to submit to the Arab political slavery, economic exploitation and denial of human rights."[64] The August 1955 mutiny had demonstrated that the time had come for Southerners to use force. Thus, Southerners realized that their only option left was to meet force with force.

THE GUERRILLA MOVEMENT BEGINS TO TAKE SHAPE IN EASTERN EQUATORIA

The guerrilla movement that rose from the aftermath of the August 1955 Torit mutiny did not start from scratch. As early as October that year, those soldiers of the Equatoria Corps as well as policemen and prison guards who had refused to surrender had begun attacking isolated military posts, especially in Eastern and Central Equatoria. For example, Lance Corporal Latada Helir, a prison guard at Lapon when the Torit disturbances broke out, grabbed two guns and fled to his village at Lopi, where he gave one to Lance Corporal Vincensio Heworu Lajok, a retired Southern soldier. Corporal John Itala, a Latuko with a box of ammunition and a rifle, joined the two combatants at Lopi.[65]

Aware that the army would pursue them, they and other colleagues fled to the mountains of Eastern Equatoria—some to Madok Mountain. From here Latada, Lajok, and other Latuko launched sporadic operations against Sudanese security forces. As Lajok described their first guerrilla activities:

> After three days Haggana [the camel corps] arrived in four vehicles asking for our whereabouts. They were told that we were at Madock (this was in October 1955) coming to Madock Lotada fired at them before they could encircle us. I and John Itita [Itira] opened fire on them. They ran away carrying their dead and wounded and left us on the mountain where we spent three days, after which we went and made our camp at Korokore Mountain in November 1955. There, some soldiers joined us. They were Lobulu (a policeman with a rifle) and Sgt. Lonyakwo Nyidong with his rifle and the prison warden called Marcelino with OLIKA. Now we have become of good strength and a good number of civilians associated with us.[66]

Joseph Lagu has corroborated Lajok's account of this first Southern military encounter with the Sudanese army. In addition to Latada and Marcelino, Lagu cites as other combatants on the East Bank of the Nile, Philipo from Torit, Lasuba at Yei, and Paul Yosia at Kajo-Kaji.[67] Latada and his followers continued their assaults on the security forces until he was killed in battle at Lobulo Mountain in Eastern Equatoria in November 1960. His death had a profound impact on guerrilla activities, and for almost three years the rebels made virtually no further raids on the army in Eastern Equatoria.[68]

Meanwhile, Lasuba and Yosia in the Yei/Kajo-Kaji area of Central Equatoria were as active as the rebels in Eastern Equatoria. The execution of Kakwa and Kuku policemen and prison guards at Koro'be Hill in Yei District after their surrender to the security forces was deeply resented throughout the Yei/Kajo-Kaji area. In Kajo-Kaji, the massacre at Koro'be Hill—and the burial alive of a Kuku soldier—rekindled memories of the Arab slave traders in the nineteenth century. According to Anya-Nya veteran Wojia Masiri, although the Kuku were determined to avenge the death of their relatives and friends, they had few firearms.[69]

Spears, bows, and arrows were plentiful but were no match for the firepower of the government's soldiers and policemen stationed at Kajo-Kaji. In an isolated incident there, Jeremiah Jale ambushed a Northern soldier, killed him, and took his gun. When Kuku freedom fighters attacked military and police posts at Kajo-Kaji for the first time on June 15, 1962, they had only a few rifles and ammunition,[70] but they set a precedent for armed struggle in the area against the security forces and Northern civilians. In 1962, the freedom fighters established a military camp at Murta, west of the town.[71] As in Eastern Equatoria, uncoordinated guerrilla activities in the Kajo-Kaji area continued until the founding of the Anya-Nya movement in August 1963.

In Eastern Equatoria, the suspension of military activities after the death of Latada Helir failed to shatter the hopes of the local population. In early 1963, guerrilla activities there were marked by renewed energy and vigor. Southern civilians, soldiers, policemen, and prison guards left their villages government employment, or military service to volunteer as guerrillas. In January, militants founded Agu Camp as the first base of operations for the Southern freedom fighters.[72]

Initially, there were twenty-four guerrillas at Agu, including Amadeo Taffeng, Lazarus Mutek, Marko, Lokuyiro, Beda Paul, Erodiene Lohuri Guzer, Bina Lokiata, and several others from the Latuko. Agu Camp was strategically located in an area easily accessible to the Latuko, Acholi, Madi, and other people in Eastern Equatoria. It was also close to the Uganda border and attracted Southern Sudanese refugees. By February, the number of volunteers had reached four hundred. This increased further as Southerners in the former Equatoria Corps, police, and prison forces defected to join the insurgents.

Eastern Equatoria had no shortage of manpower for the liberation movement; the majority of the Equatoria Corps had been recruited by the British from the Latuko and other small ethnic groups in Eastern Equatoria to balance the overwhelming numbers and warrior traditions of the Nilotic Dinka, Nuer, and Shilluk.[73] Southerners who returned from prison did not hesitate to join the liberation struggle. Their people supported them morally, financially, and—equally important—with food.[74] It was, therefore, in Eastern Equatoria that guerrilla activities began and from there they spread to other districts of the South.

SOUTHERN SUDANESE POLITICIANS FOUND AN UNDERGROUND RESISTANCE MOVEMENT

Meanwhile, an underground movement was being established in the Sudanese capital of Khartoum. Founded by Darius Bashir, the organization included Ezbon Mondiri, Lawrence Mama, George Otto, Akumbek Kwanai, Oliver Batali Albino, Isaiah Majok Akoc, and Natale Olwak. The primary function of this movement was to provide Southern MPs and politicians in exile with information. Although Southern politicians in exile may have been determined to engage in armed struggle against the Abboud regime, taking up arms was not a simple task for those without experience.[75]

Employing the most appropriate propaganda to appeal to the emotions of Southern Sudanese was of paramount importance.[76] The underground movement in Khartoum was instrumental in informing Southerners within the country about the general security situation. According to Gordon Muortat-Mayen, the aims of the movement were "to help people join the Anya-Nya, the Southern resistance movement, and also to politicize the population by informing them about what the war was all about."[77] In response, the Southerners in exile presented the following requests to the movement: "Stockpile information on resistance; Help organize the resistance; Give publicity to [the] cause and argue the case to the world."[78]

Albino Mathiang Thiep, who served as secretary for the underground movement in Bahr al-Ghazal in the late 1950s and early 1960s, also noted the aim "to secure funds for the movement, and help those convicted and enlighten the masses."[79] Members of the movement opened branches in Wau, Malakal, and Juba and raised funds. Despite the risks, in Bahr al-Ghazal about thirty thousand Sudanese pounds were collected to facilitate the flight of young students to neighboring countries, with the ultimate goal of organizing a liberation movement in exile In Northern Sudan, it was less dangerous to raise funds among resident Southerners. In fact, fund-raising in the North was very successful. Most of the money was used to recruit Southern youths to the resistance movement in exile, purchase food, and subsequently acquire arms.[80]

The underground movement in Khartoum was an effective organization whose achievements were impressive. It organized the Southern students' Sunday strike of 1960 and kept Southerners in Khartoum informed about imminent military confrontations between the rebels and the Sudanese army.[81]

SOUTHERN LEADERS IN EXILE CONCEIVE OF A GUERRILLA MOVEMENT

By the middle of 1963, the increasing number of Southern refugees in East Africa had come to the attention of the United Nations High Commissioner for Refugees (UNHCR).[82] These exiles formed a ready supply of manpower for any guerrilla movement. Southerners from all walks of life, including women, publicly expressed their desire to fight and liberate themselves from the Northern Sudanese. It was during this year that Southern politicians in exile and Southern officers who had defected from the Sudanese army, police, and prison forces formed a guerrilla movement.[83]

In 1960, Southern intellectuals and politicians became convinced that peaceful efforts to resolve the Southern problem had failed and that the time had come for Southerners to counter Northern Sudanese aggression by military force. Joseph Oduho and Father Saturnino, both Latuko from Eastern Equatoria, had a plan to organize a guerrilla movement. In December, they fled to Uganda together with other Southern politicians to lay the foundations for a Southern strike force.[84]

Then in March 1962, William Deng, Oduho, and Father Saturnino met in Kinshasa and founded the Sudan African Closed District National Union (SACDNU) (see Chapter 5). In July 1963, Oduho as president and Father Saturnino as patron of SACDNU visited Western Europe to solicit foreign recognition and acquire financial assistance. While in Rome, they conceived the idea of a military movement based in Southern Sudan as a deterrent to the Sudanese army's assaults on the Southern population. They envisioned a guerrilla movement that would require an effective propaganda machine to win the support of Southern intellectuals in exile, the Southern soldiers in the Sudanese army, remnants of the former Equatoria Corps, students in Southern schools, and others.[85]

As a first step, Oduho wrote to Southern officers in the Sudanese army, including Joseph Lagu, Jovani Andrago, Frederick Bryian Magot, and George Missen, urging them to join SACDNU and its nascent military organization. When Lagu was granted home leave in Nimule in early

1963, Oduho wrote a "personal letter" to him and encouraged him to join them so that they could benefit from his military experience.[86] Lagu later confirmed that he was indeed approached by SACDNU members at Nimule in April 1963, and that it was then that he decided to join the guerrilla forces.[87]

The leaders of SACDNU also wrote to Prime Minister Obote of Uganda asking him to win the release from prison of former members of the Equatoria Corps who had been imprisoned following the 1955 mutiny at Torit. When Obote visited Sudan in early 1963, he took up the cause. In response, General Abboud released the mutineers and dissidents in March.[88] Those released immediately joined the resistance movement, thus swelling the number of Southern guerrillas.

THE RESISTANCE MOVEMENT ASSUMES THE NAME "ANYA-NYA"

On August 19, 1963, Southern politicians and military leaders met at Oduho's residence in Kampala, Uganda, to draw up a comprehensive military plan for the guerrilla movement inside Southern Sudan. Those present included Oduho, Lagu, George Akumbek, Julius Moroga, and Severino Fuli. The name of the movement would be important because its psychological impact would affect the movement's ability to rally the people, and a number of names were proposed. Southerners in London had suggested the Azania Secret Army, but this was rejected on the grounds that "no army can be secret!"[89] Father Saturnino and Lagu proposed the Pan-African Freedom Fighters. Others argued for the Southern Sudan Liberation Movement, which Lagu would later adopt when he became the undisputed leader of Southern military operations. This name did seem to evoke the aspirations of the people of Southern Sudan.[90]

Fuli, a Madi intellectual, proposed the indigenous name of *Inyanya*,[91] the word for a deadly poisonous snake venom in Latuko, Madi, and Acholi country. Inyanya poison was greatly feared along the Nile, where people often migrated to safer areas in the interior to escape. The British district commissioner of Torit in the 1930s had issued warnings to any individual or people who extracted and used the poison.[92] Moroga, a young Moru, then proposed the name *Manyanya*, which is the Moru word for the army ant.[93] After much deliberation, the officers and politicians decided to remove the letter *m* from the Moru word *manyanya* and delete the letter *i* from the Madi word *inyanya*. The letter *a* was then placed in front of *nyanya*, forming the new word *anyanya*.[94]

Although *Anya-Nya* may have had meaning to people in Equatoria, it was scorned and rejected in Upper Nile. The people there chose their own names, which reflected the same objectives as *Anya-Nya* but had greater appeal to their own culture. For example, Philip Pedak, an intellectual from Upper Nile, refused to acknowledge the name *Anya-Nya* because it was not indigenous and accepted it only in 1965 when Anya-Nya activities became widespread in Upper Nile. The people of Upper Nile in general called the Southern military *Dej Door*; the Anyuak gave them the name *Jo Pap*; and in Western Equatoria among the Azande they were called *Aboro Nvuo*. The Dinka of Bahr al-Ghazal named them *Koc Roor*, and the Lwo called them *Ya Dom*.[95]

The structure and operation of any military insurgency require prudence, patience, and training. The movement can witness obstacles real or imaginary. Resistance to the name *Anya-Nya* was more psychological than ethnocentric, as was evident in later years when all Southerners, irrespective of ethnic backgrounds, conducted military operations under its banner.

SOUTHERN RESISTANCE IN WESTERN EQUATORIA

The circumstances that led to the rise of the Anya-Nya in Western Equatoria differed from those in Eastern Equatoria. A strike by workers of the Nzara Industrial Complex in August 1955, in response to the government's program of Sudanization, had been marked by bloodshed. The Azande people of Western Equatoria, who constituted the bulk of the workforce there, saw this violent reaction as a Northern declaration of war against them in particular and the Southern Sudanese in general. Bloodshed in Zandeland rekindled memories of atrocities by Northern slave traders.

The mutiny at Torit shortly after the Nzara strike reinforced distrust of the Northerners, whether soldiers, policemen, prison guards, administrators, traders, or merchants. The climate of insecurity in Zandeland encouraged both Azande and members of the smaller ethnic groups in traditional tributaries (the Mundu, Moru, Avokaya, Wira, and Baka) to flee in large numbers to the Congo and Central African Republic.

Activities of the Anya-Nya in Western Equatoria would likely have begun around the same time as in Eastern Equatoria except that the rivalry between Protestants and Catholics became a critical factor in the early years of the resistance movement. Father Saturnino Lohure was a Catholic but the people of Western Equatoria were predominantly Protestants. Father Saturnino wanted to consolidate his position among the Latuko, Madi, Acholi, Lokoya, and other peoples on the East Bank of the Nile before turning to the Protestant Azande in Western Equatoria. When Joseph Lagu, who was a Madi and a Protestant, defected from the

Sudanese army and joined Father Saturnino, he was informed not to associate himself with "the Westerners."[96]

The first activities of freedom fighters in Zandeland occurred during 1962 and 1963 when the students of Rumbek Secondary School went on strike; many of those from Bahr al-Ghazal fled to Zandeland, the Belgian Congo, and French Equatorial Africa (Central African Republic). Thousands of Azande went to their kinsfolk in the Belgian Congo and settled in refugee camps. It was in this context that students from different parts of Southern Sudan founded the Union of Southern Students and Youth (USSY) under the leadership of Edward Nyil Abot.[97]

The USSY was initially based at Isiro in the Congo. Later, a new headquarters was established at Bisquimbi in Zandeland. Abot named it the All South Camp because it drew students from all parts of Southern Sudan. In subsequent years, the headquarters was moved to Lerango inside the Congo for security reasons. Student recruits were trained to operate inside Zandeland. The overall commander of the guerrilla forces in Zandeland was Paul Yosia, who was later killed in a pitched battle with Sudanese troops near Kajo-Kaji in 1963.[98]

The Azande were potential recruits for the guerrilla movement for two reasons. They were numerous, and they had village communities in the Congo and Central African Republic. They were a society whose traditional centralized authority rested with an aristocratic Avungara clan organized for war. This traditional loyalty to authority had been instrumental in their resistance to foreign intruders, whether slave traders, Turco-Egyptians, Mahdists, or the British.[99]

It was on the basis of this ethnic cohesion that Azande refugees in camps in the Congo began to organize and train themselves. They were especially encouraged by promises from Southern politicians in exile that weapons would be supplied. When these were not forthcoming, they started collecting firearms in their own territory and established their first guerrilla camp at Navogo, east of the Azande town of Yambio.[100]

Azande guerrilla forces rallied behind Dominic Dabi, who was later joined by Habakuk Kefu in organizing and training guerrillas. With efficient training, though with few arms, the number of insurgents continued to increase as Azande civilians left refugee camps in the Congo for guerrilla camps in Zandeland. These camps were renowned for their cohesiveness and strict military discipline, qualities traditional in Azande society and badly needed for a growing guerrilla movement.[101]

Southern Resistance in Bahr al-Ghazal

As Equatoria prepared for war, there was much less activity in Upper Nile and Bahr al-Ghazal. John Ukech Lueth notes that in 1963 recruitment of youth into the liberation movement in Bahr al-Ghazal was insignificant (as a Jur from Bahr al-Ghazal, he had wanted to join but was considered too young).[102] Although most people in these two districts were not involved in the guerrilla activities in Equatoria, they had sympathy for their kinsfolk there. Equatoria shared a border with Uganda and the Congo, where most Southern refugees had settled with sympathetic ethnic groups. Southerners could use these areas as springboards for military operations against the security forces in Southern Sudan. Most Southerners, however, lacked military training. Former soldiers of the Equatoria Corps were instrumental in providing this, while Southern politicians promised weapons.

Conditions that precipitated revolt in Bahr al-Ghazal differed somewhat from those in Equatoria. All peoples in the South recalled with bitterness the devastation caused by Arab and Turco-Egyptian slavers in the nineteenth century, but Bahr al-Ghazal, which shares a border with the Arab Rizayqat, Humr, and Missiriyya, had a long history of conflict as a result of slave trading and skirmishes for pasture and cattle. The Dinka, Belanda, Feroge, Kreish, Ndogo, Njagulgule and others had been victims of Arab ethnic raids and pillage.[103]

The Bahr al-Ghazal was not isolated from the 1955 disturbances. In fact, a few Northern Sudanese merchants who escaped from Nzara in Western Equatoria and reached Wau, the capital of Bahr al-Ghazal, caused some panic there. This prompted the governor, senior civil servants, and the commander of the garrison to flee by steamer to the North. A fabricated story circulated that a Southerner named Nyang Dhiew, a lieutenant in the Equatoria Corps at Nzara, had killed the commander of the military post there.[104]

Meanwhile, following suppression of the mutinies at Torit and Juba, Northern troops harassed the population along the Tambura-Wau road, a vital link between Western Equatoria and Bahr al-Ghazal. They burned houses and stole property.[105] Luis Mongo Boolo, who lived at Baggari village, recalled, "We went to Wau with my uncle, while we were walking we met Northern soldiers. When my uncle stared at them, they beat him and asked him why he should stare at them. When my uncle said he was a villager they still beat him. I was watching these deeds."[106]

This state of insecurity continued into the 1960s. The student strike at Rumbek Secondary School had a profound impact on the inhabitants of the province. In December 1962, the Sudanese army's display of force, intimidation tactics, and arbitrary arrests resulted in a mass exodus.[107] Many refugees settled in Congolese border towns. They sold all their property, wristwatches, clothing, and radios to buy food and shelter. Without a quick response from the UNHCR, they would starve. Their only alternative was to return to the Southern Sudan and fight.[108]

The Anya-Nya launched their first organized military offensive against the Sudanese army on September 19, 1963, in Eastern Equatoria. A week later, William Deng, secretary general of the SACDNU, visited the Southern Sudanese people from Bahr al-Ghazal who were settled in refugee camps at Isiro in the Congo. People there had hoped that their political leaders would deliver weapons so they could return to the South to fight, but their hopes were shattered when Deng announced that military aid would not be forthcoming. The refugees pledged to go back to the South and take up spears, bows, and arrows to fight the enemy, preferring to die in defense of their homeland rather than to perish of starvation in the Congo.[109]

Deng, acknowledging the refugees' frustration, promised to send Captain Bernedino Mou to their camps to help organize and train former soldiers, policemen, prison guards, and student cadets.[110] According to Colonel Stephen Madut, who joined the guerrilla movement after the student strike at Rumbek in 1962, students from Rumbek Secondary School who had fled to the Congo were put into two categories: those from the third and fourth years were encouraged to go to school and study the Congolese syllabus in French, while Southerners from second-year to intermediate-school level were sent to the camps to be trained as NCOs and officers.[111]

The refugees at Niangara, Rindemia, and Apalemba in the Congo were coordinated by committees of politicians from Bahr al-Ghazal, including Khamilo Dhol, Akuot Atem de Mayen, and Elia Duang. The committees were instrumental in recruiting and fund-raising activities, and they supervised political activities in Kinshasa. William Deng, then based in Kinshasa, played a vital role in coordinating both civilian and military activities. In the Central African Republic, a camp was established at a place called Obo that had the same responsibilities as those inside the Congo.[112]

The first Anya-Nya activities in Bahr al-Ghazal were launched by Captain Mou, the Anya-Nya commander of the province, assisted by Captain Thomas Dhol, deputy commander, Lieutenant Henry Deng Monywir, adjutant, and Lieutenant Peter Utu Goi. NCOs included Regimental Sergeant Majors Daniel Deng Kawac and Phillip Nanga Mariik. There were forty men who were ill-equipped with a muzzle loader and a five-round rifle. Most were not sufficiently trained to match the numerous well-equipped, well-trained Sudanese army garrison at Wau. Instead, this guerrilla force relied heavily on Southerners in the town to provide information, firearms, and morale. This was the job of the underground movement in line with Deng's strategy.[113]

An attack on Wau was planned for January 1, 1964, the eighth anniversary of Sudan's independence. It was hoped that rifle and ammunition stores could be easily captured because few soldiers would be on duty. Southerners in Wau expected a quick, decisive battle in which the element of surprise would tilt the balance in favor of the Anya-Nya. Anya-Nya tactics however, were flawed, and the attack under Captain Mou ended in disaster. Mou was wounded, captured, and later executed. Most of his followers fled to the camps in the Congo. This failure demoralized recruits, and other armed groups in Bahr al-Ghazal disintegrated. The idea of attacking Tonj and Aweil was abandoned.[114]

Defeat created tension and conflict among the officers and men of the guerrilla movement. Mou was from Gogrial District in Northern Bahr al-Ghazal. His death created a power vacuum. The Anya-Nya at Gogrial wanted their own officer from the area to replace him. However, Captain Santino Ajing Daw, who was from Aweil and was a deputy to Mou, was the choice of the commanding officer for Bahr al-Ghazal.[115]

According to John Ukech Lueth, the people of Gogrial were highly suspicious about the circumstances of Mou's death. They thought that Captain Daw, who had accompanied Mou on the first assault on Wau, might have killed him over the leadership of Gogrial. They thereupon named their guerrilla company Gur Mou, meaning "revenge for Mou."[116] As in Eastern Equatoria, the element of tribalism crept in. Dinka, the majority people in Bahr al-Ghazal, were not prepared to accept the leadership of a Lwo, a minority ethnic group in Aweil. The consequence of this ethnic rivalry was the deposition of Captain Daw, who was accused of "having [the] intention to take the arms and go to [the] Aweil area."[117]

In early 1964, when Lueth joined the Anya-Nya forces in Bahr al-Ghazal, he was confronted with this conflict between the officers and men of Gogrial and Aweil. Although he was from the Aweil area, he refused to take sides. Junior officers and others in the Aweil-Gogrial area favored an amicable solution to the crisis, and Lueth, who had military training, was appointed to mediate. In the company of two junior officers, Joseph Kuol Amun and Donato Deng Kwanai, both Dinkas from Aweil, Lueth brokered an agreement, and the Anya-Nya forces in Bahr al-Ghazal were reunited.[118]

Southern Resistance in Upper Nile

The rise of the Anya-Nya movement in Upper Nile differed markedly from its inception in Equatoria and Bahr al-Ghazal. The inhabitants of this area include the Nuer, Dinka, Shilluk, Anyuak, and Murle, Nilotic peoples who keep cattle, except for the Anyuak who also cultivate the soil. These peoples have often engaged in cattle raids or interethnic warfare among themselves. Their militaristic tradition was a source of strength in the founding and organization of the Anya-Nya movement in Upper Nile.

Unlike Equatoria and Bahr al-Ghazal, the Upper Nile had a very small number of former members of the Equatoria Corps. There were only a few policemen and prison guards stationed at Malakal, but a peculiar feature of this province was that the Nuer had experience in the use of firearms earlier than their counterparts in Equatoria and Bahr al-Ghazal. During the Italian occupation of Ethiopia (1936 through 1941), the cattle-keeping peoples of the Upper Nile had acquired firearms from Ethiopia, which they used to protect their cattle and to raid each other to acquire more cattle.[119]

In 1962, after Marko Rume, the chief propagandist of SACDNU, wrote to the students at Rumbek urging them to join the freedom fighters, the fires of insurrection spread in the Upper Nile. Phillip Pedak, a politician, convinced the students as well as Dinka, Nuer, Murle, Shilluk, Burun, and Anyuak to join the guerrilla movement. The Nilotes' military prowess was exploited, and many of them volunteered. The call to "liberate the South" appealed to the young men.[120]

The Nuer religion was also a factor in recruitment. In the nineteenth century, the Lau Nuer prophet at Waat had prophesized "that his people will one day fight the Arabs and that they should be well received and supported."[121] This message rallied the Nuer for war against the Arabs; they took up arms and thousands of them joined the freedom movement. In June 1962, Pedak, living in exile in Ethiopia, recruited Daniel Nyang and assigned him the task of recruiting students and local inhabitants, particularly at Nasir and across the border at Gambela in Ethiopia.[122]

In December 1962, Nyang met with students from Rumbek Secondary School and Juba Commercial Secondary School, who enlisted in the guerrilla movement. The students were, in turn, instrumental in convincing young men in both the rural areas and the towns to join the armed struggle. Altogether Nyang recruited 111 young men. In April 1963, he established his first temporary guerrilla base at Tiergal in Ethiopia, but there remained a need to locate an easily accessible camp inside Southern Sudan.[123]

On July 2, 1963, two months before the Anya-Nya movement was formally founded in Equatoria, the pioneers of the guerrilla movement in Upper Nile—Philip Nyang; Paul Ruot, a Nuer; and Paul Adung, a Shilluk—decided that Pachalla, a place in the Anyuak country, was the most strategically located for guerrilla training and operations. It was accessible only during the dry season from January to April and was in one of the most remote parts of Anyuak country. Guerrilla operations in Anyuak territory could, however, be easily jeopardized if an Anyuak, familiar with the area and language, were to help the Sudanese security forces.[124] Paul Nyingori, an Anyauk, took command at Pachalla on July 7, 1963. With immediate effect, Nyingori established a guerrilla camp at Dhaldhim near Pachalla, and he wrote to his people at Akobo, reminding them that the people of Equatoria were far ahead of them in the liberation struggle. This news motivated many to join the guerrilla forces in Upper Nile, and the number of recruits reached more than a thousand.[125] This marked the emergence of the Anya-Nya in Upper Nile.

CHAPTER 4

GOVERNMENT COUNTERINSURGENCY METHODS, 1955–72

SUDANESE ARMY TACTICS AGAINST CIVILIANS

MANY CASES OF ARBITRARY KILLINGS COMMITTED BY THE Sudanese army and police against the people of Southern Sudan have been recorded by Southerners as well as foreign missionaries, international observers, human rights groups, and individuals resident in the South in the period 1955 through 1972. While some atrocities committed were the acts of ill-disciplined Sudanese security forces, others appear to have been politically motivated and sanctioned by the government in Khartoum.

One of the most effective strategies employed by Sudanese troops and police to intimidate Southern civilians was the destruction of houses or whole villages. This collective punishment was meted out to Southerners believed to have harbored rebels. In cases in which the Anya-Nya had battled Sudanese troops near a village, the latter would arrest, intimidate, and sometimes kill the villagers. Orders were often issued by the Sudanese military and police commanders, but on certain occasions were issued by the Northern Sudanese district commissioners in the area.[1]

In September 1956, the district commissioner of Yei District in Central Equatoria, Idris Bukhari, an Arab who presumably feared that rebels might infiltrate the town, ordered that all houses around the town of Yei, a radius of six miles, should be set ablaze.[2] The army and police burned down seven hundred huts.[3] The security forces looted money, clothes, bicycles, and other belongings during this operation. Although the civilians in Yei demanded compensation from the government, it rejected their demand.[4]

During that same month, security forces destroyed houses in the Torit District in Eastern Equatoria. The army garrison at Torit targeted the chieftaincies of Angelo Lodyongo, Marcello, and Iwani, and the villages of Madok, Lotose-Imotong, and Teretenya were burned. In September 1957, the army set ablaze the village of Lobira in Chief Marcello's jurisdiction.[5]

In May 1955, Lomiluk Lohide, the rainmaker and government-appointed paramount chief, was accused of having incited an ethnic conflict between his chieftaincy and that of Rainmaker Patrisyo Lohocyolli Lacalili. He was sentenced to six months in jail but was freed by the mutineers of Torit. After the mutineers' surrender at the end of August, Chief Lomiluk was implicated in the revolt and fled to Uganda. From there he would secretly visit his village of Haforiere in Torit District, where the inhabitants built him a house twelve miles distant so he could visit them. On one occasion, his archenemy, Layahu Longuta, led Sudanese security forces to his hiding place, but he escaped. The soldiers burned his house and searched every house in Haforiere, taking clothes, money, and other objects of value. Although ten people complained to the district commissioner of Torit, they were ignored or threatened with imprisonment.[6]

In August 1955, an investigation tribunal comprising a platoon of Sudanese soldiers, the district commissioner of Torit, and Mahaliele Nyajo, the police commander in Torit, tried and convicted Tagiri Elok, Obebe Labana, and Tugyala Elok, all Latuko, for building the house that accommodated Lomiluk. The tribunal then levied collective punishment on all the young men in the village, fining each one a hundred cows.[7]

In September 1959, when Chief Lomiluk died in exile at Kitgum in Northern Uganda, two renowned rebels, Latada Helir and Lenyakwo, who had participated in the Torit mutiny, entered Haforiere village to offer their condolences to the family of the deceased. A week after their departure, an informant accused inhabitants of harboring the two rebels. This enraged the military commander of Torit, who mustered a company of soldiers and fifty policemen. An officer told the inhabitants of Haforiere to collect all their property from their houses, and the entire village was set ablaze.[8]

In Upper Nile, the security situation was no different from that in Equatoria. The army used the same tactics to intimidate inhabitants, expecting they would disassociate themselves from the rebels. Collective punishment was levied on whole villages, especially if security forces were attacked or had received reports that Anya-Nya were in the area.

The destruction of villages rendered the inhabitants homeless and made them vulnerable to hunger, starvation, and disease. In Upper Nile in September 1963, the Sudanese Air Force destroyed the town of Pachalla after an Anya-Nya raid, while the army destroyed Wunbarkou Camp. The chief of Adongo protested but was arrested and imprisoned.[9] During 1963 through 1964, security forces destroyed twenty-eight villages with a total population of 13,750. Across the ill-defined border the Sudanese army burned down twenty-eight villages inside Ethiopia.[10]

In Bahr al-Ghazal, government troops continued to harass Southerners, forcing many to flee to the Central African Republic and the Congo. In May 1963, authorities began mass arrests at Wau and Gogrial. Local government officials were also arrested.[11]

On March 18, 1964, the Sudanese army crossed into the Congo to attack refugee settlements. They destroyed many villages on the Congolese side, resulting in "an undetermined number of deaths."[12] The army also crossed the border into the Central African Republic to harass Southern Sudanese there. In view of the insecurity, President Bokassa shut down an extensive refugee project at Mboki near Obo.[13]

ARBITRARY ARRESTS, IMPRISONMENT, TORTURE, AND KILLINGS IN EQUATORIA

The exodus of Southern Sudanese to Uganda, the Congo, and the Central African Republic alarmed the Sudanese government and its security forces. Their reign of terror had largely contributed to the Southerners' flight. General Ibrahim Abboud's government believed that former soldiers of the Equatoria Corps, former MPs, students, and other able-bodied Southerners would join the resistance. Abboud took measures not only to hamper the movement of Southerners but also to instill fear. He restricted the movement of former soldiers released from prison, who were to remain at home and report to the nearest chief or police station.[14]

The chiefs in Central and Eastern Equatoria began seeking refuge in Uganda. Chiefs Oteno Wanto, an Acholi headman who was imprisoned in 1960 and later released, Rocco T. Joakino of Torit, Nilo Angu of Parjok in Acholiland, Geldino Bongomin of Magwi, and Ali Mulukwat Totwan from Western Kajo-Kaji, all crossed into Uganda. Chief Joakino testified about how he was arrested and charged with "'collaborating with Southern rebels to overthrow the legally constituted government of the Sudan." He knew the charges were serious, and even his guards feared what would happen to him. As he was being taken to the jail, his Arab guard told him to run away. Expecting to be shot, he set off, but the guard did nothing. Before making off for the borders, he heard that the guard had been imprisoned, as had all his own family—his wife, father, mother, and brother—as well as all the local policemen of Torit.[15]

The Abboud government specifically sought to implicate chiefs and former soldiers of the Equatoria Corps. Paulino Ngijak was accused of belonging to a secret society that advocated magic to get rid of the Arabs. Korneli Meri, a local businessman who owned a truck, was falsely accused of "giving a lift to people alleged to be rebel spies" and was imprisoned.[16]

General Abboud imposed rigid censorship on news so that little or none from Southern Sudan could reach the outside world, but Southern refugees gave testimony about their experiences in the war-torn South, and many transmitted stories from informants. These accounts were denied by government authorities, who suppressed or refuted the information.

The security forces could arbitrarily shoot and kill any Southerner. Any atrocities they committed were justified by the military administration's intention to crush the rebels. In Katire, Torit District, a Northern police sergeant shot and killed a six-year-old boy playing on a rock in August 1959. Although the case was brought before the district commissioner, the policeman was not prosecuted.[17]

Loteka Lado, a Southerner from Torit, fled to Uganda during the 1955 disturbances. In August 1959, Mahaliele Nyajo, a Southern police officer loyal to Abboud's administration, kidnapped Lado and falsely accused him of murdering an individual whose name was not disclosed! Justice El Fatih Awouda, a judge of the High Court, Southern Provinces; two third-class magistrate Southern chiefs; and security officials tried Lado on July 23, 1962. He was convicted of murder and hanged on September 18.[18] In the same month, Alfonse Arop, a former official of the ministry of animal resources in Torit, was accused of "politically educating the people for a . . . United Nation plebiscite." In October Amosa Aburi, a former teacher at Gederu (in north central Kajo-Kaji) village school, and Tito Wani, a former teacher in Amosa's school, were accused of harboring Southern rebels active near the school.[19] Duku Bojo, a farmer from Kajo-Kaji who had fled to Uganda, was arrested when he returned to Sudan.[20]

Micah Luwate, a former Southern clerk in the ministry of health at Juba, was accused of providing support to the families of Southern prisoners of conscience, including political activists and missionaries. A former policeman at Juba, John Baden, who had resigned, was arrested for planning to join the Southern mutineers.[21] Many others were imprisoned without trial. Some were tortured, and others were subjected to hard labor.[22]

Two women named Veronica and Anjelika, who were nieces of Amadeo Taffeng, were shot dead because of their connection with the Anya-Nya commander in chief. Sudanese troops killed law-abiding people "as a matter of vengeance" against the Anya-Nya. Attilio Lotidak, headmaster of Imehejez Elementary School, was shot in front of his students in December 1963.[23]

From January to May 1964, the security forces raided the Taposa, Boya, and Didinga villages in Kapoeta District. The villages of Loudo, Lorema, Munita, Kikilai, Kali, Didinga Ngalam, Lobele, and Sugouro were destroyed, and 269 men, 14 women, and 13 children were killed. In Torit District, Sudanese troops raided several villages between February and May 1964, including Mura Hatiha, Lopit-Iboni, Isaloro Ofiriha, Imilai, Lobulo, Haforiere, Tuhubak, Obbo, and Pajok. The Sudanese army killed 161 men, women, and children.[24] The security forces were determined to create an atmosphere of terror throughout Eastern Equatoria, believing this would deter rebel activities. Instead, the atrocities encouraged Southerners to flee to the bush or to neighboring countries, where they subsequently joined the Anya-Nya.

Aside from the killings and arrests by the Sudanese army, the district commissioners issued orders for the security forces to carry out collective punishment on civilians believed to be harboring rebels. The district commissioner of Yei ordered Sudanese soldiers and policemen to punish civilians in areas where the Anya-Nya had ambushed security forces. They were given discretionary powers to torture and kill civilians and destroy their villages. In October 1962, when rebels ambushed the Sudanese army on the Yei-Kaya road, the latter went on a rampage against civilians. Many were shot and killed in their homes. In December, another army patrol came across a group of people feasting at Gulumbi in Chief Lita's jurisdiction. They killed five and took the others to Yei prison, where they were tortured.[25]

Indiscriminate killings continued in Equatoria. Claud Kerbetta, a court clerk at Tirangole, described the security situation in Eastern Equatoria, "The present situation in Torit [is] dangerous and explosive . . . the government has lost the confidence of the people in this area, does not trust even its own installed chiefs and has practically lost hope in bringing the situation under control. The Arab in Equatoria is a desperate man. They see their end of colonization in the South coming to an abrupt end. It is for this reason that they no longer respect the Common Law. They have become looters, murderers and ruthless exploiters. [L]ast year alone the Government Forces looted in the name of fines about 5,000 cattle from Eastern Torit."[26]

Kerbetta also told of the death of Rubong Lerwe at Lolianga, a few miles from Ikotos. Lerwe was arrested and beaten to death for harboring "anti-government elements." The security forces continued to punish civilians by burning their villages and food stores. This situation led to an influx of refugees into neighboring countries.[27]

Arbitrary Arrests, Imprisonment, Torture, and Killings in Bahr al-Ghazal

In 1962, before Southern guerrilla activities became deeply entrenched in Bahr al-Ghazal, the Sudanese army destroyed the Catholic church at Momoi as part of Abboud's policy of Islamization and Arabization.[28] In May 1963, the security forces continued their acts of torture and intimidation against Southern Sudanese in the province. Khartoum ordered mass arrests in Wau and Gogrial: all Southern local government officials were arrested, including Parmona Kelei, Valentino Akol, Toby Mawien, Richard Koc, Ferdinand Dhol, and Matthew Kuol. Meanwhile in Wau, the security forces arrested the province medical assistant, Hassan Fartak, the chief of Bagari, Musa Luigi, and Gaetano Biringi, who was detained and tortured. Southern employees in Gogrial were suspended. The movement of Southerners was restricted.[29]

In Bahr al-Ghazal, the number of Anya-Nya increased during 1964, as former soldiers of the Equatoria Corps and civilians acquired arms and ammunition to join the movement. The Sudanese army and police in the province became increasingly suspicious and harassed the inhabitants, especially after the ill-fated and disastrous attack on Wau by Captain Bernedino Mou on the night of January 1, 1964 (see Chapter 3).[30] After this attack, several hospital attendants were arrested and tortured.[31] Although they were released, their services at the hospital were terminated for supporting the Anya-Nya.[32] Security forces also arrested three clerks and detained and tortured them at the Grinti military prison. They were tried and subsequently released. In the words of one:

> They brought me into the torture hall in Grinti where I was stripped naked. Then they tied my hands and feet behind my back with wire and made me lie on my back. They filled my eyes and nostrils with paprika [red pepper] powder as well as my anal opening. They tied my head inside a sack of the same powder so that I was unable to breathe. Then they threw me on the table extending my head and feet over the table and downward, and beat me to blood while one of the soldiers shook the sack of paprika powder so that the powder would enter my eyes, nostrils, and mouth. Meanwhile a soldier continued to read a list of names . . . which I was supposed

to accuse. The more I kept silence, the worse my torture got. They threw me on the ground and began hitting me with their gun butts and stamping on me with their heavy shoes until I fainted. This procedure was repeated every two or three days.[33]

Ten people from the health department died from torture in Grinti, while twenty-two clerical staff in government departments died there as well. Their bodies were "wrapped up in strips of sack by other prisoners and were buried in unknown places."[34] In Bussere, south of Wau, staff members including two guards were arrested and tortured.[35]

Inhabitants of Mboro, Daym Zubayr, and Kpaile were flogged and beaten. Southern prisoners were tortured to confess connections to the Anya-Nya. Father Santino Locatelli described their interrogations in the Grinti military prison in Wau:

> A metal ring was placed around the head of the prisoners from whom the soldiers wanted a particular answer. Two small balls of some hard material were then placed against his temples. Then the ring was tightened, forcing the balls farther and farther into his temples until the eyes were almost pushed out. At other times instead, the metal ring was placed vertically, passing under the chin, and around the top of the head, where again a ball was inserted. . . . The spasms resulting from this torture were so cruel that . . . it was impossible to resist telling the soldiers what they wanted to hear, [whether] one wanted to or not.[36]

Security forces in Bahr al-Ghazal had discretionary powers to arrest and charge any Southerner suspected of collaborating with the Anya-Nya. Both innocent and guilty Southerners were indiscriminately arrested for minor or serious crimes or for no reason at all. In January 1964, an Arab trader at Wau implicated his servant, but when he could not prove his case, "he reported him to the police as the father of a rebel." The servant was immediately arrested, taken to Wau prison, and tortured. His ankles and wrists were tied up with wire, and his head was put inside a bag of red pepper powder. He was then beaten severely until he became unconscious. Believing he was dead, the police threw his body into the bush, but he survived. Father Valentino Saoncella, a Catholic priest at Wau, saw the victim, who was feeble and almost blind, on February 1, 1964.[37]

A Southern seminarian from the seminary at Tore in Equatoria was arrested when Anya-Nya activities there made him a prime suspect, and he was brutally flogged.[38] In Western Bahr al-Ghazal, another Southern seminarian at Raga was arrested by the security forces as an insurgent. He was beaten and later released.[39] On February 2, 1964, two Italian priests,

Giacomo Colussi and Giuseppe Velente, were arrested along with thirty Southerners at Mboro and Biseglie by soldiers from Wau. The Southerners were beaten beyond recognition and loaded into a truck for Wau. On the way, the soldiers seized any Southerners they could find and burned the villages along the road. When the Southerners and Italian priests arrived the following day, they were all subjected to intense and violent interrogation.[40] The atrocities committed against Southern Sudanese by the security forces in Bahr al-Ghazal encouraged many to flee the country.[41]

ARBITRARY ARRESTS, IMPRISONMENT, TORTURE, AND KILLINGS IN UPPER NILE

The first human and animal tragedy in Upper Nile Province, which the Sudanese government could have avoided, occurred between 1961 and 1963. In the first half of 1961, the rains failed and famine spread throughout the Bor District. People and animals living close to the Nile had access to water and survived, but those in the interior died of thirst. In July 1961, the situation dramatically changed when heavy rains caused the Nile to flood a considerable amount of territory beyond the river.[42] Many villages were destroyed by the flood waters, and pasture for animals as well as cultivation was flooded. Crocodiles and snakes roamed the area, seeking high ground. Insects, especially mosquitoes, proliferated. The floods also cut communications between villages and the commercial and administrative centers of Kongor, Palieu, Duk-Faiwel, Duk-Fadiet, Mar, and others that had to be evacuated. The waters did not subside for months. In April 1962, the Dinka and Nuer in the flat flood plains migrated to the ground on the ironstone plateau south of Bor. Many others displaced at Bor and Malakal lived in crowded camps.[43]

The floods in Bor District between 1961 and 1963 caused enormous losses in human and animal life as well as property. Two thousand people died, some twenty-six thousand cattle perished, over eight thousand sheep and goats died, and 266 villages consisting of 52,666 huts were destroyed.[44] The chiefs repeatedly reported the devastation to government authorities in Bor and Malakal, but the government sent no help. A SANU official expressed frustration, "Yet in the case of [the] Bor famine the Northern Sudanese government has deliberately refused to discharge its duty in the interest and for the welfare of the citizens." Paradoxically, the Sudanese government had on two occasions shipped relief aid to Iran following its earthquake, and to Somalia "as an expression of Arab and Islamic solidarity."[45] On November 8, 1963, the headmen and members of the Bor rural council sent a letter to General Abboud appealing for immediate relief, but received no reply.[46]

In Upper Nile, the security situation was similar to that in Equatoria and Bahr al-Ghazal. Sudanese soldiers and police were given full powers to arrest, charge, jail, and torture Southerners they suspected were supporting or sympathetic to Anya-Nya forces. They shot and killed Southerners at will. Their intent was to intimidate Southerners into not supporting or assisting the Anya-Nya.

In the Pibor, Eastern, and Lou Nuer Districts of Upper Nile, soldiers raided villages and seized cattle. Similar incidents occurred in the areas of Pachalla, Nasir, and Akobo in Nuer and Anyuak country. These violent actions drove thousands of Southerners to seek refuge in Ethiopia so that by 1963, 3,685 refugees from Upper Nile province were living there, including villagers, students, and civil servants. Many supported the rebellion and joined the Anya-Nya.[47]

Sudanese soldiers and police continued to provoke the Anyuak and Nuer along the Ethiopian border. Their seasonal movements were restricted, and they were not allowed to visit kinsfolk in Ethiopia. These restrictions created a dissatisfied and disgruntled population increasingly hostile to the Sudanese administration and the security forces, which were "instruments of repression." A tense and hostile atmosphere prevailed throughout Upper Nile.[48]

In 1963, Sudanese troops from Akobo garrison besieged the nearby Anyuak village of Nyikwar. A Southern Sudanese who was spying for the Sudanese government falsely reported to the commanding officer of the Akobo garrison that a stranger believed to be a member of the Anya-Nya had visited the village. The alleged stranger was Chief Akodho of Objale village, who lived on the Sudan-Ethiopian border and who had gone to Nyikwar to visit part of his family.[49] The commanding officer sent a platoon to arrest and bring in all the inhabitants for interrogation. When the security forces failed to obtain the information they sought, they selected thirty people, including the chief, whom they blindfolded, tied to trees, and finally shot in cold blood. A similar mass killing was carried out the following year in the village of Gang Lual. On January 3, 1964, Sudanese soldiers burned the house and storage facilities for grain at Gang Lual.[50]

Relatives were often arrested by the security forces as a punishment, especially if one was suspected of having collaborated with the rebels. Chief Medho Cam and his people were repeatedly threatened; fearing arrest, he fled to Ethiopia. His daughter, who was in primary school, was arrested and held as a hostage.[51]

The pregnant wife of Gaich Duach was arrested and severely beaten in an attempt to force her to reveal her husband's hideout. The case was not investigated.[52] Security forces did not discriminate between the guilty and the innocent: the Southerners were their enemies. The government was determined to destroy the Anya-Nya movement by any means: intimidation, arbitrary arrests, torture, public executions, or random killings.

After the Southern guerrilla forces in Upper Nile briefly overran Pachalla in September 1963, the town was bombed, twenty-eight surrounding villages were burned, and the mission house used by "agricultural practitioners" was destroyed.[53] Sister Ermella Cariolato, who had worked thirteen years in Malakal hospital, testified that a member of the governor's family in Upper Nile confirmed that the governor had ordered the bombing and machine-gunning of the villages because of suspicion that they harbored Anya-Nya or people sympathetic to them. In addition to Pachalla, several villages were destroyed in Pibor toward the end of 1963.[54]

Meanwhile, inside Ethiopia Sudanese troops penetrated Southern refugee settlements and burned twenty-eight villages. The soldiers entered Ethiopia on the pretext that they were pursuing Southern refugees who had links with guerrilla activities in Upper Nile.[55]

On February 15, 1964, in Malakal prison, the inspector of prisons requested a dresser to provide treatment for seriously ill Southern prisoners, but when Albino Gambela was sent to the prison, the inspector prevented him from giving treatment. Eventually, an Arab medical doctor named Salah brought a total of seven prisoners back to the hospital for treatment. These prisoners were among eighteen Southerners whom the security forces had arrested earlier in the forests of Nasir District to extort confessions. The prisoners were suspected of being Anya-Nya. The doctor discovered that most of the prisoners in Malakal prison had been badly tortured, "They bore the signs of having been flogged and from head to foot there were one great burn. . . . Their hands and feet stank for gangrene." Some of them died a few days later.[56]

In 1964, in the Tonga area of Upper Nile, floods destroyed crops and villages and many cattle died of disease. Despite this catastrophe, government authorities at Malakal did not send any aid. Throughout the province individuals were afraid to express their views about the political situation. A Southern Sudanese clerk in Upper Nile described the situation thus: "The Southerners have no trust in the Authorities or in the Government. Nobody can control the Arabs or defend the population from their vexations. . . . Instead of redressing an unsustainable position the Government Officials refuse to consider that there might be errors in their behavior with the Southerners. They want to keep up their prestige even if they must do it by sheer force. This is not only the opinion of the population, but above all of all those who have seen the situation."[57]

The Massacres of Juba, Wau, and Malakal

The worst atrocities of the civil war were to come under the repressive civilian government of Prime Minister Mohammed Ahmed Mahgoub, who came to power in June 1965, and whose policy was "chasing the rebels and disarming them so as to maintain law and order as an essential step towards settling the Southern problem."[58] According to Eliaba James Surur, the policies of the Khartoum governments, whether military or civilian, toward the people of Southern Sudan were the same—political subjugation, oppression, and repression—and Mahgoub's administration was bent on destroying the South.[59] The security forces were now given more powers, and in early July, Mahgoub ordered massacres of Southern Sudanese. According to John Ukech Lueth, Sudanese troops "went berserk from one village to another, terrorizing" civilians. Those who suffered the most were in Equatoria, and this repression continued throughout Mahgoub's administration.[60]

July 1965 was to witness the most serious bloodbaths in the major Southern towns, the primary goal being to eliminate educated Southerners believed to be instrumental in spreading propaganda. The bloody work began at eight o'clock on the night of July 8 and continued into the following morning, when security forces at Juba went on a rampage in the Southern residential neighborhoods of Malakia and Kator, burning down houses and shooting and killing men, women, and children—all innocent civilians.[61] According to one witness, the massacre resulted from a fight between Northern soldiers and Southern civilians in the house of a prostitute. When a Southerner stabbed a Northern soldier to death, the other soldiers fled to the main barracks and reported the incident. This enraged the soldiers at headquarters, who were supported by others at the airport and the police at their headquarters.[62]

According to Surur, himself a survivor of the Juba massacre, Arab soldiers in Juba had targeted him, Daniel Tongun, and other Southern politicians and professionals to be shot and killed. For two days they shot Southerners indiscriminately in hopes of killing their targets, since they were unable to identify them personally. The soldiers even shot and killed patients in the operation theater of Juba Civil Hospital. On the morning of July 9, when they examined the numerous dead bodies all over Juba for the men they were seeking, to their surprise they did not find them, although they had succeeded in killing some Southern politicians.[63] And so they continued searching for them throughout the day.[64]

Many Southerners had taken refuge in Surur's house in the neighborhood of Malakia when a group of armed soldiers came to the house looking for him. As Surur described the incident:

The others [soldiers] came straight to me, and then because I was small in body, in stature, they say, "*Ya wolet, abu pitak wenu?*" [literally "Young boy, where is your father?" in Arabic] . . . And then I began to think, what is this? And I quickly answered [them], I said, Oh, my father, Let me go and see him inside. And then I discovered that these were people coming actually to shoot *me*. And straightaway I went in. Instead of coming back to them, I escaped through the back door of my house and ran away. But then, when they learned that that very man you asked where's your father, is the man, you should have shot him straight . . . but you have allowed him to . . . run away, he ran through the door, and that's how I ran to Congo, and stayed . . . until we came back in 1972.[65]

Members of the Southern Front (an organization of Southern intellectuals founded in 1964) conservatively estimated the death toll at Juba at fourteen hundred.[66] Lueth believed the number of people killed to be about two thousand,[67] while Clement Mboro, president of the Southern Front, estimated the numbers at around fifteen hundred.[68] Some civilians also drowned in the Nile while trying to escape. The massacre prompted the Southern Front to issue a statement in the *Vigilant* expressing despair over the future of Southern Sudan under an Arab-dominated government. As they asserted, the Northern government and army did not believe peaceful negotiations would solve the problem of the South. Their solution instead "depends on how quickly the Arab government through its Army of occupation can complete its massacre of over 1,400 Southern civilians by the Army; [this] cannot but stand as indisputable proof [of] our contention that the Northern Army under the orders of the government is carrying out a genocide and systematic extermination of the Negro population of the Southern Sudan."[69]

Nor was the massacre in Juba an isolated incident. In Wau the following day, July 10, a nephew of Chief Cier Riang was being married in his house only a few yards from the Technical Intermediate School, where Sudanese troops were stationed. Most of the wedding guests were from Gogrial.[70] Unexpectedly, Sudanese soldiers surrounded the house. An eyewitness and survivor of the massacre described how the army cordoned off the house and began shooting into it. While those inside hit the floor to escape the bullets, a group of soldiers "went into the fence and started pulling out the men from their hiding [place] and shooting them with a revolver."[71] The women, however, were spared. Seventy-six people were killed, most of them from the educated Southern elite.[72] Among the dead were Victor Bol, deputy governor of Bahr al-Ghazal,[73] Dr. Babiti, the province veterinary officer, and the executive officer in Wau—the most high-ranking civil servants.[74] The only survivors had hidden on the ground pretending to be dead. The security forces put all bodies, dead and alive, on a military truck to be transported to Grinti barracks. On the way, those still alive slipped out the rear of the truck unnoticed.[75] Similar killings were subsequently carried out in Juba, Malakal, and Torit. According to Dr. Dominic Akec Mohammed, "These were all designed really to eliminate the educated Southerners. . . . [Sudanese soldiers] used such occasions where all these intellectuals would be found gathered together."[76]

According to Mboro, when he heard the news of the massacre in Juba, he personally decided to fly there to investigate the incident. On his way, he stopped in Wau on July 11, where upon his arrival, Dr. Benaiah Surur, a medical doctor, informed him of the wedding massacre. Although the army had accused those at the wedding of being associated with the Anya-Nya rebels, Mboro maintained that all of them had been intellectuals or professionals. Deeply distressed, he shouted loudly to the Southerners around him, "All of you who are here . . . I am Clement Mboro . . . all of you leave the town, and go to the forest . . . go and save your lives."[77] On arriving in Juba, Mboro met with government authorities, who briefed him about the killings. Upon returning to Khartoum, he held a press conference to express the gravity of the situation in Juba. According to Mboro, he risked his life in doing so because the Khartoum government did not want the general public or the international community to know anything about the massacres.[78]

The massacre of Southerners at Juba and Wau precipitated panic among members of the Southern Front, even in Khartoum. The atrocities had one thing in common: "The operations seemed to have been carried out to kill educated Southerners in the area."[79] The Southern Front in Khartoum pressured the government to investigate the massacres, particularly at Juba, where the death toll was highest. It also published a memorandum to Prime Minister Mahgoub "to deplore and protest against the slaughter of Southern citizens by the Arab army in the South."[80] The memorandum stated that while government sources put the number of massacred at Juba at four hundred, their own sources put it at one thousand, but whoever was correct, the incident was a "national disaster" that was clearly carrying out a government policy that "has . . . come to mean butchery of Southern civilian population in towns and villages." The statement further chronicled the systematic burning of villages in Northern Shilluk and the murder of villagers, including women and children, all of whom were "unarmed innocent law-abiding citizens," and it described how villages now stood deserted. The Southern Front condemned the massacres as a "policy of extermination of our people."

The Southern Front also resolved to send a delegation to Juba, including its president Clement Mboro, Gordon Muortat, Hillary Paul Logali, and Luigi Adwok, to see the security first-hand.[81] The delegation arrived at Juba in the middle of July. As Muortat described the situation, "We saw [a] very bad scene . . . people were massacred. People were sprayed with bullets while running about. . . . Many people got drown[ed] in the Nile . . . and there was a very bad incident where four to five workers of sanitation [health workers] were put in a house, and the house was set on fire. Four to five of them were burned alive. We saw all those terrible things. . . . We saw the army rampaging the streets, shooting anybody." The delegation remained seven days collecting information before returning to Khartoum. During this period, many Southerners bravely came forward to provide information, even though the government was spying on them.[82]

As the airplane carrying the delegation was returning to Khartoum, they grew suspicious that upon landing the security forces would search their luggage for the information they had collected. Fortunately, another Southerner passenger offered to carry the documents. According to Muortat, "We told him that as soon as the plane touched down, you take these documents of ours, and just vanish." The young Southerner took the documents just as the police commander of the Khartoum airport arrested the delegation, who were taken to police headquarters for interrogation. Their luggage was thoroughly searched, and the police reluctantly released them.[83]

On July 12, the Southern Front central executive committee decided to inform international organizations that "there is a Nazi-type of extermination policy being carried out in the Sudan by the Arab army of occupation on the unarmed and helpless Negro population in the Southern Sudan,"[84] and they asked the Organization of African Unity and the United Nations Human Rights Commission to intervene. They also sent letters to Uganda, Kenya, Egypt, Ghana, Nigeria, and Algeria.[85]

Sudanese troops also stepped up operations against civilians in Bahr al-Ghazal in early 1966. In Kayango, thirty-five miles northwest of Wau, security forces shot and killed civilians and burned houses. The *Vigilant* described how they arrived in the village at 4:30 in the morning and began searching out the villagers in their houses, but a young man returning late from a dance saw them and began blowing a trumpet to warn the villagers of the impending danger. Alerted by the disturbance, people at once left their homes and fled into the surrounding bush. The soldiers found and killed a ten-year-old boy and started setting the houses on fire. Throughout the day they continued searching the surrounding forests for survivors. In the evening they happened on an elementary schoolmaster and shot and killed him.[86] The security forces also "picked [up] the people by night" and killed them.[87] Students were always singled out. The people of Equatoria suffered most. In the interior "there were only two options: either remain in the city, and be subjected to torture [and] arbitrary killings or run away."[88] In Bahr al-Ghazal, the people "had to run into the countryside."[89] However, sanctuary in the countryside was safe only during the rainy season, when the roads were impassable to Sudanese troops. In the dry season the soldiers could travel far and wide. In the Nyamlell area of Bahr al-Ghazal, Sudanese troops arrested all the teachers and slaughtered them on the banks of the river, and at a place called Agwat in Aweil District the soldiers killed many people.[90]

GOVERNMENT PEACE CAMPS IN THE SOUTH

In 1966, the government adopted a policy of "collectivization" at Juba, Wau, Malakal, and Torit. The security forces were ordered to go into villages and arrest the civilians, who were to be resettled along the roads or in the main administrative towns. The primary purpose of this policy was to enable the security forces to patrol these areas without fear of assault by the Anya-Nya in the countryside. "This was anti-insurgency theory whereby you isolate the population from the guerrillas so that they starve because they would not get food."[91] People were brought to the towns, where there was no employment or amenities essential for daily life. Many died of hunger or disease as a result. When Sultan Ring Lual's people in Bahr al-Ghazal, numbering 250,000, were ordered to move to Northern Sudan in 1966, this uprooting of a whole population from their ancestral settlement and transfer to a strange new environment proved disastrous. Children, women, and old men died in large numbers, and most of their cattle perished.[92]

The Sudanese government called the concentrated camps of Southern civilians in the towns "peace villages." They argued they were providing "security, a dispensary and occasionally an elementary school—not just a *khalwa* [Islamic primary school]."[93] In Equatoria, where the army established thirty-three peace villages, the people had traditionally lived in small villages and they disliked conditions in the large towns. Most resented this policy, even though they were provided with security, some kind of education, and health services.[94]

Peace villages were established on the sites of former villages. The Sudanese government spent one million Sudanese pounds, establishing these villages, with a budget drawn from the local and national governments.

The military authorities supplemented this budget with unspecified amounts of money. The program was very expensive and drained the government treasury. By November 1966, 13,830 people had been resettled in peace villages in Juba District; 8,000 in Kapoeta District; 4,450 in Torit District; 11,000 in Maridi District; 7,500 in Yambio District; and 4,195 in Tambura District. Each man was given four Sudanese pounds to construct a house for himself and his family, provided with food rations, given seeds, and encouraged to grow crops. Rations were discontinued after the men had harvested their first crops.[95]

Southerners who went to the peace villages were escaping harsh conditions in the bush, where there was no proper shelter or clean drinking water, and where hunger, starvation, and disease prevailed. Although they envisaged better conditions in the peace villages, such expectations were often shattered when they realized "there wasn't really enough food to feed them."[96] They were in effect hostages closely watched by the security forces lest they join or give support to the Anya-Nya in the bush. They were told that "if you want food, take us back and show the hiding places of the people who were left behind, because these people are rebels."[97] The people in these camps had two choices: either stay under strict security observation or flee to the countryside. The peace village program was designed to divide the Southerners[98] and isolate the Anya-Nya from the people who provided them with political, military, and moral support.

The peace villages and concentration of large numbers of Southern civilians in towns also provided breeding grounds for epidemic diseases such as cholera and smallpox. In March 1971, hundreds of people died from cholera along the Nile in Bor District. On June 22, the *Guardian* reported that 1,345 Southerners had died of cholera. The disease spread to Moru District, where it killed several hundred Southerners before spreading among the Azande in Western Equatoria.[99] In Eastern Equatoria the epidemic spread along the Juba-Torit road, through the villages of Ngangala, Liangari, and Lirya and into Torit District and the villages of Ifotu, Imurok, and Ofiriha, where hundreds died.[100] These diseases "were looked upon by the Khartoum regime as God-sent allies."[101]

The Southern Sudan Association, which was made up of Southern intellectuals living in London, appealed to the World Health Organization (WHO) and others for funds, cholera vaccine, doctors, and medical assistance, but the Sudanese embassy in London and the government in Khartoum "reported to the World Health Organization in Geneva that there [was] not a single case of cholera anywhere in Sudan."[102] The government sought to conceal information that would compel the WHO and other organizations to deliver funds, vaccines, medical supplies, doctors, and food to the helpless people in the South. The government was anxious not to be accused by the iinternational community of human rights abuses.[103] Paradoxically, however, Sudanese authorities in the South were "vaccinating their own soldiers against cholera while ignoring the population in the South."[104]

On November 1, 1970, Lawrence Wol Wol, the political representative of the Southern Sudan Liberation Movement, presented a memorandum to the Afro-Asian Peoples Solidarity Organization council meeting in Tripoli, Libya, in which he summed up the atrocities committed against Southerners by Sudanese security forces. From the beginning of the "reign of terror" in Southern Sudan, more than half a million men, women, and children had died, "either shot dead, burnt alive in their huts or . . . from famine and disease." Another half million had fled to Uganda, Congo, Kenya, Ethiopia, and the Central African Republic, where they now languished as refugees. Those remaining in Southern Sudan were left "hiding in jungles and mountains. Their plight is indeed pitiful. They live permanently in fear and are always on the run. Besides being killed by Soviet bullets daily, thousands die from disease and famine." Almost six out of ten newborns were dying of disease, while thousands more children perished every year from malnutrition. Additional thousands were dying from exposure to the elements. Moreover, "Arab pilots in Russian MiGs have destroyed every single home, cattle, goats and sheep in many parts of the country. Hospitals and schools have either been destroyed, closed or turned into military barracks. The entire population is a dying one, their conditions are pathetic. They have no permanent shelter, but hide under mosquito-infested trees and in caves."[105]

The Sudanese government had used force to instill fear into every Southerner: burning villages, looting property, making arbitrary arrests, imprisoning villagers, committing individual and mass killings, and withholding food and medical supplies from victims of floods and disease. These actions clearly illustrated the government's determination to subjugate the people of the South to the point at which they had only two alternatives: surrender or pursue guerrilla warfare. The Southern Sudanese chose the latter, and the war continued for seventeen years.

CHAPTER 5

GENERAL ABBOUD'S RESPONSE

REPRESSION, ISLAMIZATION, AND ARABIZATION, 1958–64

GOVERNMENT REPRESSION AND THE FLIGHT OF SOUTHERN SUDANESE

WHEN GENERAL ABBOUD CAME TO POWER, his foremost goal was to end the rebellion and resolve the problem of Southern Sudan. Since a state of emergency had already been in full force between 1955 and 1958, Abboud was simply tightening the military's grip on the South. Northern Sudanese troops were deployed throughout Southern Sudan, and military garrisons and posts were established along the borders of Ethiopia, Uganda, Kenya, the Congo, and the Central African Republic.[1] Indeed, between 1960 and 1962, the number of Northern Sudanese in the South surpassed that of any other time since Southern Sudan was opened to outsiders in the mid-nineteenth century. According to Bona Ring, sending large numbers of Northern troops to the South was a policy traceable to the 1955 disturbances at Torit. Since then the army, the police, and the guards had been more an army of occupation than a national security force.[2]

Meanwhile, over Radio Omdurman, the government-owned station, the military government in Khartoum began broadcasting (in local Southern languages) messages about government reprisals against Southern dissidents who threatened Northern merchants, administrators, and security forces in the South. In addition, Northern traders based in Eastern Equatoria spread rumors of Southern guerrilla attacks on isolated government posts, thus reinforcing Northern Sudanese determination to strangle the Southern guerrilla movement.

Once General Abboud had firmly established his military administration in Khartoum, he instructed his governors in the three Southern provinces to frustrate or crush any Southerners who demanded federation. For example, the governor of Equatoria Province, Ali Baldo, made it clear to the chiefs in his province that anybody mentioning the word "federation" would be shot. Meanwhile, with regard to the general security situation in the South, Abboud launched a military operation he named *Nadafa Junub*, which literally means "cleansing the South." This military campaign was primarily aimed at destroying the sanctuaries of the Southern rebels along the borders of Sudan's neighbors. Thus, Southern villages along these borders were burned down, forcing many villagers to cross into Uganda, Kenya, Ethiopia, and the Congo seeking refuge.[3]

According to Clement Mboro, during Abboud's regime widespread killings took place throughout the South. He summed up Abboud's policy toward the South as "outright control of the situation, destruction of the Anya-Nya, and the establishment of the rule of law."[4] And one way of gaining control was to impose the Islamic religion and the Arabic language on the people of the South.

ABBOUD BEGINS IMPOSING ISLAMIZATION/ARABIZATION ON THE SOUTH

General Abboud came to power as a Muslim military man devoted to pursuing Islamization and Arabization in the South. He was willing to pursue this peacefully if possible, or by force if necessary. Abboud's determination to spread Islam in the South was really a continuation of Northern Sudanese religious zeal. In 1957, a few months after the Christian mission schools had been nationalized, Sayed Ali el-Mirghani, leader of the Khatmiyya Islamic sect, "declared that his sole ambition and desire was to see Islam spread throughout the Southern provinces."[5] Only time would determine the extent to which Abboud would realize his religious dream as he now set about implementing his policies with respect to the courts, the administration, the schools, and the Christian missionaries.

After consolidating its position in Khartoum, the military government became more aggressive in implementing its policies of Islamization and Arabization. Until 1960, the Southern provinces had traditional courts administered by native chiefs under the Chief Courts Ordinance of 1931, section 7 (1), "to administer the native law and custom in the area over which the Court exercises its jurisdiction, provided that such native law and custom is not contrary to justice, morality and order . . . [t]o administer the provisions of any Ordinance which the Court may be authorized to administer in its warrant or regulation."[6]

Although the chiefs had thereby enjoyed a degree of freedom for at least thirty years in administering local laws and customs, Abboud's government now stripped them of this function. Its primary objective was to undermine Southern traditional laws and customs in maintaining justice, law and order, and harmony among the various ethnic groups. Abboud's administration wanted to replace African laws with Islamic laws as part of its program of Islamization in the South.[7]

To do so, the Abboud regime was prepared to use peaceful means of coercion. Since the great majority of Southerners were directly responsible to local chiefs, it was politically expedient to convert the chiefs to Islam. And so the government forced chiefs to choose between Islam and loss of their positions. Some chiefs who had enjoyed prestige as traditional leaders preferred to maintain the status quo and so obeyed the government. Those who converted to Islam were hurriedly transported to Khartoum by special airplanes chartered by the government and made much of, while Radio Omdurman broadcast their names.[8] The aim was to convince Southern Sudanese that their local authorities had already embraced Islam, but Southern Sudanese still failed to convert or to embrace Arabism. Instead, in the face of repression, large numbers of Southern Sudanese fled into exile in neighboring countries.

General Abboud also perceived that to realize his dream of Islamizing the South, it would be necessary to decree the use of Arabic in government offices. This was expedient, since Arabic had been the official language for many decades, but in the South, English was the official language in government offices as well as the medium of instruction in all schools. This language policy was detrimental to Southerners' aspirations for equality with their Northern counterparts, as it put them "50 years back since English would not help [them] any longer."[9] This was a blow, particularly to the Southern intelligentsia.

Introduction of Arabic in government offices automatically barred Southerners (who could not speak or write it) from employment in those offices, as well as in the army and the Ministry of Foreign Affairs. Southerners viewed this policy as a means of subjugating them culturally and subsequently forcing them into "political slavery."[10]

The government even encouraged Northern Muslim merchants in the South to carry the Koran with them wherever they went. The intent was to convey the impression even to illiterate Southerners that Islam was spreading southward. A Northern Sudanese inspector of local government in Upper Nile, in a speech to a gathering of Southern Sudanese officials and village elders, reaffirmed the military administration's position on Islam, "We are not interested in seeing you praying and fasting. Our main aim is to see that you call yourselves Muslims and then convert your people so that they in turn can convert their present children who are Christians, that Christianity is a foreign religion and should have returned to Europe with the colonialists."[11] Thus, Northern Sudanese Muslims, whether government officials, petty traders, or merchants, were expected to be agents of Islam. Administrators could spread Islam by issuing orders, while businessmen could influence Southerners in their everyday contacts.

The Government Imposes Islam in Southern Schools

At the same time, the government undertook renewed efforts to spread Islam through the educational system. Although the civilian government of Abdalla Khalil had nationalized all mission schools in 1957, by the time Abboud took power in November 1958, there had been no marked improvement in education standards in Southern elementary or intermediate schools. Southerners had not opposed nationalization because they thought that it was government policy to unify the educational curriculum so they could progress along the same lines as their Northern counterparts. Now Southerners felt that the Northern Sudanese simply wanted to "retard education, isolate and insulate the Church, and to impose Islam" on the three Southern provinces.[12]

In 1957, Khalil's government had created the Department of Religious Affairs to oversee programs that reflected Islamic doctrine and its subsequent spread to the non-Arab and non-Muslim parts of Sudan. In the 1958 to 1959 fiscal year, the government had allocated a budget of more than 173,000 Sudanese pounds to the department, which were earmarked for promoting Islam in the South. In a speech to the Legislative Assembly in early 1958, Khalil reiterated his "Government's concern to support [Islamic] religious education." This included building schools for Islamic studies in Southern Sudan.[13] The Department of Religious Affairs projected that during the period 1958 through 1965, eighteen Islamic intermediate schools and one secondary school would be built in the South.[14]

In 1958 and 1959, with lavish funds allocated to the Department of Religious Affairs, a program of building *ma'ahads* (Islamic institutes) and *khalwas* (Koranic schools) in Southern Sudan was implemented. In Equatoria, Governor Baldo opened many mosques and spent money extravagantly; even "to provide for Islamic concerts." Khalwas were built in almost every town in Equatoria, and every child was expected to attend irrespective of his or her religious background. A student who did not receive religious instruction from a *khalwa* had very little chance of entering Malakal Secondary School (which was run in Arabic), even if he scored high in other academic subjects. Meanwhile, in Bahr al-Ghazal, the great majority of students who pledged to embrace Islam were granted free education, an obvious attempt to attract more Southern students to Islam.[15]

While the military government ssought to open mosques, *khalwas*, *ma'ahads*, and secondary schools in the South, it also promoted Arabic in Southern religious and academic institutions. Nationalization of the mission schools had given the government the power to dictate use of Arabic for instruction in any academic institution. Arabic, the language of the Koran and other Islamic scriptures, now had to be taught to Southerners so they could understand the teachings of Islam and consequently embrace it. Thus, it was a matter of policy for Abboud's regime when his governors in the three Southern provinces resolved: "The South must be Islamized and Arabized in order to achieve political unity of the Sudan, i.e. to arrive at the formula: one country, one language—Arabic and one religion—Islam."[16] Implementing this policy necessitated abrogating religious freedom and linguistic rights, restricting political participation, and undermining economic and educational progress in Southern Sudan.[17]

In 1960 through 1961, knowledge of Islam and the Arabic language became a requirement for admission to Southern schools. Juba 1 Boys Intermediate School used Arabic as the medium of instruction, and Southern students who passed the Arabic language exam were admitted into the school. They were expected to be as proficient in Arabic as their Northern counterparts. They also had to pay fees of fifteen Sudanese pounds, an amount few Southerners could afford. By 1962, out of 169 students in the intermediate school, only ten were Southerners.[18] In 1961, Juba Girls Intermediate School (later renamed Abboud's Intermediate School) was opened, with a first intake of forty students. Of that number, only one Southern Sudanese girl was accepted because she had Muslim parents. These two examples from Equatoria were matched by others in Bahr al-Ghazal and Upper Nile.[19] Southern students who were admitted into the schools were urged to memorize the Koran on the pretext of learning Arabic.

To ensure that the religious background of every student was known, parents and children had to declare their religious affiliation upon enrolling in school.[20] Children of parents professing African traditional religions who wanted to accept the Christian faith were either beaten or "threatened with loss of education if they [went] to church on Sunday."[21] Meanwhile, an official of the Ministry of Education in Khartoum admitted that the children of Christian parents were usually told there was no room for them. All these religious and linguistic measures were introduced in the Southern schools in conformity with Abboud's policy of "one religion, one culture and one language—one nation."[22]

Southern Sudanese argued that when Abboud imposed Arabic in the South, they recognized the importance of a standard national curriculum, but they were frustrated with the government's failure to tailor the teaching of Arabic to various educational levels. Southerners criticized Abboud's government for refusing to provide easily adaptable methods for learning Arabic, and its lack of vision in educational programs led to a decline in education standards in all government schools in the South. Religious institutions such as *ma'ahads* and *khalwas*, whose main function was to propagate Islam, lacked clear academic goals and did not emphasize the academic subjects that Southern students needed.[23] In fact, both secular schools and Islamic religious institutions in the South lacked the standard educational guidelines used by inspectors of schools in the North. Materials for Arabic instruction were also lacking.

SOUTHERN STUDENTS STRIKE AGAINST GOVERNMENT POLICY

Abboud's policies of repression, Islamization, and Arabization in the South were aimed at stifling the educational system. Freedom of speech and expression were suppressed, while Arabic was declared the medium of instruction in all Southern schools as well as the official language of administration. The real turning point came in February 1960, when the Sudanese government sought to further circumscribe activities of Southern Christians by declaring the Muslim Friday to be the day of rest, replacing Sunday, the Christian Sabbath, which had been the official holiday for Christians and Southern employees.[24] This decision had profound political and educational ramifications, and it began a new phase in Southern politics. Southern students and the general public viewed it as a declaration of war.

Students at Rumbek Secondary School saw this as a way to impose Islam on them. Having already written a letter of protest to General Abboud in 1959,[25] they were now the first to go on strike in opposition to his government.[26] When Dunstan Wai, a student at Rumbek during the strike, later complained that the food, "especially the quality of the bread and beans" was bad, the government responded by sending troops to the school.[27] Students were "beaten, ill-treated, and jailed." Northern Sudanese merchants were said to have led "the security forces into the parade of students, and handpicked those whom they thought were ringleaders." In fact, some Northern merchants "knew the students' behavior better than the headmasters and the masters at the schools." In essence, the Northern merchants served as the "eyes and ears" of Abboud's government in the South.[28] The student protests prompted the security forces to close down the Rumbek School; three ringleaders were arrested, tried, and sentenced to ten years imprisonment, later reduced to three. Several other students were arrested and detained for many months "under cruel treatment."[29] The government's intent was to frighten the students and deter similar strikes, but their efforts had other results.

The only two Southern secondary schools, Rumbek and Juba Commercial, were now joined by all the intermediate schools in the South; these played a vital role in the resistance with their large student populations.[30] Lawrence Modi Tombe, a Southern student about to enter Rumbek Secondary School in 1960, witnessed the strikes, which he termed "a spontaneous response from all over the Southern Sudan." He was also one of the ringleaders identified as starting the strike at Okaru; they were almost dismissed from the school.[31]

The year 1961 witnessed a series of political events resulting from the Southern students' strike of the previous year. Prominent Southern politicians had fled the country in December 1960. Politicians in East Africa and the Congo now wanted to use the schools as vehicles for political propaganda. Students at Rumbek Secondary School, reopened after the strike, were now sent information by the politicians. Essentially, "all of them were calling for the popular rise against the military government."[32] Politicians including Bismark 'Bungit, a Kuku, Pangarasio Ocheng, an Acholi, and Marko Rume, a Kuku, played a significant role in publishing and distributing political documents reflecting Southern aspirations for self-determination. Southern students themselves were instrumental in enlightening Southerners on political issues.[33]

In 1962, tensions between Southern students and politicians and Abboud's government intensified. The political literature the students were receiving from East Africa regarding self-determination for the South reinforced their political consciousness. They were becoming increasingly aware of the program of Islamization and Arabization, and in their daily academic life they were feeling pressure from the Department of Education. Arabic was emphasized, and students were required to memorize verses of the Koran while learning the language.

In that same year, further student demonstrations erupted in a number of Southern towns. Demonstrations began at Juba Technical School after a Southern student was insulted by an Arab teacher, a common occurrence in Southern schools. At Kator Intermediate School in Juba, an Arab schoolmistress told a Southern student, "Out of your black skins we shall make soles for our sandals."[34] Southern students at Mboro and Rumbek elementary schools in Bahr al-Ghazal went on strike for three days in defense of their religious freedom after some of their classmates were lashed for attending a church service. This strike received sympathy at Wau Technical School, where students went on a two-day strike. The intermediate schools at Tonj, Kwajok, and Bussere also protested, observing a symbolic one-hour strike.[35]

The demonstrations at Juba prompted Southern students at Torit, Malakal, Mundri, Loka, Rumbek, and Wau to go on strike in defiance of the state of emergency, and they now left school and returned to their villages. This alarmed the military government, which reacted swiftly by transporting yet more troops to the South with the primary aim of inciting "a reign of terror in order to prevent any eventual reaction by the people."[36] Some forty thousand Southerners fled to neighboring countries. The government tried to convince students who remained to return to school by a "welcome of 15 to 40 lashes."[37]

In October, the students of Rumbek Secondary School spearheaded a general strike in Southern Sudan. Lawrence Tombe later testified that the activities of Southern politicians in exile had stirred the students to act. Political documents smuggled into the school called on the students to run away and join the liberation movement in exile.[38] Stephen Madut, another student at Rumbek, later stated that Marko Rume, who was propaganda chief for the Sudan African National Union in exile, played an important role in distributing political literature that had a profound psychological impact on the students. In one document, Rume indicated that a foreign force was preparing to invade Sudan and overthrow the government.[39] Such statements, true or false, were a source of inspiration to the students.

The Rumbek strike of 1962 was met with force by the Sudanese government. John Ukech Lueth, a student at the time, later asserted that the school was surrounded by Sudanese soldiers with guns pointed at the students all the time. Some students spied on their colleagues to obtain information about the Southern resistance movement in exile.[40] The students who left Rumbek en masse went to neighboring countries. Tombe and some of his colleagues, for example, left Rumbek and went to Uganda,[41] while others fled to the Congo, where they were later recruited into the Anya-Nya movement.[42]

Dr. Hilary T. Elonai, a former student of Juba Commercial Secondary School in the early 1960s, vividly recalls the tense situation on campus when they heard that students of Rumbek Secondary School had gone on strike. At the time, the government was expelling foreign missionaries from the schools and replacing them with uneducated and ill-trained Arabic-speaking teachers from the North. According to Elonai, "the teachers treated students like dirt," and there were even fist fights between them. Armed soldiers became necessary on campus to keep the peace. Stubborn students were often rounded up by the soldiers and sent to the military barracks in Juba for punishment.[43]

In this "poisoned and explosive" atmosphere, the students received a letter from the Southern Sudanese politicians in exile informing them that a strong Anya-Nya force stood ready to take back Juba and liberate the South from the North. It further warned the students that they were in danger of elimination themselves to prevent them from serving as the future leaders of the South or joining the Anya-Nya forces. The letter had a profound impact on the students at the school. They decided to express their grievances in a letter of their own addressed to President Abboud in which they demanded the soldiers be removed from campus, Southerners be treated as equals, and freedom to choose their religion without being pressured into Islam. If their demands were not met, the students would refuse to attend class. Copies were sent to Abboud, the minister of education, the governor of the province, and the headmaster of the school. The authorities reacted quickly. To forestall a possible riot, the school was immediately shut down and the students were transported back to their homes by truck. Many of them subsequently found their way into neighboring countries, Uganda in particular, with the intent of joining the Anya-Nya.[44]

Thus, between 1960 and 1962, Southern university and secondary school students and civilians fled to neighboring countries in large numbers.[45] The strikes also had a profound impact on Southern intellectuals and politicians, whom the government presumed had incited the agitation. For instance, Father Paulino Dogale, a Sudanese priest at Rumbek whom the government "accused of masterminding the protest," was given a prison sentence of twelve years, later reduced to five.[46] Yet these strikes, like the Sunday strikes of 1960, were effective politically as well as being detrimental to Abboud's government because they were seen as a symptom of insecurity and political instability. However, they did not change government policy toward the South as far as Islamization and Arabization were concerned. Instead, the regime only tightened its grip, with the objective now of ending Christian missionary activity.

REPRESSION OF FOREIGN MISSIONARY ACTIVITY

While the military government pursued its program of Islamization and Arabization in the South, it also put barriers in the way of Christian missionary expansion. As early as 1959, the Abboud regime refused permits to foreign Christian missionaries.[47] As stated by the permanent undersecretary of the Ministry of the Interior, "As for [the] application to open Mission Station at Nyangwara, Nyangiya, among Toposa and a station among the Boya tribe, it is the policy not to allow establishment of new Stations."[48] In fact, Khartoum rejected all attempts to transfer mission stations from one area to another. The missionaries at Tore in Yei District, eighty miles west of Juba, had requested permission to relocate within the province but were denied.[49] The acting governor of Equatoria summed up the policy in a confidential letter sent to the assistant governor and district commissioners in his province, "Visiting Mission areas, schools, religious centers . . . should from now onwards be included in your trek programme and . . . any new buildings, institutions, new comers etc . . . should be carefully enquired into and reported to Province Headquarters at once. . . . In case of disclosing any unauthorized religious schools, no action should be taken without reference to this Headquarters."[50]

Dr. Kamal Baghir, a Northern Sudanese Muslim who headed the Department of Religious Affairs, echoed the government's religious policy in the Arabic newspaper *Al-Rai Al-Amm* in September, 1959: "The nationalization of the Mission schools was an important step in the direction which recognizes cultural unification . . . and we, of the Department of Religious Affairs are ready to do our duty. We have begun with the opening of Islamic centres in the Southern Provinces and we will not cease to work . . . in the direction until we have realized the cultural Islamic unity which we seek."[51]

On December 3, 1959, a Khartoum meeting of Interior and Education officials issued a joint communiqué stating, "The Ministry of the Interior, together with the Governors of the Provinces and the Ministry of Education, will present a draft of reforms of the administrative and general laws required to obviate all the foreseeable cases (regarding education, missionary activity, trade, industry, agriculture, buildings, etc.) to the Attorney General, in order to put an end to the activities of the Missionary Societies, since they have proved a great disadvantage to the country."[52]

These decisions were translated into action between 1959 and 1964. The government reserved its *"full right* to exercise powers of regularizing religious institutions" (emphasis in original) without damaging the interests of the nation and its citizens. According to the interior minister, "regularization" would not apply to Christian catechumenates or prayer centers if the government was satisfied these were purely places of worship.[53]

This order about "regularizing" religious institutions was received calmly by Dominic Ferrara, the apostolic prefect of Mupoi in Zandeland.[54] Mgr. S. Mazzoldi, the vicar apostolic of the Bahr al-Gebel, expressed gratitude for the government's "respect of the principle of religious freedom," and promised that no reading, writing, or academic subjects would be taught in the catechumenates, only "prayers and religion." Relations between the government and missionaries thus seemed to improve, but this impression was short-lived.

When, in February 1960, the Sudanese government declared Friday instead of Sunday to be the official holiday in the South, prompting student strikes throughout the region, Governor Baldo of Equatoria grew worried. Fearful that any gathering of Southerners could foment trouble, he decreed it "a violation of the law to hold public meetings in the open where more than three persons are assembled." As Baldo spelled out his policy toward the foreign Christian missionaries:

> We note with certitude as clear as the sun that the origins of all the misfortunes and contrarieties in our way is the Roman Catholic Church and that the greater part of these evils come from it, although we have pardoned them for many things that should have required hard and energetic treatment. . . . Notwithstanding all this, the Catholic priests do not quit their corrupt politics and they do not make their best effort to co-operate with our present scopes, to respect our national feeling and the scopes for which we work. They do not cease to instill their poison and create the spirit of racial division and of hate between the children of the one and the same country, and even tempt others to mistrust the authority and law in some cases. . . . In front of all this, the wisdom and security of the nation and the interests of the citizens demand with one voice, that this evil which is represented by the Catholic priests should be rooted out: there is no other way to save ourselves than to kick out all the Italian priests, and put the situation in the hands of the Sudanese priests who are only a small number. The time has been reached when we must adopt this measure which is both imperative and useful.[55]

Because Baldo believed that the missionaries were responsible for the strikes in the schools, he accused them of initiating all kinds of evil among the people of the South, but his announced preference for Southern priests over foreign missionaries was only propaganda. He knew that the Sudanese priests could be more easily controlled in their proselytization efforts than the foreigners.

Hassan Ali Abdalla, permanent undersecretary of the Interior, reiterated government policy to the governors of the Southern provinces in July 1960, "The policy of restricting the activity of the missions in the religious sphere, in order to protect the country from the danger of their success, is now entering upon a decisive phase after full enquiries on various matters . . . I ask the Governors to keep this policy secret, so that the missionaries do not learn anything of our intentions, and are thus unable to find any counter-measures to our policy or to mobilize the world press and thus try to make an impression upon us."[56]

In forging ahead with its policy of Islamization, Abboud's regime was thus concerned about world opinion, particularly in the Christian West. Any negative publicity in the world press could severely damage his government's image.[57]

IMPLEMENTATION OF ABBOUD'S POLICIES IN THE SOUTH

Abboud's determination to spread Islam was reflected in Arabic newspapers. On March 9, 1960, the weekly *Anba el Sudan* commented: "This religion [Christianity] continues to expand in the South notwithstanding the measures adopted by the government in its regard. . . . It is the duty of the government to call into the South Islamic missionaries from India and Pakistan and from other Moslem countries."[58] Northern officials and politicians consistently echoed government policy. In a May 17, 1960, article in *Al-Rai Al-Amm*, an anonymous Northern official endorsed the policy of "one Religion and one country. . . . I read in *Rai El Amm* of the orientation given by Islam in the South. You cannot imagine my joy by reading the news, not only because I am a Moslem but because I have a well founded faith that the problem of the South will be solved when Islam will be propagated in the Southern Provinces. I congratulate the Director of Religious (Islam) Affairs for this important initiative: go ahead with courage."[59]

Such statements were common. Southerners were rarely bold enough to express their own views in Arabic newspapers to counteract this propaganda. Instead they presented their opinions in their own newsletter, the

Voice of Southern Sudan, or in petitions to the Organization of African Unity or the United Nations. In June 1960, interior undersecretary Abdullah introduced a measure by which all parents in the South were required to provide written consent that they approved their children's choice of religion (such consent was also required for their children's baptism). The vicar apostolic in Khartoum told the undersecretary that the Catholic Church would allow the children of Catholic parents to "attend Church services and listen to religious instructions given at church or outside the church" because they already had their parents' oral consent.[60] On June 28, Abdulla told Bishop Baroni that written parental consent was applicable only to "certain localities where religious beliefs did not yet take deep roots and where it [would] be misleading to take things for granted." Therefore, if Catholic parents wanted their children to follow their own denomination, they had to provide written consent "in accordance with the law of the land."[61] Bishop Baroni objected that "pagan" and Christian parents were being put into the same category.[62]

In Equatoria, Governor Baldo issued tougher measures to stifle Christian missionary activities. In a letter to all missions, he emphasized that missionaries had to obtain government permission before establishing catechumenates, seminaries, or other religious schools; any that had been illegally opened without approval had to be legalized forthwith or closed within a month.[63] Baldo warned against admitting minors to such schools without a witnessed "consent form" signed by the father and "available for inspection by any Government representative." Missions also had to wait for written approval before they could open any new schools. These measures were aimed at limiting missionary activities in both the religious and educational spheres.[64] Baldo also told foreign missionaries in Juba, Torit, and Mupoi that their bookshops, printing presses, and flour mills must cease to function by the end of June 1960 because these were businesses, not religious activities.[65] It therefore became difficult for missionaries to engage in minor transactions without a trader's license. Instead they had to "confine their activity to purely religious work."[66]

In addition, to prevent Southerners and Christian missionaries from working together, the whole South was declared a "closed area." Foreign missionaries could not enter except with special permits. This decree made it hard even for Southerners living outside the region to enter it.

In 1959 and 1960, Abboud's government achieved a few of its goals in Southern Sudan: the charitable, medical, and quasi-educational activities of the missionaries were all brought to a halt in 1960, while a new immigration law preventing reentry of foreign missionaries into Sudan further discouraged new medical centers, orphanages, and educational institutions.[67] This was only the beginning; further repressive measures would soon follow.

THE MISSIONARY SOCIETIES ACT OF 1962

On May 15, 1962, the Abboud government formally promulgated the Missionary Societies Act. Although the act expressed the government's desire to regulate the activities of foreign missionaries in Southern Sudan, it stated it did not wish to interfere with "the right of any person to profess any religious denomination or sect." The act spelled out the government's position on missionary activities in the South: "No missionary society or any member thereof shall do any missionary act in the Sudan except in accordance with the terms of a license granted by the Council of Ministers. Such license shall be in the prescribed form and shall specify the religion, sect or belief of the missionary society, and the regions or places in which it may operate and in addition may impose whatever conditions the Council of Ministers may think for either generally or in any specific case."[68]

Thus, any foreign or Sudanese individual wishing to teach Christianity to Southerners had to obtain a license from the minister of the interior specifying where and how long operations would take place. The license was valid for one year and was subject to withdrawal or denial of renewal by the interior minister.[69]

The act also made it difficult for Christian missionaries and their adherents in the South to spread the gospel. A priest could be accused of contravening the regulations if he sat under a tree and "read his breviary." A priest could come into direct confrontation with the government if found doing any of the following: "Distributing clothes to needy people; Supplying medical care to the sick; Offering help to an abandoned leper; Visiting a fellow missionary." The Act also included a "provision that no person under the age of 18 may be baptized, even with his parents' consent."[70]

In essence, the Missionary Societies Act was intended to frustrate Christian missionaries in Southern Sudan. At the same time, the government continued to increase the budget of the Department of Religious Affairs. Public funds were diverted so that it could implement its programs. In 1958 to 1959, the budget allotted to the department was 173,222 Sudanese pounds; for 1960 to 1961, 284,950 Sudanese pounds; and for 1961 to 1962, 328,165 Sudanese pounds.[71]

Abboud Expels Foreign Christian Missionaries

On November 15, 1962, the military government introduced yet another measure: the Regulations for Missionary Societies. These "imposed innumerable previous approvals for even the most necessary actions, including repairs in one's home."[72] They were but a prelude to the mass expulsion of Christian missionaries. One hundred fifty foreign Christian missionaries were now expelled from Southern Sudan. Some were detained, while others served various prison terms before their expulsion.

Of the 150 missionaries ordered to leave, seventeen belonged to the United Presbyterian and Reformed churches; they were expected to depart by January 19, 1963, leaving only sixteen missionaries to serve nine mission stations. Eugene Blake of the United Presbyterian Church and Marion DeVelder of the Reformed Church (both American missionaries) issued a joint statement to Abboud's government, hoping to defuse its suspicion and to make a clear distinction between Christianity and the West: "We hope that the fact that Christianity is not a Western religion will enable the Sudanese government to reconsider its action on the basis of the fact that in their service to the people of the Sudan the missionaries represent the worldwide Christian community."[73]

The expulsion provoked immediate international protests from Christian organizations and governments, particularly in the West. For the first time in Sudan's history, its government policies were being brought to light, which had far-reaching consequences for the government's image.[74] In response to allegations in the foreign press, Abboud decided to go on a diplomatic offensive. For example, on January 24, S. A. M Salih, the Sudanese press and information officer at the Sudanese embassy in the United States, defending his government's actions, wrote in the *Catholic News*:

> The policy of the Republic of the Sudan has always been, and shall always be, freedom of religion and worship for all our citizens without discrimination. Thus the sole purpose of the Missionary Societies Act 1962 is . . . to regulate the activities of all missionaries in the Sudan and guarantee freedom of religion and worship for all. . . . [T]he people of the Sudan always and at all times, welcome the good teachings and preaching of Christianity which are based on love, brotherhood and peace. All Sudanese and foreigners alike, both Moslems and Christians, agree to the fact that religious fanaticism has no place in the Sudan where mosque and church are equally respected and where the people are brought up under healthy religious practices.[75]

Salih further argued that since 1957 the government had nationalized the mission schools because it wanted to achieve national integration in "education throughout the country." The government thus deemed it politically expedient to expel some missionaries who had come into the country to establish educational institutions (mission or private) because they "were no more needed for the job." He also accused missionaries of indulging in Sudanese politics with the intent of influencing the country's political destiny.[76]

CATHOLIC REACTION TO THE EXPULSION

Expulsion of the Christian missionaries from Sudan, most of whom belonged to the Catholic Church, was deplored by Pope John XXIII, who directed Archbishop Joseph McGeough (who had visited Sudan earlier on a special peace mission) to express "profound grief" for the four hundred seventy thousand Christians in the South who were deprived not only of priests to minister to them, but also of their rights of religious freedom. The Church had indeed been hard hit: between November 1962 and January 1963, twenty-one lay brothers, seventeen priests, and twenty-three sisters were expelled. Only twenty-one lay brothers, twenty sisters, and sixteen priests were left to serve two hundred twenty thousand Catholics in the South. The foreign Catholic missionaries remaining were insufficient for the eighteen mission stations and twenty bush chapels scattered across the region.[77]

The Verona Fathers order was affected more than other Catholic groups: about one third of their missionaries were expelled. The Reverend Anthony Todesco, one of the expelled missionaries, deplored the plight of Christian missionaries in speeches he delivered in the United States and Italy and at the Vatican. It was "obvious . . . that the Moslem government is determined to suffocate the Church and all Christianity in the Sudan in order that only Mohammedanism will survive," he wrote.[78] Bishop Ireneo Dud[79] of the Catholic diocese of Wau told Todesco in a letter that he had only one priest left at each mission. Todesco in turn feared that "too few priests" were left to cater to the spiritual needs of Catholics in the province.[80]

Fathers E. Sloane, W. Dowds, P. Kok, and A. Myers, who belonged to the Mill Hill Fathers mission at Malakal in Upper Nile, were among those ordered to leave in 1962. Upon arrival in Nairobi, they were met by Archbishop Guido del Mestri, the apostolic delegate; they reported that in a space of two months, some thirty-six priests and nineteen sisters and brothers belonging to their order in Upper Nile had been expelled, leaving their two missions in the Malakal apostolic prefecture to close. Only seven Mill Hill Fathers were left to provide Christian ministry to sixty-five hundred Catholics.

The Reverend Lawrence Endrizzi, who had served in Sudan for ten years, received a letter dated November 6, 1962, and delivered to him by the commandant of police in Equatoria, reading: "I have been directed by the director of Passports, Immigration and Nationality to warn you to leave the country within a period of six weeks from today. The reason being that the purpose for which you were allowed to enter the Sudan no more exists. You are hereby requested to send to this office within two weeks a written undertaking to the effect that you will leave the country within the prescribed period of six weeks."[81]

This statement is representative of the many orders that were issued to the foreign Christian missionaries. As Endrizzi, who left on December 15, later expressed his views about the expulsion, "The preaching of the Gospel of Christ is no longer desirable by the Republic of the Sudan. The practical application of the Gospel teaching is against the law. . . . Strongly enforced restrictions have been placed on the people of the country and on Catholic and Protestant Missionary Society so as to effect the discontinuance of Christianity in the Republic of the Sudan. The ultimate aim of the Sudanese government is to Mohammedanize the entire Southern Sudan which is predominately Christian and pagan."[82]

ISLAMIZATION AND MUSLIM PROPAGANDA IN WAKE OF THE EXPULSIONS

The first phase of expulsion between November 1962 and January 1963 paved the way for further steps in the Islamization program. Islam no longer faced a formidable Christian presence in the South. In Equatoria, for example, the Department of Education laid down a plan to admit Southern Christian students to the *ma'ahads* to train them to become agents of Islamization. On June 16, 1963, A. M. Sharaf El Din, the province education officer at Juba, wrote to the inspector of local government (with copies to all executive officers in Equatoria) providing the names of eighty Southern Christian students: "Attached herewith is a list of boys who are accepted in Torit and Yambio *Ma'ahad* Intermediate Schools. . . . Will you please arrange for their transport to their schools chargeable against Department of Religious Affairs, Khartoum . . . the boys had demanded to enter the *Ma'ahad* Schools and were accepted."[83]

The military government wanted people to believe that Southern students with Christian names had voluntarily joined Islamic schools to learn the Koran and become religious teachers and scholars. The Department of Religious Affairs was to ensure the building and maintenance of the schools and to subsidize the education of these Southern students in the *ma'ahads*. Southern students thus faced a dilemma: either "to reject Islam and abandon education or to accept education and become Moslems."[84]

Moreover, the Sudanese government now accused Father John Travella, a foreign missionary, of spreading rumors among the Southern Sudanese of impending "disorder and violence."[85] These accusations were linked to Father Saturnino Lohure and William Deng's newly founded organization, the Sudan African National Union, which the government accused of seeking to destabilize the country's political system, carry out acts of sabotage, and destroy life and property. Similarly, Father Andria Torcce in Wau was accused of arranging to transport a number of Southern Sudanese by car to neighboring countries where they could join the Anya-Nya guerrilla forces. Investigation of the incident supposedly revealed a clandestine operation by the missionaries in Bahr al-Ghazal in constant contact with Southern freedom fighters inside the country and with their headquarters outside Sudan.[86] Meanwhile, a Southern priest named Peter was alleged to have instigated schoolgirls at Tembura to go on strike. Three Italian missionaries were accused of assisting the students in planning the strike. Angelo Convleri, a foreign priest at Wau, was said to have gone into Wau Technical School by night and instigated the students to strike the following day.[87] The intent of this government propaganda was to establish some evidence (whether genuine or bogus) that would be convincing to the international community in the event the government decided to expel all foreign missionaries.

ABBOUD RIDS SUDAN OF THE REMAINING FOREIGN MISSIONARIES

Finally, on March 4, 1964, the government ordered the expulsion of 214 missionaries consisting of three ordinaries, seventy priests, forty-three lay brothers, and ninety-eight sisters[88] from eight Catholic and Protestant missionary societies.[89] The minister of the interior defended the government's action in a statement released to the Central Council of Ministers in the Constituent Assembly:

> I should like . . . to assure this Assembly . . . that the government is very keen to maintain the freedom of worship in all parts of the country and that every citizen has the full right to perform his religious natural right which we sincerely respect and honestly recognize. . . . The freedom of

worship provided by the laws and which the government pledges to maintain does not mean the exploitation of simple minded citizens in the underdeveloped parts of this country in order to create disunity and hatred and open a door for anarchy and disrespect of the fule [rule] of law so that instability may prevail and the sovereignty of the state will be at stake. . . . It does not also mean that the government will be oblivious and negligent to its fundamental responsibilities.[90]

The minister of the interior reassured Southern Sudanese that the government did not oppose their profession of Christianity but instead preferred that native Southern missionaries should "take over all the duties which those foreigners used to perform in the field of religion." He advised Southern Sudanese not to listen to rumors spread by subversive elements. Rather, they should feel comfortable in pursuing "their private and public affairs"; there was no reason for government interference in their religious practices.[91]

This statement was received with dismay and despair by Catholic missionaries. On March 8, 1964, before leaving Sudan, they refuted the allegations against them in a letter to the interior minister:

> Before leaving this country, we write you not to express our feelings which—you may imagine—are feelings of people who have been shocked by . . . unprecedented and unintelligible events; but we write to fulfill our duty as responsible Church Authorities. . . . [A]s the responsible heads of those [local] Churches for several years, we know perfectly well all our Missionaries, namely the Priests, Brothers and Sisters who are now deported together with us. . . . We are consequently in position to speak for them, and even more, we are bound by justice and charity to defend their good reputation when their behavior is correct, just as we would avow their faults, were they factual and detrimental.[92]

The missionaries denied any involvement in the country's politics or in undermining law and order. They argued that they were concerned solely with teaching Christian doctrine and principles for the benefit of Southern Catholics and that they had always closely cooperated with the different governments of Sudan, whether civilian or military.[93] The missionaries also knew they had no hope of swaying the government to reverse its decision. And so they departed.

Meanwhile, Southern intellectuals argued that the Sudanese government's accusation of Christian missionary involvement in politics was meant "solely to divert and mislead public opinion" about crucial issues facing the country. They believed that Christianity and the Christian missionaries in Southern Sudan were "only victims of Arab religious chauvinism." To Southern intellectuals, the interior minister's statement about the expulsion was simply "Arab propaganda and double talk," which African and world leaders should not pay attention to; Islam was an obstacle because the Sudanese government saw it as the sole basis for national unity.[94]

The expulsion of Christian missionaries received worldwide attention. The London *Times* feared that the Sudanese government's decision was calculated "to remove witnesses of ruthless (if futile) military repression of which there is already evidence." Foreign observers should be admitted "to see that coercion does not become mere brutality."[95]

The Church Missionary Society (CMS) in England also deplored expulsion of the missionaries and urged the press to publicize the real political situation in the country. In a letter to the *Times*, John V. Taylor, CMS general secretary, cautioned the press not "to mask the far more serious issue of the political class [clash] between the Arab-North and the African-South." He argued that this clash should be viewed in historical context; the problems of Sudan could not be resolved "by imposition of one culture upon another." The general secretary was optimistic that men of wisdom and vision could engage in dialogue to reach a "peaceful settlement" to the problems facing the country.[96]

The Catholic priests in particular were more active than the other Christian denominations in gathering support from the Christian community around the world. Catholics in other countries sympathized with the expelled foreign missionaries. West Germany, whose citizens were not affected by the expulsion, showed support for Christians in Southern Sudan: German Catholic organizations and dignitaries put great pressure on the Foreign Office in Bonn to intervene.[97] Other West German Catholic organizations joined the movement and made representations to the Sudanese ambassador.[98]

In his six years in office, General Abboud endeavored to remove the Christian threat in the South by introducing stringent laws that not only made the propagation of Christianity difficult in the region, but also eliminated the foreign missionary presence. The government increased the budget for the Department of Religious Affairs, which built mosques and other Islamic institutions designed to produce Southern Muslims literate in Arabic and capable of propagating Islam to the Southern people, but Abboud's programs of Islamization and Arabization in Southern Sudan became counterproductive as Southern students went on strike across the region, with thousands fleeing into exile. Meanwhile, his use of force to suppress and try to crush the Southern resistance movement resulted in hundreds of thousands of Southern Sudanese fleeing into Uganda, Kenya, the Congo, and the Central African Republic. It was also under Abboud's administration that the Anya-Nya resistance movement was established and consolidated and became a force to be reckoned with. And it was continued Anya-Nya resistance that ultimately led to Abboud's overthrow by the dissatisfied and disgruntled civilian population in Khartoum on October 24, 1964.

CHAPTER 6

EMERGENCE OF SOUTHERN SUDANESE POLITICAL MOVEMENTS, 1960–72

SOUTHERN SUDANESE POLITICIANS FOUND A POLITICAL ORGANIZATION IN EXILE

THE MILITARY ADMINISTRATION OF GENERAL IBRAHIM Abboud had targeted Southern intellectuals and politicians for arrest, imprisonment, or even possible assassination. When, in December 1960, a few days before Christmas, Southern politicians learned of a secret government plan to arrest them, they quickly crossed the Sudanese border into Uganda, where they found safe sanctuary. Here they founded the Sudan Christian Association (SCA) the following year. Its objectives were disguised since Uganda at the time was heading toward independence and the association did not want the authorities to learn about its activities lest the Sudanese government point a finger at Uganda for providing sanctuary to Southern Sudanese rebels. As the name of the association suggests, its members wanted to solicit material and monetary support from Christian organizations and communities in East Africa and overseas. It also wanted to draw the world's attention to the persecution in Sudan under Abboud's military and Islamic regime. Because the association's role was clandestine, it restricted its activities "to the task of raising funds for refugees in neighbouring countries and improving their living conditions."[1]

In February 1961, William Deng joined Joseph Oduho and Father Saturnino in Uganda, where he and Oduho published *The Problem of*

Southern Sudan. This was the first attempt by Southern intellectuals to present the political, social, economic, and religious problems confronting the South.[2] In July, Oduho, Deng, and Father Saturnino met in Kampala, then visited Kenya and the Congo to explain the Southern problem.

The following January, Father Saturnino and Oduho attended the All African Peoples Congress in Lagos, Nigeria, where they met African heads of state and government and held a press conference.[3] In February they returned to Leopoldville (later Kinshasa) in the Congo, where they were later joined by Deng and where they founded the Sudan African Closed Districts National Union (SACDNU).[4] Father Saturnino was named "patron" (political advisor) of the organization. Although Oduho was given the title of president, he was but a figurehead; as Joseph Lagu later asserted, "The power was in the hands of Father Saturnino."[5] Deng was named secretary general.[6] This was the first Southern exile political organization, and they "declared to the world that they knew they were going to struggle for independence."[7]

The SACDNU reached out publicly to Southerners, and by June 1962 it had attracted most of the Southern political refugees. Father Saturnino and Oduho then visited Congo-Brazzaville and the Central African Republic to gather support. They next carried their diplomatic offensive to Europe, seeking both recognition and financial aid, but their efforts were unsuccessful, and they returned to East Africa with sympathy but no tangible support. Nonetheless, this was their first diplomatic move outside Africa, and they were determined to organize other campaigns to win assistance from Western countries and the Vatican.

At the same time, Deng in his capacity as secretary general of SACDNU sent a letter to the United Nations secretary general. This was followed by a twenty-eight-page petition to the UN, which was subsequently presented by Deng to the UN General Assembly in New York in April 1963.[8]

SOUTHERN POLITICIANS FORM THE
SUDAN AFRICAN NATIONAL UNION

The SACDNU was the first Southern Sudanese political movement "to organize their resistance to the Northern Arab domination."[9] Although its name was "supposed to speak for itself," it failed to do so since few outside Sudan knew what a "closed district" was. Thus, it adopted a new name: the Sudan African National Union (SANU), presumably to resonate with KANU (Kenya African National Union) in Kenya, and TANU

(Tanganyika African National Union) in Tanganyika (later changed to Tanzania), both of which had also been founded in exile.[10] SACDNU as a political organization was abandoned in favor of SANU because of the former's ineffectiveness. SANU as the new political organization was then able to achieve what the Southern politicians could not under the designation of SACDNU. In essence, the SACDNU failed in its political endeavors because:

> ... it neither reflected much of the southern Sudan nor was there anything in it that could implicitly reflect the southern Sudanese struggle. In its functions the movement followed in the steps of the SCA (Sudan Christian Association) with the additional task of providing material help to the fighting men in the southern provinces. ... What seemed strange was that, despite its commitment to the cause of the fighting men, the SACDNU was not able to establish close ties with the leaders of the fighting forces nor was it able to supply any weapons for the guerrilla forces. In addition, southerners within the country did not have a clear idea of the existence of the movement in exile. The difficulties at this phase of the movement were clear. No country showed any sign of interest in the southern problem, thus the movement was not able to get help. Besides this, the movement did not start by laying down a clear ideological commitment which might have enlisted the support of one of the big powers at a time when the cold war was at its peak.[11]

The same Southern politicians who had founded the SCA and SACDNU filled in the top positions of SANU.[12] Father Saturnino remained patron, Oduho president, Deng secretary general, and Marko Rume served as vice president.[13] Although SANU's political role in place of SACDNU was not clear at the beginning, particularly to Southerners within Sudan, it was the first political organization to establish a "harmonious relationship between the political wing and the fighting forces" in the South.[14]

SANU's propaganda became widespread within and outside Southern Sudan. In 1963, it founded a news journal called *Voice of Southern Sudan*, which was published in London until it was discontinued in mid-1964.[15] Joseph Lagu later testified that Rume, the propaganda chief of SANU, was instrumental in disseminating valuable political and military information to Southerners both inside and outside Sudan.[16] SANU's major tasks were "political propaganda, raising funds for the movement after the welfare of southern Sudanese refugees in the neighboring countries and trying to consolidate itself. SANU ... made great strides in explaining the aims of the movement to the masses in the southern Sudan and exposing the policies of the Sudan government towards the south to the world at large."[17]

Between November 1962 and July 1963, Father Saturnino, Deng, and Oduho lived in East Africa, where they devoted themselves to organizing the political and military structures of SANU.[18] Although the three Southern leaders initially worked together harmoniously, they eventually fell out.

In April 1963, when Lagu defected from the Sudanese army and joined the liberation struggle, he "found out that the three leaders were not even on good terms. . . . They were writing hostile letters to one another. . . . There was a measure of cooperation between Father Saturnino and Oduho, but there was really no harmony. . . . William was staying in Leopoldville [Kinshasa], Joseph Oduho in Kampala, and Father Saturnino was in Aru."[19] Because Oduho feared that Lagu might be arrested by the Ugandan authorities, he advised him to stay with Father Saturnino in Aru. Soon Lagu became aware that "tribalism was breaking" the movement. In fact, at a "certain stage I [Lagu] became angry and disappointed with" the chauvinism of Oduho and Father Saturnino.[20] (Father Saturnino and Oduho were Latuko from Eastern Equatoria, while Lagu was a Madi of the same province.) Such ethnic conflicts within Southern Sudanese political organizations would become a critical issue in subsequent years.

On October 15, 1963, the Ugandan authorities learned of SANU's political activities inside the country. Oduho was arrested and accused of "managing an unlawful society and raising an army." He was sentenced to nine months imprisonment but was soon released.[21] SANU, in any case, succeeded in opening branch offices in Ethiopia, Kenya, and the Congo; an office was also opened in the United Kingdom. These branch offices were intended as organs to agitate for a plebiscite in the South as a first step toward self-determination. Of these, Ethiopia became the base from which SANU operated and designed military plans and agitation for the plebiscite.[22]

In early 1964, the main office of SANU was transferred from Kinshasa to Kampala in Uganda, where the political climate "was more accommodating." Here, the leaders of SANU felt the need once again for a name more appropriately reflecting the aspirations and goals of the Southern Sudanese. A number of suggestions were put forward, including the South Sudan Land Freedom Army (SSLFA), the Azania Secret Army (ASA), and Anya-Nya. The first known disagreement between Oduho and Deng became manifest in a letter Deng sent Oduho regarding suggested names: "If by contention you mean to say that [Anya-Nya] is the official name, then it should have been discussed, the three names: ASA, SSFLA and Anya-Nya *REMAIN UNOFFICIAL AND SHOULD BE LEFT TO THE ARMED FORCES WHO ARE DIRECTLY CONCERNED*. . . . If SSLFA is adopted as the official name, I cannot see how it can divide the South any more than can ASA and Anya-Nya . . . names may not divide but actions such as yours certainly can."[23]

The rift in SANU was caused not only by arguments over the suitability of a new name but by a financial crisis as well. Since the founding of SANU, money had been channeled to the movement in various ways. Funds were raised from Southern Sudanese in exile, while monetary and material contributions came from the Catholic Church. There was no central bank account. Instead, each of the three leaders received money from his benefactors and spent it in ways he deemed worthwhile for the movement. Father Saturnino was receiving money from the Catholic Church but never made it known to Oduho or Deng.[24]

Ethnic differences also played an important role in the tension that developed between Father Saturnino and Deng. The old Equatoria Corps had been dominated by soldiers recruited from Equatorian ethnic groups. Father Saturnino thought that people from the other two provinces of Bahr al-Ghazal and Upper Nile would be inferior soldiers; Equatorians were the best potential soldiers and hence "most worthy of support." The problems this attitude caused aggravated the disagreement between Father Saturnino and Deng over the timing of the first guerrilla operations in Southern Sudan.[25]

Ultimately, the three Southern leaders were incompatible. Father Saturnino, though a Catholic priest, was an ambitious man, aspiring privately to be the leader of an independent Southern Sudan.[26] The Catholics were behind him; they "always wanted their man [Father Saturnino] to lead."[27] The priest, however, chose to operate "behind the scene as 'patron' of the movement, rather than openly assume leadership" of SANU.[28] These problems, whether ethnic conflicts, personality clashes, or personal ambitions, adversely affected the political and diplomatic activities of SANU. Oliver Batali Albino, a Makaraka from the Yei District of Central Equatoria, and a member of the Anya-Nya movement and later the Southern Sudan Liberation Movement, expressed his frustration with Deng, "Tribalism and regionalism are obviously being sustained to enhance individual ambitions. Another discouraging attitude to those who would work for reorganization is that 'this is SANU which we formed, if you like it join us, if you don't then start your own party and let us see.' . . . The present leaders are partly responsible for our people's sufferings because disunity among us are what the Arabs are working for."[29]

In the midst of these squabbles among the leaders of SANU, in September 1964, Oduho called for a first National Convention to reorganize SANU,[30] which was subsequently held in Kampala from November 7 through November 16.[31] Oduho hoped the convention would reaffirm him as president, thus empowering him in his rivalry with Deng.[32] However, Lagu did not want Oduho to be elected unopposed, and so he solicited Aggrey Jaden, the deputy secretary general of SANU, to challenge Oduho. Jaden agreed after Lagu promised that he "would influence the Dinka to vote for him [Jaden]."[33] When the votes were counted, Jaden had won by a single vote.[34] Thus Jaden became the first elected president of SANU in November 1964. Philip Pedak (from Upper Nile) was appointed vice president, Father Saturnino remained patron, and Oduho was named secretary for legal and constitutional affairs.[35]

After appointing his "cabinet," Jaden consolidated the diplomatic front, appointing SANU representatives to the Soviet Union, the United States, Tanzania, Kenya, Ethiopia, the Central African Republic, and the Congo. In his swearing-in ceremony as president, Jaden spelled out the philosophy of SANU, "Countrymen and brothers, at this stage of our movement, it is now absolutely important that more than ever WE NEED UNITY OF AIMS. To be united does not mean to abolish differences of opinion or points of view . . . but it is very necessary that we must be united in our common and final goal which is independence from the North. . . . We must try to bury our personal, tribal, or sectional interests for the sake of our beloved country. . . . Only unity will be our strength."[36]

In the meantime, before the National Convention, Deng had "been in touch with the Sudan government."[37] When the Abboud regime collapsed in October 1964, the caretaker government of Sirr al-Khatim al-Khalifa "announced policies which seemed to provide prospects of a negotiated and peaceful solution" to the Southern problem.[38] According to Gordon Muortat, such overtures seem to have convinced Deng this was an opportunity for him and others to return to Sudan. In a letter to al-Khalifa, Deng indicated that Abboud's military government had forced some of them into exile and that its collapse had paved the way for Deng and others to return home. He asserted that he wanted a political solution to the problems in the South, but most importantly, he wanted the Sudanese government to accept the consistent Southern demand for federation. On this basis Deng struck a deal with the government in which he was "promised a kind of autonomy for the South with himself as the Vice President of the Republic."[39] Deng did not attend the convention, knowing he would be defeated.[40] Instead he decided to leave SANU and return to Sudan, where in February 1965, he founded a rival group that came to be designated SANU-inside in contrast to Jaden's SANU-outside. Philip Pedak, SANU's vice president, defected to him.[41] According to Albino, these two political entities "were different organizations rather than wings of the same organization."[42]

Aggrey Jaden's term started off well on both the domestic and foreign fronts, but although Oduho accepted defeat in the election, he refused to recognize Jaden's new government even though offered a cabinet position, arguing that "Jaden could not lead a revolutionary movement because he was unknown."[43] However, before Jaden could further consolidate his position, Father Saturnino, who had gone to Europe during the elections, arrived back on the scene. When he learned that Oduho had "conceded defeat," he told him to denounce the election.[44]

Religion was a factor in Father Saturnino's cooperation with Oduho (also a Catholic), especially after formation of the new SANU government under Jaden. That "the Catholics always wanted their man to lead" was already clearly evident before the elections: Father Saturnino had been patron of SANU while Oduho was president. After the 1964 election, the Catholics were completely opposed to Jaden because they wanted Oduho to lead the movement. Because SANU was in need of financial support, Father Saturnino and his Catholic supporters hinted that "the Vatican or certain force[s] connected with the Catholics would give certain financial aid to the movement."[45]

Although SANU was shaken by the struggle between the camps of Father Saturnino-Oduho and Jaden, SANU-outside enjoyed the support of a large number of Southerners.[46] The politicians who had begun the Southern struggle for independence in the early 1960s obviously did not want to follow Deng back to Sudan, despite their differences of opinion.[47]

EMERGENCE OF THE SOUTHERN FRONT

In 1964, following the fall of the General Abboud's military government, Southern politicians and intellectuals still living in Khartoum founded the Southern Front as a political organization. Its politics were clandestine, and its members included Gordon Muortat-Mayen, Darius Beshir, Bona Malwal, Clement Mboro, Abel Alier, Alfred Lubari Ramba, Hillary Paul Logali, Lam Chec, and Arkanjelo Wanji. This organization also supported Anya-Nya activities inside the South through fund-raising.[48]

When Mboro was appointed interior minister in the government of Prime Minister al-Khalifa, he remained a loyal member of the Southern Front. As he put it, "I was Minister [of Interior] by day and Anya-Nya at night."[49]

Meanwhile, leaders of the Northern political parties in Khartoum were debating whether negotiations with the Southern political organizations should be conducted outside or inside the country.[50] The Southern Front played a vital role "in persuading the external organizations to support negotiations inside the country." Darius Beshir, president of the Southern Front, "used to shuttle between East Africa and Khartoum"[51] in an effort to persuade Jaden and Oduho to negotiate for peace; Gordon Muortat, however, was opposed.[52]

What became known as the Round Table Conference took place in Khartoum between the major Northern political parties (Umma Party, National Unionist Party) and representatives of SANU-outside, SANU-inside, and the Southern Front in March 1965. The delegates were there to discuss crucial political issues such as federal status for the Southern region and the unity of Sudan at large, but ethnic differences were already at work before the conference opened. Some members of the Southern Front, particularly the Dinka, deserted it for Deng's SANU-inside Party. Thus a rift was created in the Southern Front similar to the split of SANU into its "inside" and "outside" factions the previous year.[53] Muortat led the Southern Front delegation to the conference, while SANU-outside sent Elia Lupe, Jaden, and Daniel Jumi Tongun. The Uganda government sent Felix Onama to provide a "guarantee for the safe return of SANU members who came from outside."[54]

During the deliberations, a deadlock developed between Deng's and Jaden's factions. The Southern Front mediated, and it was decided that the SANU delegation would be led by Deng and Elia Lupe, a strong supporter of SANU-outside. The Southern Front had its own delegation of nine. Thus, the Southern Sudanese were represented by three delegation heads at the Round Table Conference, again exhibiting ethnic conflict, personal ambition, and the usual personality clashes.[55]

THE ALF/SALF SPLIT AND MERGER

The disagreements between Father Saturnino and Oduho's camp and that of Jaden prompted the two leaders of the former to dissociate themselves from Jaden in June 1965 and declare their faction the Azania Liberation Front (ALF). In response, Jaden formed his own political organization, the Sudan African Liberation Front (SALF).[56] The wrangling between ALF and SALF on one hand, and between the Southern Front and Deng's SANU-inside on the other, frustrated the Southern Sudanese refugees in East Africa. The situation was further compounded by the brutality of the new government of Prime Minister Mohammed Ahmed Mahgoub, which in June 1965 succeeded the caretaker regime in Khartoum. In fact, the North was more determined than ever to gain full control of the South.

In this unfavorable political climate, the Southern Sudan Students Union (SSSU) of East Africa formed a commission in July to bring about a compromise between Oduho's and Jaden's factions.[57] After investigating the issues threatening to destroy the Southern political and military organizations, it reached two important conclusions, "William [Deng]'s SANU inside the country which aims at federation is in confusion with the actual SANU which works to liberate the South. The difference should be made clear by change of name. . . . Since SANU is not fighting to liberate the whole Sudan there should be a name given to the land we are fighting to liberate and the name should be born in the party."[58]

According to Lagu, when he visited Eastern Equatoria (in 1967) he learned that the Southern Sudanese refugees in East Africa were urging Jaden "to step down in favor of Oduho because by then the Catholic Church was the one ready to support [us] . . . our Anglican Community [was] reluctant to support [us] for military purposes."[59] By this time, Jaden's movement was bankrupt financially and proving difficult to sustain. Thus Jaden agreed to step down as president of SALF and merge his party with Oduho's ALF. Both parties accepted the name ALF as the political and military banner of the Southern Sudanese people—Oduho became its president and Jaden was named vice president.[60]

Between January and July 1966, Oduho traveled some 450 miles in Eastern Equatoria, holding meetings with those who had not fled to neighboring countries. In July, he organized an executive meeting of ALF, during which he quarreled with Father Saturnino over receipt of financial aid from foreign benevolent organizations; aid destined for Oduho had instead been diverted to Father Saturnino. Because Oduho's leadership was being undermined, he became frustrated and left for Kampala. Father Saturnino, however, remained in Eastern Equatoria. This was yet another cause of instability in ALF.[61]

Joseph Lagu, then a lieutenant in the Anya-Nya, was disappointed with the ALF-SALF merger and left for Northern Uganda, where he transferred his family from Lira and resettled it at Gulu. Father Saturnino, realizing Lagu's potential, sent an envoy, Father Delino, a Madi priest, to enlist Lagu's support for his political and military agenda.

Lagu for his part realized there was tension among the Latuko people themselves.[62]

Meanwhile, in Uganda, President Milton Obote's government had turned against the Southern Sudanese politicians and combatants. According to Gordon Muortat, Obote became hostile under pressure being exerted on both Uganda and Kenya by the Sudanese government. Mahgoub persistently accused the two neighboring countries of not only hosting Southern refugees but also harboring insurgents. Obote did not want his diplomatic image or his relations with neighboring countries tarnished.[63]

Obote's hostility forced the Southern leaders in Uganda to flee to neighboring countries. Elia Lupe escaped to the Congo, while Oduho fled to Southern Sudan. Upon arriving at Dito (near Torit), he declared it the capital of Southern Sudan, but Oduho was losing support from his own people. While still in Kampala, he had been expected by the Latuko to deliver military supplies to them, but when he turned up empty-handed, his people lost confidence in him.[64] He was even briefly arrested when Lazarus Mutek, a Latuko chief, accused him of adultery,[65] further damaging his credibility. He consequently left for Nairobi in Kenya.[66]

The movement was further shaken when Father Saturnino, returning from Europe where he had been buying arms and soliciting financial assistance, was unexpectedly killed by Ugandan soldiers in Northern Uganda on January 23, 1967. Ugandan politicians seem to have been implicated in his death. At the time, the political parties in Uganda were affiliated with Christian religious denominations. Obote had come to power with support from Protestants in the country, while Catholics supported the opposition Democratic Party. Thus Father Saturnino was deemed dangerous because of his support from Southern Sudanese Catholics and for his direct links with the Vatican and other Catholic communities in the world.[67] The year 1967 thus started badly.

THE SOUTHERN SUDAN PROVISIONAL GOVERNMENT IS FORMED

At this point, Jaden decided to intervene to save the Southern liberation movement.[68] Between February and August 1967, he toured Central Equatoria extensively, attempting to rally government-appointed chiefs to support him. Nine chiefs pledged support for the liberation of Southern Sudan. Jaden also solicited the support of Lupe and Kamilo Dhol, a Dinka from Aweil and former senator in the Sudan government.

On August 15, Jaden convened a meeting at Angundri in Western Equatoria that drew together, for the first time in Southern history, all the civilian and military leaders.[69] It was attended by three hundred delegates from the three Southern provinces,[70] although the Azande, who had already formed their own Sue River Republic, and the Moru, who had their own grievances, refused to attend.[71]

In his speech to the delegates, Jaden "sketched the history of the struggle and condemned the many causes of disunity such as personal ambition, desire for gain, tribalism and politicking."[72] His primary aim was not to form a party or a front, "but a government in which all the elements of southern leadership would be united."[73] Delegates reiterated their determination to create a new movement, which became known as the Southern Sudan Provisional Government (SSPG).[74] They further passed resolutions to transfer movement headquarters back into Southern Sudan, dissolve competing organizations, unite the military and political wings, and hold an annual convention.[75]

The various Southern guerrilla factions were merged into a single national army, which became known as the Anya-Nya National Armed Forces (ANAF).[76] The convention also spelled out a clear foreign policy: "close cooperation with all liberation movements in Africa for the liberation of southern Sudan from Arab rule; opposition to imperialism, communism and racism; support for all international peace movements; support for a greater East African Common Market; opposition to religious or racial prejudices and discrimination among the members and supporters of SSPG, and with this understanding the desire to negotiate and cooperate with any Arab Government."[77] The SSPG strongly voiced its determination to uphold "true African unity" and vowed it would "relentlessly resist with all means at her disposal the Arab Colonialism in the Southern Sudan until full independence and dignity is achieved by the Southern people."[78]

The Angundri convention took place in an atmosphere where democracy could be exercised. To prevent ethnic conflicts within the new SSPG, its members implemented the idea of equal representation of people from the three Southern provinces. Jaden (from Central Equatoria) became president; Kamilo Dhol (from Bahr al-Ghazal) became first minister for communications; Michael Tawili, a Kakwa and MP for Yei (Central Equatoria) became minister for social affairs; and George Kwanai, a Shilluk from Upper Nile and a journalist, assumed the post of minister for information.[79] Although Jaden emphasized equal representation among the Southern Sudanese in his new government, the composition of his cabinet reveals there were more people from Equatoria (his own province) than from Bahr al-Ghazal or Upper Nile.

The reasons for the convention's success were threefold. First, Southern leaders such as Father Saturnino and Oduho, whose personalities had clashed in previous movements, were not present; Saturnino was already dead; and Oduho was at Dito in Eastern Equatoria. Second, for the first time, both political and military representatives had been brought together to hammer out important guidelines for the liberation movement. And third, delegates to the convention came from all three Southern provinces, and there was harmony rather than tension among them.[80]

It was not long before problems developed. In late 1967, Gordon Muortat, as the new SSPG's foreign minister, was sent to Uganda and Kenya on a diplomatic mission. In his absence, a fight broke out in a military camp commanded by Nanga Mariik, a Dinka Anya-Nya officer from Rumbek. An Anya-Nya contingent opposed to Mariik's leadership arrested him, but loyal supporters smuggled him out and transferred him to SSPG headquarters at Bungu. Akuot Atem, as defense minister, thereupon ordered his release.[81]

On a previous occasion, while on a military mission to Angundri Mariik had encountered Gabriel Kau, a former minister of justice in Oduho's ALF, and arrested him; these two are believed to have had an earlier conflict in Rumbek over some cattle. When Kau was now brought to Bungu, Atem took pity on him and instead rearrested Mariik, who was put in detention. This military development later led to armed clashes between the supporters of Mariik from Rumbek and forces loyal to Jaden and Atem. Fighting spread as far as the border of Zaire, and a few soldiers loyal to national headquarters were killed. This tense situation prompted Jaden to issue an order to Atem not to release Mariik. Jaden and Muortat then went to Uganda and Kenya to discuss political and military issues with Israeli officials.[82] In their absence, Akuot ordered the execution of Mariik and three other Anya-Nya officers. Jaden now became highly suspicious of Atem and refused to return to his headquarters.[83]

At this point, Jaden suddenly told his cabinet that a relative was sick and he needed to visit him. He was accompanied by a military escort on what would be his last day in the SSPG. Abandoning the leadership, he left for Kampala. Jaden's erratic behavior came as a shock. According to Muortat, "We were really worried because there was very good unity among the soldiers, among the political group. . . . All that was being awaited was military help."[84]

Jaden's abrupt departure from the SSPG prompted its cabinet to hold an emergency meeting at which Muortat was "elected to go and talk to him." Jaden and Muortat were old friends, and it was believed that

Muortat might succeed in convincing Jaden to come back. Muortat went to Kampala and for two days exerted every effort to persuade Jaden. As Muortat later recounted, he said to him, "Mr. President, why did you leave? . . . What happened? . . . The situation is very delicate and it is a turning point in our history . . . we have now just received help and if you don't go back, then everything will be upset." Jaden confided to Muortat that he was upset with Atem, who had carried out the executions without his consent, and with Lagu, who he believed was undermining his authority.[85]

Jaden thought he was becoming increasingly unpopular and thus was not being an effective leader. Since he was from Central Equatoria, where he drew much of his support, other parts of Southern Sudan did not see themselves as an integral part of the SSPG. Jaden and his supporters had been suspicious that Dhol, his vice president, and followers were planning a coup,[86] and there had been speculation that Jaden planned a cabinet reshuffle that did not reflect the principle of equal representation of the provinces.[87] On the military front, Jaden's ambition for greater success had been unrealized. The traditional squabbling between the Nilotes and Equatorians had added more fuel to the fire; arms procured by the movement were to be divided up on the basis of equal representation, which meant the loss of a substantial amount of arms and ammunition from Equatoria.[88]

Although Jaden's SSPG lasted only a short time, it achieved some major goals: "The SSPG laid down policies and a programme which on paper at least offered a better chance of generating a sense of national identity and purpose than the policies of any previous administration. Given time, the government might have succeeded in establishing an administration in which all elements of the South could have worked together in harmony and mutual respect."[89]

The departure of Aggrey Jaden from the SSPG affected its machinery. Many officials and military men deserted, and the direction of the movement as a whole remained unclear for some time.[90]

THE NILE PROVISIONAL GOVERNMENT

In September 1968, the cabinet of the SSPG, under the chairmanship of Vice President Dhol, proposed that the second National Convention, expected in August, be held instead at Abba (Ibba) in Zaire in December. The SSPG decided to call for the National Convention primarily "to name the country . . . [t]o submit to the Convention the draft Constitution . . . [t]o give chance to all Southerners who have the liberation at heart to discuss their country's affairs."[91]

The convention was delayed until the following year because the organizing committee wanted Southerners from inside Sudan, in other African countries, and in Europe to attend. Finally on March 19, 1969, at Balgo-Bindi, in the Congo (Zaire), Dhol officially opened the convention. Jaden and Oduho, who had brought the liberation movement almost to the brink of collapse because of their squabbling for power over the previous four years, did not attend.[92]

The political atmosphere was conducive to critical discussion of issues in a frank manner. A motion was introduced to discuss a new name for Southern Sudan before independence was achieved. Many names were suggested, and the debate for the most appropriate name lasted several hours. In the end it was resolved that since the word "Nile" was "the only unifying factor to all parts of the South" as all tributaries flowing through the Southern villages emptied into it, the name Nile should be adopted, and the governing body assumed the name Nile Provisional Government (NPG).[93] In an atmosphere of friendliness, the convention passed a few resolutions:

> The assembled representatives declared that the three Southern Sudan Provinces of the Sudan and its people [are] under a separate state called the Nile, and the people Nileans. Its boundaries [are] declared identical to the original Southern Sudan. The Nile Provisional Government, its armed wing, the Anya-Nya National Armed Forces and the civil population, shall prosecute with determination the war of Liberation for national Independence and Freedom. The Supreme governing will of the Nilean people shall be vested in the National Legislative, Executive and Judicial bodies. . . . The Convention re-affirmed that the seat of the Nile Provisional Government shall always be situated inside the Nile State, and that only the Provisional Government operating inside the country is the constitutional, legal, and authoritative body of the Nile State in its internal and external affairs.[94]

The delegates also reiterated the need for close cooperation between the Nile state and African nations in an effort to guard against "Arab genocide and racial subjugation." They declared all other Southern political parties or movements in exile illegal and condemned any further attempt to split the Southerners.[95] The convention also drafted and passed a constitution, "An executive body of 8 persons, two amongst whom are the president and vice president elected on separate and secret ballot, and the rest appointed by the President in consultation with an Adhoc advisory committee; a legislative body referred to as National Liberation Council representatives plus the executive members and 12 other nominees. The constitution divided the country into nine (9) administrative units called

Regions, and also provided [for] Defence, Legislative, Executive and Judicial matters. For Defence, it provided for a unified National Army Forces (ANAF)."[96]

The Nile state constitution guided the delegates at the convention when by secret ballot they elected Gordon Muortat as president and Marko Rume as vice president.[97] Muortat appointed young men to his cabinet: Arkanjelo Wanji as foreign minister, Joseph Banak as information minister and attorney general, and David Koak as defense minister.[98] But the cabinet did not reflect equal representation of the three Southern provinces as stipulated by the National Convention of 1967.

The NPG started well as a democratically elected government with young and dynamic leaders, but like Southern organizations before it, it was not immune to rivalries. Muortat appointed Major General Amadeo Taffeng Lodongi commander in chief of the ANAF and Emmanuel Abur as chief of staff. A few months later, Taffeng got permission from Muortat to visit a sick daughter as a disguise for a plot to overthrow him.[99] Taffeng went to his home area on the East Bank of the Nile and declared the formation of the Anyidi Revolutionary Government. He was joined by Rolf Steiner, a soldier of fortune, who advised Taffeng "that if he could keep away from the Nile Provisional Government . . . the German government had agreed to supply him with arms so that he could fight separately against the Arabs." Steiner now not only vigorously campaigned against the NPG but also convinced Muortat's military commanders to stage a coup. Steiner's grand plan was to become overall commander of the Southern Sudanese rebel forces.[100]

Steiner's plot for a coup was hatched while Muortat was on a diplomatic mission to Uganda and Kenya. As early as August 1969, "an article appeared in the *Uganda Argus* that the Nile Provisional Government had been overthrown,"[101] a rumor propagated by elements opposed to the new government. While Abur was acting chief of staff and Dhol acting president, Taffeng sent Michael Loruwe to persuade officers of the NPG to overthrow Muortat. The officers were divided over the issue, and in an armed clash Loruwe was shot and killed.[102] Taffeng thereafter remained aloof from the liberation struggle until Lagu overthrew the NPG.

Between March and September 1969 Muortat made contact with the Israeli embassies in Kinshasa, Kampala, and Nairobi. On some of these missions he negotiated financial as well as military assistance. In fact, Israeli officials in Kampala were more receptive to Muortat's appeal for military assistance than they had been of previous Southern Sudanese approaches, but they remained skeptical about agreements with the NPG civilian leadership.

At the same time that Muortat was in touch with Israeli officials in the Congo, Uganda, and Kenya, Lagu was also secretly contacting the Israelis in Kinshasa and Kampala. Like the Israelis, he was skeptical about the Southern civilian leadership. As a trained military officer, he had become convinced that uniting the armed forces of the Anya-Nya under a central command was of paramount importance. It was partly for this reason that he contacted the Israelis, and he succeeded in acquiring military assistance from them.[103]

This provision of arms to Lagu upset Muortat and his provisional government. Muortat thought that Lagu was stabbing him in the back and undermining the NPG. In frustration, he announced that he wanted to dissolve the NPG to pave the way for Lagu's ascendancy to power. Officers loyal to Muortat, however, dismissed the idea, arguing that Lagu had always had the tendency "to resist the orders of the Provisional Government" and should therefore be branded a rebel.[104] They wanted Muortat to give them permission to "attack Lagu's headquarters and take the arms so that the foreign government [Israel] is not given a choice." This move was calculated to draw the attention of the Israelis to the delicate security situation in Southern Sudan, which directly affected the rank and file of the ANAF. The primary aim of the officers loyal to the NPG was to create a military situation in which the Israelis would be compelled to divert arms to the Provisional Government."[105]

Although Muortat faced a dilemma, he refused to attack Lagu's camp. According to him, if factional fighting broke out among the Anya-Nya soldiers, it would likely "lead to the complete collapse of the movement" and also to withdrawal of Israeli assistance to Southern Sudan. In this complex state of affairs, he preferred to step down from the presidency and hand power to Lagu. Since this was opposed by Anya-Nya officers loyal to him, a deadlock ensued.[106]

THE EMERGENCE OF THE SOUTHERN SUDAN LIBERATION MOVEMENT

Muortat now complained to the Israelis in Kampala about the diversion of arms to Lagu's camp. Instead of apologizing, officials at the Israeli embassy reassured Muortat in a meeting that they could supply the NPG separately if he was not ready to cooperate with Lagu. Muortat decided to send a delegation under his fforeign minister, Arkanjelo Wanji, to the Israelis in Kampala. The delegation included Emmanuel Abur and Michael Mut.[107]

While Wani proceeded to the Israeli embassy in Kampala, the other two commanders went to Lagu's headquarters, where new Israeli arms had arrived. Shortly after the delegation returned, forces loyal to Lagu planned a coup against Muortat. After surrounding Muortat's residence, a military contingent led by Colonel Paul Aweil announced to him that the NPG had been overthrown and that he had "better give up power." In Muortat's words, he declared "there is no power in the bush.... I have no power to hand over."[108] In the interest of Southern unity, Muortat agreed to dissolve the NPG and pledged his readiness to cooperate with Lagu and his Southern Sudan Liberation Movement (SSLM). This transfer of leadership from Lagu to Muortat took place in July 1970.[109]

In later years, John Ukech Lueth, who was a lieutenant at the time of the NPG, admitted that he was one of the officers loyal to Lagu who planned and executed the bloodless coup. The rank and file of the ANAF were disillusioned with the civilian leaders of the NPG. The politicians had promised military supplies from foreign powers, including Israel and France, but these promises had not been kept. Dissatisfaction led to support of alternative leaders under Lagu, whose power and popularity were increasing among the Anya-Nya.[110]

Meanwhile, Lagu had consolidated his position in the military and was ready to lead the SSLM and its military wing, the ANAF. In his words, "When Taffeng learned that he had taken over power from the Nile Provisional Government he paid allegiance to him, but was later retired." This marked the end of the Anyidi Revolutionary Government under Taffeng.[111] When Samuel Kabashi of the Sue River Republic heard of the NPG's demise, he also declared his allegiance to Lagu. In essence, Lagu "became the undisputed leader" of the SSLM.[112]

Although Muortat had agreed to dissolve the NPG and had handed power to Lagu, he remained incensed with the Israelis, whom he blamed for having planned the coup, but he had also conceded defeat, and rather than stay in Southern Sudan or go to a neighboring country, he left for Britain in April 1971 and never returned.[113]

Thus, from the outbreak of the 1955 Southern disturbances until 1970, there had been no effective Southern liberation movement or government. At various times, quasi-liberation movements had emerged, consolidated, and disintegrated. Although they differed in structure and composition, their philosophies were similar: the liberation and total independence of Southern Sudan from the Arab and Muslim North. But ethnic conflicts, personality clashes, and power struggles prevented these movements from creating a unified front to challenge the better organized and equipped Sudanese army. It had taken Lagu nearly seven years before he could amalgamate all Southern liberation movements or pseudo-military factions into a single, formidable organization: the SSLM. But the same problems of personality clashes, personal ambitions, and ethnic conflicts that had worked against the unity of the Southern Sudanese would also be reflected in the rise, centralization, and decentralization of the ANAF.

CHAPTER 7

REORGANIZATION AND CONSOLIDATION OF THE GUERRILLA MOVEMENT, 1963–71

EARLY LEADERSHIP CRISIS IN THE ANYA-NYA

THE LEADER OF THE ANYA-NYA MOVEMENT AT its founding was Father Saturnino Lohure, who according to Joseph Lagu had more power than Joseph Oduho, the nominal president of the Sudan African Closed Districts National Union (SACDNU, afterward the Sudan African National Union [SANU]).[1] John Ukech Lueth has corroborated this. Father Saturnino organized those Latuko who had defected from the Equatoria Corps. He was an ambitious priest who wanted to be not only the political leader but also the commander in chief of the Anya-Nya.[2]

Father Saturnino's attempt to seize both political and military control of the movement was challenged by officers from ethnic groups in Eastern Equatoria, such as the Madi, Acholi, and Lokoya, who all supported Lagu. Father Saturnino commanded the loyalty of his Latuko parishioners and also of Sudanese abroad, especially among Catholics in Uganda and the Congo. He had also won support at the Vatican during his visit in 1963, and it also provided monetary assistance to SANU.[3]

Thus, from its founding in September 1963, the Anya-Nya had a leadership crisis created by the rivalry between Oduho and Father Saturnino. According to Lagu, the priest knew more about using demolition devices for bridges than did Lagu himself, who had been trained in the Sudanese army. Father Saturnino's military skills, coupled with his religious connections, gave him an advantage over Oduho, who had been a schoolteacher before fleeing to Uganda in December 1960. "There was also a measure of cooperation" between them for they were, after all, both Latuko.[4]

Lagu was occasionally frustrated when these two Latuko exhibited their tribalism and refused to cooperate with him, a neighbor but a Madi, over military organization, training, and operations. To avoid getting entangled, he devoted his energies to consolidating his position in the movement and organizing his own people, the Madi. While this helped to ensure his personal security, it also compromised his primary aim of achieving unity among all the ethnic groups of Eastern Equatoria before expanding the activities of the Anya-Nya to Central and Western Equatoria. At the same time, Lagu was fully aware that the largest proportion of the Anya-Nya was Latuko, and he needed their support not only in Eastern Equatoria, but also to expand the insurgency to other parts of the South.[5]

When Lagu joined the Southern freedom fighters in June 1963, Father Saturnino regarded him as a potential military leader. After establishment of the Anya-Nya, Lagu was made defense minister and was directly responsible to Father Saturnino, who wanted to be the commander in chief. In Lagu's words, "It was with him that I wrote the orders for action."[6] This arrangement, however, was loosely defined.

Father Saturnino Relocates Anya-Nya Headquarters

Although the Anya-Nya began in Eastern Equatoria and was led by Latuko, there was a dilemma regarding the location of its headquarters. Strategic military advantage outweighed any attachment to an ethnicity or location. Suppression of the 1955 Torit mutiny had led to insecurity requiring the presence of the Sudanese army; if Anya-Nya headquarters were established in Eastern Equatoria, it would be exposed to very high risk from Sudanese troops. Moreover, the political leaders of SANU were scattered in three countries: Oduho was in Kampala, William Deng in Leopoldville (Kinshasa), and Father Saturnino in Aru, a small town inside the Congo near the Ugandan border.[7]

Lagu could not plan and execute military operations in Eastern Equatoria in particular, and Southern Sudan at large, from Uganda. Therefore, as defense minister of SANU, he joined Father Saturnino at Aru, whence they could safely traverse the territory between the Congo and Western Equatoria. Indeed, the terrain at Aru was crucial in its choice as movement headquarters, for it provided ample hiding places for Anya-Nya camps to avoid detection by the Sudanese army and air force. It was thus at Aru that Lagu and Father Saturnino established the military organization of the Anya-Nya.[8]

Although Aru was a strategic location from which the Anya-Nya could launch guerrilla operations into Western Equatoria, Father Saturnino decided to abandon it and move instead to Eastern Equatoria to set up Anya-Nya headquarters among his kinsfolk, the Latuko. He did so for two reasons: He was more familiar with the territory in Eastern than in Western Equatoria, and he also felt secure among the Latuko, whom he could easily train and supply with weapons. He was thus opposed to a similar military organization being established in Western Equatoria.[9]

Father Saturnino's objective was to set up a well-organized military force that could first liberate the whole of Eastern Equatoria and then move into Western Equatoria, but this decision pitted the Bari people of Central Equatoria against the Latuko of Eastern Equatoria. In fact, the Bari, Azande, and Moru of Western Equatoria were outraged that military activities were to be confined to Eastern Equatoria to the neglect of other parts of Southern Sudan, but despite these ethnic conflicts, the new military organization did not collapse. In the spirit of patriotism, the Southern insurgents constantly reminded themselves of their enemies, the Arabs, who for more than a century had caused the inhabitants of the region misery, whether through enslavement, destruction of property, arrest, torture, imprisonment, or execution.[10]

HENERICK ROSSI TRAINS THE ANYA-NYA

Henerick Rossi, an Austrian soldier of fortune, joined the Anya-Nya movement in Eastern Equatoria in 1964 and provided advice and military training. He proposed that Southerners create a state of general unrest involving student demonstrations and civil disobedience in the South, arguing that "when the parents condemn their children, then the public is not ready for war, but if they support their children then they [are] ready for revolution." This advice was taken seriously by Marko Rume, vice president of SANU and its chief propagandist, who wrote to students in the South urging them to "come up for the military training and that arms [would] be dropped by air and that student leaders should report to Kampala to political leaders."[11] Rossi advised the Anya-Nya to launch operations against Southern towns to boost morale, saying that they already had enough men and officers drawn from the police, prisons, and the army to do so. William Deng, secretary general of SANU, fully agreed.[12]

Lagu, however, was pessimistic about such a military plan. He thought that any attack on Southern towns would "demoralize the people." He insisted that training was a prerequisite to a first offensive against the Sudanese army. Lagu therefore began a course of basic training for the Anya-Nya lasting almost six months.[13] But Rossi did not give up: he predicted that an Anya-Nya assault on Southern towns could provoke the Sudanese security forces into launching a counterattack against the Southern civilian population in which many would die. This would, in turn, "drive the Southern intellectuals and villagers into the movement."[14]

Obstacles stood in Rossi's way, "The need of a guerrilla to be in his own area to avoid being spotted or betrayed . . . the indigenous people will hardly support guerrilla leaders who come from far. Thus hindering the expansion and involvement of local people. . . . Most of [the] Southern police and Warders [had] already been dismissed when many started to escape with weapons despite [the fact] that very few Southerners were police and prison guards."[15] These problems seemed real in the infancy of the Anya-Nya, but in subsequent years, with strong leadership, they were resolved without much resistance from fighters and civilians alike.[16]

Rossi also stressed the importance of propaganda in warfare. He wanted the Southern people to publicize all atrocities committed against them by the Sudanese government. This was particularly important for two reasons: first, it would raise the morale of the people, and second, it would tarnish Sudan's national and international image with far-reaching potential consequences for the government. Rossi thought that "after outbreak of hostilities in the Sudan even the Uganda Govt. will be forced to react and that searches and arrests will take place. To avoid this he advised on hiding documents, dispersing, and not to live in one building or one part of the city. In Rural [sic] areas he advised that the people should move away from along the roads. On intelligence, Rossi advised that the easiest and shortest way for . . . collecting information is through Khartoum."[17]

The flow of information from Khartoum was facilitated by two Southerners located there. Henry Bago was an employee of the United Nations who smuggled information through the diplomatic bag to Kampala, where leaders of SANU were based, while Captain Peter Joane, a pilot for Sudan Airways, also carried information from Khartoum to SANU and the exiles in Uganda.

THE POLITICS OF LIBERATION

In September 1964, Southern politicians based inside Southern Sudan—Father Saturnino Lohure, Aggrey Jaden, Joseph Oduho, and Ezbon Mondiri—organized a meeting at Tul near Torit, where Lagu was "given the responsibilities to organize the Anya-Nya."[18] Instead of being appointed commander in chief, he was given the awkward title of chief organizer/chief instructor of all Anya-Nya forces and was placed under Mondiri, a Moru from Western Equatoria who was appointed defense minister.[19] Lagu was a farsighted officer who wanted unity among the people of Eastern Equatoria before political and military activities were carried out in Western Equatoria.[20]

After this meeting, Mondiri asked Lagu to tour the South with him, but Lagu declined because he "was already assigned the duty of chief organizer/chief instructor" and wanted to remain in Eastern Equatoria. According to Lagu, he refused because Mondiri had his own agenda,[21] but Lagu also had his own ambitions. In any case, Mondiri was a civilian, and Lagu did not consider him competent to head ALF's ministry of defense.[22]

Instead, Severino Fuli, a Madi politician in the Anya-Nya, accompanied Mondiri on the long journey to Anya-Nya camps in Central and Western Equatoria. After visiting Kajo-Kaji, Yei, and Aba, they proceeded to Maridi. In his journeys, Mondiri assured the civilians and Anya-Nya that "they were fighting for the same cause." He informed the soldiers particularly of "the new politics and regulations of the ALF [Azania Liberation Front]," and he acquired firsthand information about the living conditions of Southerners. In early February 1967, Mondiri arrived at his home in Lomilingwa in Moruland.[23] According to Lagu, the moment Mondiri reached Lomilingwa, "he declared that that was the headquarters of the Anya-Nya."[24] From here he could solicit the support of the Azande, Moru, Mundu, Avukaya, Baka, and Wira. Lagu believed that Mondiri had his own plan to assume leadership of the Anya-Nya forces.[25]

According to Gordon Muortat, Mondiri was the first to attempt to transform the Anya-Nya into a national army under a central command with regional commanders in the three Southern provinces. He began in Central Equatoria, where he integrated the Anya-Nya forces in the Bari and Yei areas, where the Bari, Kakwa, and Kuku had related languages and traditions. His plan was to extend this arrangement to Western Equatoria, incorporating the Moru, Mundu, and Azande into the movement.[26] He would then extend the military arrangement to Bahr al-Ghazal and Upper Nile, beginning with Tonj and Rumbek in Southern Bahr al-Ghazal and proceeding to other parts of the province, but before he could implement this program, he quarreled with Anya-Nya commanders in the province who were undermining his authority. Their insubordination shattered his hopes and destroyed his long-term goal of reorganizing Anya-Nya forces under one chain of command.[27]

Upon returning to Lomilingwa, Mondiri also quarreled with Ezbon Jodi, a Moru whose ambition was to become overall commander, or at least commander of Anya-Nya forces in Western Equatoria. He had a large following among the Moru and placed Mondiri under house arrest. Jaden and his military supporters intervened and released Mondiri, who, however, lost confidence in the Anya-Nya movement and left for Nairobi, where he remained a political refugee until 1972.[28]

While Mondiri was pursuing his own military advancement in Central and Western Equatoria and Southern Bahr al-Ghazal, Lagu was busy training and arming the Anya-Nya in Eastern Equatoria and working closely with Father Saturnino. They launched their first military assault against the Sudanese army on November 26, 1966, destroying bridges on the Juba-Nimule and Juba-Torit roads. Their strategy was to impede the movement of Sudanese troops to garrisons in Eastern Equatoria from their headquarters in Juba—standard guerrilla tactics of "hit and run" to frustrate a superior enemy that was well equipped and well trained.[29]

Then on January 23, 1967, Father Saturnino was killed by Ugandan soldiers in Northern Uganda on his way back from Europe. Although deeply demoralized, Lagu was convinced that he could keep the support of Father Saturnino's Latuko. At the same time, Oduho, who was living at Dito near Torit, tried to convince the Latuko to transfer their allegiance to him, but most of them were reluctant to desert Lagu. In Kampala in 1966 through 1967, Oduho had promised the Latuko weapons, uniforms, and financial assistance. When he failed to deliver, he lost his credibility with his own people. Lagu, on the other hand, continued to gather support from the peoples of Eastern and Western Equatoria until the Southern Sudan Provisional Government (SSPG) was formed under Jaden in August 1967.[30] Absorbed with military plans between 1965 and 1967, Lagu did not extend his influence over the activities of the other Anya-Nya forces in the Bahr al-Ghazal and Upper Nile. Here the Anya-Nya remained highly decentralized, and there was no coordination of military information between them and Lagu.

Jaden Reorganizes the Anya-Nya

In August 1967, Aggrey Jaden became the first elected Southern leader as president of the newly formed SSPG. Although Jaden was an intellectual and politician without significant military experience, he had a vision for reorganizing and consolidating the Anya-Nya forces. Briefly as leader of SANU in 1964 and of the Sudan African Liberation Front (SALF) in 1965, he had contacted senior and junior military officers and the rank and file of the Anya-Nya movement. But his leadership of SALF was short-lived, and he did not play an effective role in reorganizing and consolidating the Anya-Nya until his election as president of the SSPG.[31]

Jaden's program involved ending the highly decentralized and ethnocentric Anya-Nya operations. He seems to have acknowledged and admired Mondiri's efforts during 1965 through 1967, but he also realized that reorganizing the Anya-Nya required coordinating military operations and the distribution of weapons, uniforms, food, and financial resources.[32] To accomplish this objective, Jaden appointed Amadeo Taffeng instead of Lagu as commander in chief of all the Anya-Nya forces in Southern Sudan.[33] According to Lagu, Jaden appointed Taffeng because he thought that Taffeng, a Latuko, "was the most powerful" military man and consequently should have overall command of Anya-Nya forces.[34]

Jaden also renamed the Anya-Nya the Anya-Nya National Armed Forces (ANAF) to reflect its national mission, and appointed Akuot Atem, a Dinka politician from Bahr al-Ghazal, as defense minister of the SSPG.[35] The military command consisted of Taffeng as commander in chief; his deputy, Ali Gbatalla from Western Equatoria; and Lagu as chief of staff, a position he resented and which was to have a profound impact on the Anya-Nya movement in later years.[36]

A new group was created within the military hierarchy known as the general staff. It comprised the senior Anya-Nya officers, Colonels Emmanuel Abur from Bahr al-Ghazal, Samuel Abujohn from Western Equatoria, Frederick Brian Maggot, and others. Jaden's primary aim was to create a chain of command that could operate effectively in all three Southern provinces.[37]

Jaden did not want Anya-Nya fighters to operate strictly in their own ethnic localities. Instead, he wanted all ethnic groups integrated into the ANAF so that Latuko could carry out military operations in Zandeland or Dinka of Bahr al-Ghazal could fight in Eastern Equatoria. This idealistic military strategy was designed to promote harmony among all Southern Sudanese, an opportunity for ethnic groups to recognize differences and yet respect commonality in a struggle to liberate Southerners from their Northern foe.[38]

Jaden was also keen to create what he called the National Mobile Force. This was a multiethnic unit that could operate in any part of the South. In fact, one such unit was dispatched to Upper Nile and operated there until Anya-Nya officers overthrew Muortat and Lagu became the undisputed leader of the Anya-Nya in early 1970.[39]

In Bahr al-Ghazal, the process of amalgamating Anya-Nya forces under a central command had begun in 1966 and continued until Jaden became SSPG president. Anya-Nya battalions at Tonj, Aweil, Gogrial, and Wau, and battalions such as the Railway Battalion and the Anti-Demolition Battalion were commanded by Anya-Nya officers but not under an overall provincial commander. During Jaden's term of office, the Northern Command, which comprised the districts of Aweil and Gogrial, was formed. The Fertit and Jur battalions in the Western districts and the battalions at Wau and Tonj had their headquarters at Ted-Adhol.[40] By June 1967, unity among the Anya-Nya forces in Bahr al-Ghazal had been achieved.[41] Philip Nanga Mariik, a high-ranking officer, was appointed commander for the whole province.[42]

The Anya-Nya also had access to arms and ammunition stored in a military depot at Angundri in Moruland in Western Equatoria, nearly six miles from the Sudan-Congo border. Here Anya-Nya forces from all parts of the South were represented, and tensions among the various ethnic groups were temporarily resolved.[43] Jaden's political acumen, coupled with Anya-Nya reorganization, helped to create an atmosphere conducive to military operations.

MILITARY CRISIS IN THE ANYA-NYA CENTRAL COMMAND

While military reorganization was taking place in Equatoria and Bahr al-Ghazal, in Upper Nile a serious military crisis was developing in the Anya-Nya leadership. Rivalry between Paul Aweil and Daniel Kozi led to the latter's death. Shilluk officers in the Anya-Nya engaged in "a string of coups" that almost destroyed the movement in the province, but the National Mobile Force, dispatched to Upper Nile, contained the interethnic conflict.[44]

As the reorganization, amalgamation, and consolidation of the Anya-Nya continued, Lagu remained angry about the appointment of Taffeng as commander in chief. He recognized this as a demotion for himself since he had served briefly in Jaden's SANU as commander in chief of the

Anya-Nya forces.[45] Muortat has confirmed that Lagu was furious about serving under Taffeng, who was illiterate and whose only claim to power was the allegiance of the Latuko.[46] As Lagu later put it, "I was disappointed with the whole movement and kept out of it. I could not envisage myself working under illiterate generals. I know Taffeng was appointed commander in chief because he commanded strong tribal loyalties in Western [sic] Equatoria but I had a strong influence at this time all over the Anyanyas. . . . The people of Eastern Equatoria recognized me as the only military leader."[47]

From 1967, Lagu set out to undermine Taffeng. He refused to take orders or cooperate in military matters. This insubordination frustrated Taffeng's military administration. Privately, Taffeng complained about Lagu's arrogance but considered Lagu "his son," for he was old enough to be his father. He never expressed outright hostility toward Lagu and continued carrying out his own duties in the ANAF in the spirit of patriotism until the SSPG's fall in 1968.[48]

Although Lagu recognized Jaden as leader of the SSPG, he was ambivalent about the politicians inside Southern Sudan. Since 1963, when he had first joined the Anya-Nya forces, he had witnessed continuous squabbles over power among the Southern politicians. He believed that the vendettas and maneuvers for personal power had weakened the guerrilla movement, and he argued "that the politicians should step down and allow military men to run the affairs of the movement."[49]

Indeed, Lagu had begun laying the foundation for his subsequent leadership of the ANAF. In June 1967, after the Six-Day War, Lagu wrote to Israeli prime minister Levi Eshkol, congratulating him on the victory of Israeli forces over the Arabs. He told the prime minister that he was also fighting the Arabs in Southern Sudan and that if Israel supported him and the Anya-Nya forces, he would pin down the Sudanese army, making it difficult for Sudan to send troops to support Egyptian forces in Sinai and along the Suez Canal. But before Eshkol could address the Southern problem, he died of a heart attack.[50]

The new prime minister, Golda Meir, immediately sought to support the Southern Sudanese and made arrangements for Lagu to travel to Israel in late 1969. His visit marked the beginning of close relations between the Israelis and Southern Sudanese. From then until the signing of the Addis Ababa Agreement in 1972, the Israelis consistently sent military assistance to the Anya-Nya and provided it with military and political training.[51]

As Lagu trained, organized, and equipped the Anya-Nya forces with the powerful support of Israel, his prestige and power increased, while

Jaden became suspicious about his intentions. Despite tensions within the leadership throughout 1967 and until 1968, the strength of the Anya-Nya forces continued to grow. Ethnic groups hostile to each other before the emergence of the SSPG began to cooperate in the common cause. In a demonstration of unity, the headquarters of the ANAF and civil administration of the SSPG were established at Angundri in Western Equatoria. There all ethnic groups in Southern Sudan were represented.⁵²

At Angundri, representatives of these ethnic groups could "negotiate and buy guns and send them to their respective areas."⁵³ But Anya-Nya units from Bahr al-Ghazal were in an awkward position at Angundri. First, "there was a lot more hostility among the people" toward the people of Bahr al-Ghazal.⁵⁴ The principal representatives of the Anya-Nya at Angundri were Bari, who were hostile to Nilotes from Bahr al-Ghazal in their territory. Although the people of Central Equatoria were better equipped militarily than their counterparts in Bahr al-Ghazal because of their proximity to sources of arms in the Congo, they were overwhelmed and alarmed by the influx of a large number of Nilotes.⁵⁵

In fact, the Bari were highly suspicious about amalgamating the Anya-Nya forces for the entire Southern Sudan, believing this was designed to transfer arms they had secured from Zaire to the people of Bahr al-Ghazal. Even Jaden and other leaders from Central Equatoria began to leave Angundri. "They didn't trust that this union would be of benefit to them." Nonetheless, some Equatorians had already been sent to Bahr al-Ghazal with forces from other ethnic groups "based on the theory of having a territorial army, and then a strategic, more conventional army."⁵⁶

As elections for a new government in Southern Sudan approached in August 1968, suspicions among the Bari increased. The people of Equatoria considered Khamilo Dhol, a Dinka from Bahr al-Ghazal, a rival to Jaden, and they believed that since Bahr al-Ghazal was more populous than Equatoria, it would win any democratic election.⁵⁷ Jaden's sudden and mysterious disappearance from Angundri for Kampala was partly the result of such fears. As John Ukech Lueth later explained, "The important politicians of Central Equatoria felt themselves as if they were not going to be a part of the system because of the volume of people [Nilotes]."⁵⁸

GORDON MUORTAT AND THE
NILE PROVISIONAL GOVERNMENT

In the election of April 1969, Gordon Muortat Mayen was elected president of the new Nile Provisional Government (NPG), but his election was not well received by many ethnic groups in Equatoria. There was tension between the Anya-Nya of Central Equatoria and Nilotes from Bahr al-Ghazal. This affected the military structure and strength of the ANAF. Some deserted the movement, while others took weapons to their villages. Many Anya-Nya refused to fight and instead moved to refugee camps in neighboring countries. During this crisis, Michael Loruwe, encouraged by politicians from Equatoria, led a contingent of Equatorian Anya-Nya against the headquarters of the NPG at Balgo-Bindi (near the Sudan-Congo border) to eliminate the Nilotes.[59]

Loruwe's forces captured an outpost of Anya-Nya loyal to the NPG. Fighting between the Equatorian Anya-Nya and Bahr al-Ghazal Anya-Nya continued for two months. The kinsmen of the Nilotes from Bahr al-Ghazal were unable to reinforce them because they were attacked on their way to Western Equatoria.[60] Allan Reed, an American reporter for NBC, observed "great hostility between the Zande and the Dinka" in the two years before he traversed Zandeland in 1971.[61]

This fighting between the Anya-Nya forces of the two provinces was disastrous. The Anya-Nya from Bahr al-Ghazal were caught between two enemies: Both Sudanese troops and the Bari Anya-Nya frequently attacked them. As Lueth put it, "We were just like in prison." The difficulties, he said, were "generated by the politicians from Equatoria, who had left the executive of the Southern Sudan Provisional Government. They wanted the people of Equatoria to believe that the only government that could be formed in 1969 was one that would be dominated by the people of Upper Nile and the Bahr al-Ghazal."[62]

During skirmishes between the two Anya-Nya factions, Lagu remained aloof. He continued to consolidate his position, especially by receiving military equipment from the Israelis through Uganda, Ethiopia, and Zaire (Congo). He also established a secret headquarters at Owing-ki-Bul in Eastern Equatoria. From there, Anya-Nya from different parts of the South were trained and redeployed to their respective areas with arms and ammunition.[63]

Lagu, unlike Jaden, wanted Anya-Nya forces to operate only in their own localities, which were familiar to them and where they would receive support from local inhabitants. He continued to preoccupy himself with restructuring, retraining, and arming the Anya-Nya forces, particularly from Eastern and Western Equatoria and Upper Nile. During this time, Lagu emerged as the dominant military officer whose position no other senior Anya-Nya officer in Southern Sudan could challenge.[64]

Meanwhile, the election of Muortat as president of the NPG was opposed by senior Anya-Nya officers, including Michael Towili and Samuel Abujohn, both from Zandeland, Frederick Maggot of the Bor

Dinka, Akuot Atem from Upper Nile, and Taffeng, a Latuko. Taffeng now openly broke with the NPG. He and Maggot subsequently moved to Eastern Equatoria and formed the Anyidi Revolutionary Government. At the same time, in Western Equatoria, Abujohn and Towili formed the Sue River Republic.[65] This was described as a "pan-Zande movement," whose long-term goal was to link up with the Azande in northeast Congo and the Central African Republic,[66] but this dream proved unfeasible, and the project was abandoned by its founding members.[67]

In late 1969, when Taffeng realized that Lagu had emerged as the most powerful individual in Eastern Equatoria, he and Maggot abandoned their Anyidi Revolutionary Government and offered their loyalty to Lagu; Abujohn also "pledged his loyalty." Simon Jada, an Anya-Nya officer who commanded a big Bari following and was operating in Central Equatoria among his Bari kinsfolk, also joined Lagu at Owiny-ki-Bul.[68] To unite the Anya-Nya commanders from throughout the South, Lagu established the Anya-Nya High Command Council in October.[69] Lagu and his Israeli military advisors then went to Kenya and subsequently to Ethiopia, where he was able to organize "support for Upper Nile straight from Ethiopia."[70] Lagu had now almost achieved his objective. By late 1970, he had gained control of the whole of Eastern, Central, and Western Equatoria, and of Upper Nile; Bahr al-Ghazal, however, remained under the control of Muortat's supporters.[71]

Joseph Lagu and the Southern Sudan Liberation Movement

While these developments were taking place, senior Anya-Nya officers loyal to Muortat's NPG were becoming dissatisfied with his empty promises of arms from the Germans, French, and British because the "bulk of people coming from Bahr al-Ghazal and Upper Nile" had no weapons. Anya-Nya officers in Bahr al-Ghazal were aware of Lagu's growing military strength, and they preferred to turn to him rather than continue to pledge loyalty to a political leadership that had never fulfilled its promises.[72]

The most effective means of overthrowing the politicians of the NPG was by a coup. Thus, Lueth, Dhol, Abur, and Aweil arrested Muortat and announced the NPG's overthrow by Bahr al-Ghazal Anya-Nya officers. A military delegation was immediately formed comprising Lueth, Major Kawac Makwe, Colonel Abur Nhial, NPG chief of staff Major Frederick Fadul, and Colonel Makur Thou, all of whom pledged allegiance to Lagu. He told them in turn that "we will only give you arms if you declare, as of today . . . no fighting will ever take place between you and any other Southerners . . . leave alone the people from the Bari-speaking tribe." The Bari people at headquarters were given a similar warning. A declaration of principles was signed by the former belligerents, thus paving the way for unification of the ANAF.[73]

As Anya-Nya officers and men came to Lagu's headquarters to offer their allegiance, he found himself the "undisputed leader" of the ANAF.[74] In July 1971, he brought together Southern military and political leaders in a conference that established the Southern Sudan Liberation Movement (SSLM), with Lagu as its political leader.[75] He also became the commander in chief of all territorial forces in Southern Sudan and restructured the chain of command to improve their fighting efficiency. In addition, he appointed Colonel Abujohn from Zandeland as deputy commander in chief and regional commander of Western Equatoria.[76]

Because Lagu, unlike his predecessors, was opposed to amalgamating Anya-Nya forces under a single overall command, preferring that each ethnic group carry out military operations in its own locality, Anya-Nya forces from Bahr al-Ghazal could no longer operate in Central Equatoria, although there was still a military depot for weapons and other supplies at Angundri in Western Equatoria. By the same token, Anya-Nya forces from Upper Nile could no longer receive military supplies only from Owiny-ki-Bul and then return to their region. Thus, the idea of a territorial army or the National Mobile Force introduced under Jaden was abandoned.[77]

Instead, Lagu decentralized the Anya-Nya forces. Each of the three Southern provinces now had its own brigade.[78] In 1970, Lagu created the Annual Command Council Conference to review the achievements, problems, and issues pertinent to the SSLM. By October 1971, the high command of the SSLM comprised the following officers: Lagu, commander in chief, ANAF, and leader of the SSLM; Brigadier Joseph O. Akuon, deputy commander in chief, ANAF, and regional commander of Upper Nile; Colonel Emmanuel Abur, regional commander of Bahr al-Ghazal; Colonel Frederick Maggot, chief of staff and secretary to the High Command Council, and Lt. Colonel Habakuk Soro, regional commander of Western Equatoria.[79]

The military reforms in the Anya-Nya stemmed from the fact that Lagu, unlike his predecessors, was in an advantageous position. While political leaders such as Jaden and Muortat had received a formal education, they had limited military knowledge. On the other hand, military commanders such as Taffeng, Lazarus Mutek, and Ali Gbatala in Western Equatoria had no formal education or military science training. In fact, they were "only officers from the ranks . . . and therefore what they had to give to the soldiers in the form of training was limited."[80] Lagu's military experience, both from the Sudanese army at the Military College in Khartoum before he joined the Anya-Nya in June 1963 and within the movement itself, made him unique.[81]

Lagu attracted a big following among the Southern Sudanese because he had something to offer them. His fluency in the Southern languages of Madi (his own language), Acholi, Dinka, and "Southern Arabic" enabled him to communicate directly with many Southerners regardless of their ethnic backgrounds. The fact that Lagu was the son of a police constable who had served in various parts of the South further increased his popularity and prestige among Southern Sudanese.[82]

Lagu claimed that his policy was to "talent-spot" any Southerner and build him into an effective fighter. He cited an Israeli commander who had told him that "the essence of good leadership is the ability to talent-spot others . . . and having done that, build them. . . . It is not good leadership to lock knowledge in the drawer, but [to] pass it to other people." Lagu asserted that it was on this basis that he "put more emphasis in training and building others irrespective of their political views" or ethnic affiliations.[83]

Lagu had created a command structure less prone to a centrally organized coup than those of earlier organizations.[84] The lack of swift transportation across the length and breadth of the South and the shortage of support facilities made it difficult to coordinate information and soldiers in a coup. The rank and file of the ANAF were content with the training and equipment they received from Owiny-ki-Bul as a result of Lagu's leadership. This state of affairs continued until Lagu opted to negotiate a peace agreement, the process of which began in late 1971 and ended in March 1972.

CHAPTER 8

EXTERNAL POLITICAL AND MILITARY INVOLVEMENT IN SUDAN'S CIVIL WAR, 1960–72

SOUTHERN SUDANESE ACQUIRE WEAPONS FROM VARIOUS SOURCES

TO BEGIN A GUERRILLA MOVEMENT WHOSE OBJECTIVE WAS to destroy the government and its military authority in the South was not an easy task. The Anya-Nya had to take up arms against a numerically superior Sudanese army that was well trained and well equipped. The Southerners, who had few financial and material resources, had to start a liberation movement from scratch. After the 1955 mutiny at Torit, the Southerners—former servicemen in the Equatoria Corps and the police, prison, and wildlife forces—needed arms before they could launch any real challenge to the Sudanese army. Consequently, the Anya-Nya forces and weapons varied according to the political, economic, and military circumstances in each locality or region of Southern Sudan.

The majority of Southern civilians owned only spears and bows and arrows, which they used in guerrilla "hit-and-run" tactics in isolated skirmishes against Sudanese security forces throughout Southern Sudan. Thus, the first weapons of the Anya-Nya were spears, bows and arrows, *pangas* (machetes), and swords.[1] Although these were far inferior to the rifles of the Sudanese army, the patriotism of the Southern people was a source of strength in their resistance. Guerrilla warfare's element of surprise in dense vegetation also worked in their favor. A classic example was when Jeremiah Jale surprised an Arab soldier on the outskirts of Kajo-Kaji with a bow and arrow, instantly killing him and confiscating his gun.[2]

Henerick Rossi, the "helpful Nazi" who offered to train the first Southern freedom fighters, emphasized the digging of trenches across roads, which, if covered with grass, could immobilize enemy trucks. Once the trucks were stopped, freedom fighters could use machetes and spears to defeat their enemies. In the absence of boats, Rossi taught Southern guerrillas how to cross a river with a rope. Such practical aspects of guerrilla warfare were taught at Agu Camp in Eastern Equatoria in the early 1960s.[3]

In Bahr al-Ghazal at Khor Ghana on the Wau-Raga road, inhabitants armed with spears and swords attacked a police station at night. In the ensuing fight the policemen exhausted their rudimentary weapons. The attackers killed most of the policemen and captured British rifles.[4] Such incidents were frequent. Although traditional weapons were no match for the firepower of the army, the Southerners were determined to fight.

In some cases, civilians possessed firearms before the 1955 mutiny. Southern servicemen in the Equatoria Corps and the police, prison, and wildlife forces who later defected to the Anya-Nya movement carried with them their rifles and ammunition. At Kajo-Kaji, a medical assistant, Manasseh Yeinio, who worked for the Kajo-Kaji hospital, donated his rifle to the guerrillas in 1962. This was one of the few rifles acquired by the guerrillas there.[5] In Western Equatoria, civilians and former servicemen who possessed rifles donated them to the insurgents. As a symbol of good faith, donors were given receipts.[6] Some civilians at first refused to surrender weapons but were forced to do so and given a symbolic receipt.

The guerrillas collected any firearms they could find, irrespective of age or condition. By the end of 1963, guerrilla training camps such as Nyangara and Bangidi in the Congo had acquired weapons for training. The rifles included muzzleloaders, breechloaders, magnums, light British rifles, Remingtons, Manchesters, and shotguns.[7] In Western Bahr al-Ghazal, a transit camp was established at Ngo Sulugu to collect firearms from donors. Guerrilla forces were provided basic training with various types of weapon before being sent to the major training camps of Nyagara and Bangidi.[8]

Meanwhile, in Upper Nile, the Anyuak, Nuer, Murle, and Burun people had had access to firearms since the 1930s when the Italians invaded Ethiopia.[9] The Italian defeat of the Ethiopian army led to the proliferation of arms throughout Upper Nile, where the border peoples had easy access to them. They collected rifles from the Ethiopians for their own protection against the cattle raids of the neighboring Nuer, Murle, Shilluk, and Dinka. At the time of the 1955 mutiny, the Anyak, Burun, Murle, and Nuer therefore already had a supply of firearms. When the Sudanese army assaulted the police and prison headquarters at Malakal on August 21, 1955, these locals were able to repel them.[10]

The Southern Sudanese explored every avenue, peaceful or otherwise, to acquire firearms from the Sudanese police, prisons, or armed forces. When two Sudanese policemen, one a Nuba and the other an Arab, became very drunk while guarding a post at Kajo-Kaji, a Kuku mob rushed to the scene and beat them severely. According to Wojia Masiri, the Arab was killed but the Nuba was spared. During this incident, the Kuku confiscated the police rifles.[11]

In Bahr al-Ghazal, incidents similar to the one at Kajo-Kaji were common. In November 1963, Ferdinand Goi went to the police station at Bussere and falsely reported that a fight had broken out two kilometers away and that two people had been killed.[12] Two policemen were immediately ordered to accompany him to the scene. On their way, Goi "tricked them and killed them both." He confiscated their rifles and their uniforms.[13]

In August 1964, a Dinka woman at Wau, who was a close friend of Sudanese troops in the town, invited four soldiers to her house along with four Southern women to entertain them. When they got drunk, "each with a lady beside him," she took all their firearms, wrapped them in a mattress, and carried them into the forest where the Anya-Nya had established a camp.[14]

Defections of Southern policemen, prison guards, and soldiers from the Sudanese army also provided arms and ammunition to the guerrilla movement. As early as 1955, when some soldiers of the Equatoria Corps refused to surrender, they carried their firearms and ammunition to the guerrilla movement. Thus freedom fighters such as the prison guard Helir Latada, who ambushed Sudanese troops in Eastern Equatoria; Lasuba and Paul Yosia, who launched guerrilla attacks at Kajo-Kaji-Yei; and George Hilal, who defected from the police with a British rifle and two hundred rounds of ammunition, were examples of former servicemen who contributed weapons to the movement.[15]

FUNDS FOR THE ANYA-NYA MOVEMENT

Southern Sudanese at home and abroad worked hard to raise funds for the Anya-Nya. This was done secretly through political agents. Between 1959 and 1964, an underground movement in Bahr al-Ghazal raised funds for the Anya-Nya and its political wing in exile. Funds facilitated the travel of Southern students inside Sudan to Anya-Nya training camps in the Congo. Some funds were channeled to the political leadership in exile through missionaries or Southern runners.[16] General Joseph Lagu later stated that this was a "people's war," and Southerners "collected money and gave it to their local Anya-Nya who bought arms for their local Anya-Nya. . . . It was the effort countrywide of Southern Sudanese."[17]

In some cases, funds were acquired through Anya-Nya attacks on trucks of Northern Sudanese traders and merchants in the South. Anya-Nya officers, such as Santino Ajing Daw and Ferdinand Goi, launched isolated ambushes on commercial trucks and captured three thousand Sudanese pounds.[18] Such exploits also boosted Anya-Nya morale.

Within Southern Sudan, money for the Anya-Nya was raised in a variety of ways. The local inhabitants were asked to pay taxes in the form of food, grain, or cattle. In Bahr al-Ghazal, John Ukech Lueth became the first Anya-Nya officer to take cows from Aweil to the Central African Republic to be sold. The profits were used to purchase weapons from the remnants of the Simba insurgents and Congolese soldiers who had hidden firearms and ammunition in their houses. All these transactions were carried out secretly without the knowledge of the Central African Republic authorities.[19]

Aside from the sale of cows, every man was urged to pay a poll tax; in monetary terms it was fifty dollars, and in material form it was fifty pounds of grain. In return, the Anya-Nya provided security to the local inhabitants. However, the Anya-Nya also cultivated grain to ensure a constant supply of food for themselves and civilians. During the dry season, the Anya-Nya would travel far and wide in the Dinka area collecting taxes. They were reasonable in assessing taxes. Assets were the decisive factor, and as a result there was mutual understanding between the political agents of the Anya-Nya and the Southerners.[20]

Southerners explored every avenue to raise money in support of the Anya-Nya. In Western Equatoria, game was a lucrative source of income. Each camp had a department that "dealt in big game and seasoned meat and skins."[21] Skins of crocodiles, pythons, and leopards as well as rhinoceros horns and elephant tusks were in high demand. These were bartered for clothes, medicine, bullets, and firearms. Sometimes the Anya-Nya raided government hospitals and dispensaries for medicine and equipment. Along the Southern borders of Sudan, black markets dealt in firearms, ammunition, medicine, and clothes.[22]

Although wildlife products provided revenue, in some cases Anya-Nya officers embezzled the money. Colonel Habakuk Kefu Soro, a former Anya-Nya officer in Zandeland, provided this testimony, "Our commander asked all the camps to contribute money and ivories for him to take to Congo to buy arms and ammunition; however, when these were contributed he went but bought beautiful clothes, shoes, [a] Radio recorder for his wife and family. The clothes that he brought to his wife caused the wives of the soldiers to insult their husbands that they called themselves Anya-Nya while the real Anya-Nya is [the commander] who brought nice clothes to his wife while they were suffering with ropes on their buttocks."[23]

Funds were also raised from sources outside Southern Sudan. Father Saturnino Lohure was instrumental in raising funds in the early years when the movement was struggling to organize, restructure, and acquire military equipment. He made contacts through the Catholic Church to solicit financial and material support.[24] According to Gordon Muortat, Father Saturnino received substantial sums from Catholics who were sympathetic to the Southern Sudanese in their struggle against the Muslim Northerners. He then used these funds to purchase arms and ammunition on the black market along the Sudan-Congo border as well as the Congo. He acquired sufficient weapons from mercenaries and the Simba insurgents to equip two thousand Anya-Nya on the East Bank of the Nile, mostly Latuko.[25] This explains why sporadic activities began in Eastern Equatoria before spreading to other parts of the South.

Fund-raising activities outside Sudan were also carried out by Southern civilians, particularly prominent politicians and their agents. In East Africa, Southern exiles formed the Southern Christian Association (SCA). A similar organization was established along the Sudan-Congo border.[26] Enoka Digga Amena later testified that the insurgents received money from the SCA to purchase the arms that enabled them to launch the first attack on Kajo-Kaji on November 15, 1962.[27]

In refugee camps and villages in neighboring countries, financial committees of Southern Sudanese raised funds. Anna Poni Wani-Buluk (the author's mother) was instrumental in fund-raising activities among Kuku refugees in Gulu in Northern Uganda. This money was handed over periodically to an Anya-Nya political agent, Modi Lojuru, who toured the camps. He also traveled between Uganda and Morta, Anya-Nya headquarters in Central Equatoria.[28] Meanwhile, the chief political representative of the Anya-Nya in Kampala was Angelo Vuga, who oversaw collection of funds and coordinated efforts to acquire financial and material assistance.[29]

Sudan and Uganda Frustrate the Anya-Nya

Although fund-raising activities in Uganda were carried out clandestinely by Southern agents, the Ugandan government accused Southern refugees of participating in rebel activities inside its territory. Milton Obote, prime minister from 1962 to 1966 and president from 1966 to 1971, tried as early as 1963 to restrict the activities of Southern refugees in support of the Anya-Nya. General Ibrahim Abboud's government also constantly accused Southern refugees in Uganda of being "wholly responsible for the rebellion in the South" and urged Uganda to extradite them.[30]

General Abboud sent his minister of the interior, Mohamed Ahmed Irwa, to attend Uganda's independence anniversary on October 9, 1963. While there, Irwa held talks with Ugandan interior minister Felix Onama about the rebellion in Southern Sudan and security problems along the border. Following this visit, in October and November 1963 Ugandan security forces raided the residences of Southern politicians, other prominent Southerners, and members of the SCA.[31]

Joseph Oduho, then president of the Sudan African National Union (SANU), and Severino Fuli, a Madi politician living in exile in Uganda, were arrested. Oduho was charged by Ugandan authorities for "non-compliance with the conditions of his permit to stay in Uganda and later with raising or helping to raise an army to invade the Sudan." As the number of Southern Sudanese in Ugandan prisons increased, Abboud exerted more pressure on Uganda, Ethiopia, and the Congo to "extradite and frustrate the refugees."[32] In some incidents, Sudanese troops crossed into Uganda to pursue Anya-Nya. In other cases, Sudanese troops cooperated with Ugandan soldiers in an effort to "eliminate Anya-Nya activities" inside Uganda.[33]

Between 1965 and 1969, when Obote and Mohammed Ahmed Mahgoub were in power, the Ugandan army and Sudanese soldiers often carried out joint military exercises against the Anya-Nya.[34] It was in one such operation that Father Saturnino was killed in January 1967 while passing through Uganda on his return from Europe, presumably by Ugandan security forces. Father Saturnino's death was a blow to Southerners in general and to the Anya-Nya liberation movement in particular.[35] In Khartoum, however, the death was received with great joy and relief by the government, which immediately dispatched "a special letter of appreciation to the Uganda government for her cooperation with the Sudan to fight the South rebels."[36] That same month, the Ugandan government took a tougher stand against foreign Catholic priests that it accused of supporting activities of the Anya-Nya. Ten foreign priests had their immigration passes and permits revoked.[37]

When Southern leaders such as Father Saturnino and Oduho (in 1960), William Deng (in 1961), and others fled into exile in Uganda, they identified themselves much more with the Democratic Party leadership there than with Obote's Uganda People's Congress. The Democratic Party had religious affiliations with the Catholic Church, while the Uganda People's Congress was mainly affiliated with the Protestants. Thus, these Southern politicians received spiritual and moral support from Catholic priests based in Uganda. When Obote became prime minister in 1962, he was uncomfortable with the delicate alliance between the opposition party and Sudanese Catholic refugees in Uganda. He thought that "an independent Southern Sudan could back the opposition," which is why he opposed the Southern Sudanese.[38]

From November 1966 onward, the Ugandan security forces harassed Southern Sudanese refugees in their camps, subjecting them to harsher living conditions and preventing delivery of food and other humanitarian assistance. By early February 1967, the number of refugees in Uganda had reached forty thousand. Although they lived in deplorable conditions, with poor sanitation and a lack of clean drinking water and food, they preferred to die in the camps in Uganda rather than return to Southern Sudan.[39]

Although the Ugandan authorities took drastic steps to frustrate the Southern refugees in mobilizing financial as well as human resources for the Anya-Nya, they were not entirely successful. Southern refugees struggled to support their families but were still able from their meager earnings to support the Anya-Nya movement. In the border town of Arua and elsewhere in the interior, Southern refugees worked as truck drivers, waiters, factory workers, building or road construction workers, and at other nonprofessional jobs. Some Southern youths attended school and worked on a part-time basis to raise funds. Seminarians, who got little financial assistance from the Catholic Church, were yet able to contribute to the struggle. The money raised in these activities, however, was not sufficient to have a significant impact on the battlefield. Most of the funds were directed to buying medicine and medical facilities.[40]

THE ANYA-NYA ACQUIRE
WEAPONS FROM THE SIMBA

Following its independence from Belgium in 1960, the Congo[41] suffered economic mismanagement and widespread corruption, leading to an intense political, economic, and military crisis by 1964. In response, the Simba (Lion) guerrilla movement arose in opposition to the government. They received diplomatic and military assistance from Burundi, Congo-Brazzaville, Tanzania, Egypt, and Algeria. The government of Congo-Brazzaville allowed them to establish training camps inside its territory, while Tanzania received a variety of arms from China, which it shipped to the Simba.[42]

In late 1964, the Simba captured the city of Stanleyville (later renamed Kisangani), trapping more than 1,600 Europeans. In response, Congolese prime minister Moise Tshombe solicited diplomatic and military assistance from the United States, Belgium, and Britain.[43] Early the following year the combined forces of the Congolese National Army and foreign mercenaries defeated the Simba insurgents.[44]

This Congolese political and military crisis opened up opportunities for the Anya-Nya for military assistance. Anya-Nya officers and men used every military tactic to acquire modern firearms and ammunition from Congolese regular forces and mercenaries, and from the Simba insurgents. According to Lagu, the Anya-Nya purchased weapons and ammunition from those Simba who fled to Southern Sudan following their defeat at Kinsangani. The defeated Simba were desperate. They needed money for food, clothing, shelter, and medicine.[45]

This situation was familiar to Anya-Nya whose families had settled in the Congo, Ethiopia, and Uganda. Thus when the Simba insurgents fled to Southern Sudan, the Anya-Nya knew they would be receptive to trading their weapons for the necessities of life. In most cases, Simba voluntarily sold their arms; in other instances, the Anya-Nya "cheated the Simba in some places . . . they pretended to be the regular Sudanese army, and disarmed the Simba." This tactic was successful because the Simba could not distinguish between the regular Sudanese army and the Anya-Nya. None of the Simba spoke local languages, let alone Arabic or English.[46]

Some Southern Sudanese were so desperate for arms that they joined the Congolese army and fought alongside South African mercenaries against the Simba. These activities occurred along the Sudan-Congo border, without the knowledge of the Congolese military leadership.[47] The Anya-Nya mercenaries generally received arms from the Congolese, "and it was always in an agreement with the local commander on the spot." In essence, the Anya-Nya were given arms to fight against the Simba, and if they captured more arms and ammunition or looted the property of Simba insurgents, they kept the spoils for themselves. Thus, the Congolese crisis provided the Anya-Nya forces in Western and Central Equatoria with arms that strengthened the movement.[48]

In late 1964, massive arms supplies were flown to the Simba insurgents along the Congo-Sudan border from China, the USSR, Eastern Europe, Algeria, Egypt, and Sudan.[49] These weapons were intended to strengthen the Simba in their war against what the Eastern Bloc deemed American political and military hegemony. Large quantities of this military hardware were transported across Southern Sudan. These weapons could be transported through Sudan because the caretaker government of Prime Minister Sirr al-Khatim al-Khalifa (from October 1964 to June 1965) had a socialist orientation and was therefore sympathetic to the Simba, who had embraced the communist ideology.[50] In one particular incident, when the Anya-Nya intelligence network learned that Russian-made weapons were en route from Juba to Simba insurgents in Eastern Congo, they ambushed the convoy between Yei and the Congo border.[51]

The large quantities of arms and ammunition from this convoy bolstered the military strength of the Anya-Nya.[52] The guns included a variety of German-made weapons and other light firearms, American FLL rifles, and Chinese- and Russian-made weapons, including antitank and antiaircraft pieces. According to Allan Reed, an American reporter for NBC who traveled with the Anya-Nya in Southern Sudan in 1970 to 1971, the collapse of the Simba guerrilla movement in Eastern Congo was instrumental in the later success of the Anya-Nya.[53]

Anya-Nya Weapons from Mercenaries and the Congolese Government

The Anya-Nya also acquired weapons from white mercenaries after the latter had crushed the Simba rebellion. They had no grudge against the Anya-Nya, and, in fact, had very cordial relations with them. The Tshombe regime had equipped the mercenaries with modern weapons, which enabled them to capture large quantities of arms and ammunition from the Simba. These they either bartered or sold to the Anya-Nya. The mercenaries bought ivory, leopard skins, rhinoceros horn, and crocodile skins, which the Anya-Nya possessed in substantial amounts and which could be sold in the world market at great profit.[54] Some traders made a fortune as middlemen between the Anya-Nya and mercenaries inside the Congo. They received ivory, skins, and money from the Anya-Nya and took them to the Congo. In return, they carried truckloads of arms and ammunition from the mercenaries to the Anya-Nya operating along the border.[55]

In addition to these efforts by Southern Sudanese civilians and the Anya-Nya to acquire funds and military hardware for the liberation struggle, they also attempted to contact the Congolese government. Although Father Saturnino had solicited financial and material assistance, particularly from the Catholic Church in the Congo and Uganda early in 1965, Southern military and civilian leaders made more formal diplomatic contacts with the Congolese leadership later that year. As president of the Sudan African Liberation Front in 1965, Aggrey Jaden went to Leopoldville to meet Tshombe to solicit military assistance.[56]

Jaden was well received by Tshombe, who promised military assistance only on the assurance that a military commander directly responsible to the Congolese government would ensure that these arms were delivered to the Anya-Nya inside Southern Sudan. To that end, Lagu was recalled from military duties in the South to join Jaden in Leopoldville and "discuss military matters with the Congolese authorities."[57] Lagu went by Congolese military helicopter to the Sudan border, where he was given a little military assistance, including radio facilities that could enhance Anya-Nya communications. Soon thereafter he received a few airdrops of weapons at the border. He also helped establish a training camp for the Anya-Nya at Garamba Park inside the Congo.

When Mahgoub became Sudanese prime minister in June 1965, Khartoum sought to establish closer relations with the West, and this had diplomatic and military repercussions for the Anya-Nya movement.[58] The military assistance that Jaden and Lagu had secured from the Congolese government dried up. Lagu had to abandon his military activities in Garamba Park and move to Eastern Equatoria, where he devoted his efforts to gathering together and training the Madi, Acholi, and Lulobo. He also raised funds among the local populations and searched for arms on the black market and elsewhere.[59]

THE SUDANESE GOVERNMENT
INDIRECTLY ARMS THE ANYA-NYA

The various Sudanese governments, whether civilian or military, allocated a special budget to the armed forces to sustain the war in the South against the Anya-Nya. Khartoum had been more inclined to use force to resolve the "Southern problem" since its outbreak. Thus, throughout the governments of Ismail el-Azhari and Abdalla Khalil (1954 to 1958), Ibrahim Abboud (1958 to 1964), Mohammed Mahgoub and Sadiq al-Mahdi (1965 to 1969), and General Jaafar Mohammed Numayri (1969 to 1985), force was considered the only way to completely destroy the Anya-Nya movement.

Successive regimes judged the Anya-Nya to be ill-trained, poorly organized, deficient in conventional warfare tactics, and equipped only with primitive, ancient weaponry. The government in Khartoum, on the other hand, was armed with light semiautomatic rifles, machine guns, grenades, rockets, land mines, antitank and antiaircraft pieces, artillery, explosives, armored cars, military trucks, jet fighters, and helicopter gunships. These weapons were purchased from Britain, Germany, Yugoslavia, China, Czechoslovakia, and the USSR. Some were also donated by sympathetic Arab countries, including Egypt, Saudi Arabia, Libya, and Algeria.[60]

A variety of weaponry did not necessarily enhance the effectiveness of Sudanese troops in the battlefields of the South, because the Anya-Nya were using guerrilla hit-and-run tactics against fortified military posts or well-guarded military convoys. They effectively employed the element of surprise, causing panic and confusion among the enemy. According to Reed, the NBC reporter, they "made a series of attacks on Sudanese army posts, armed only with their crude traditional weapons. . . . They managed to capture a few guns and with these went on to make bigger raids."[61] Thus, when Anya-Nya forces launched their first raid against Sudanese government military posts in Eastern Equatoria on September 19, 1963, they captured one British-made rifle at Katire township and one Bren gun and five British rifles at the Sudanese military post at Chukudum.[62] In November 1966, Lagu and a platoon of Anya-Nya ambushed a Sudanese army convoy destined for Juba, destroying an armored car and capturing a considerable amount of arms and ammunition.[63] In Central Equatoria, the Anya-Nya successfully ambushed and dispersed the Sudanese troops at Kobo-be and Keriwa and captured all the rifles, including German weapons and British rifles and ammunition.[64] In April 1970, Anya-Nya from the Nuer clashed with Sudanese troops at Panom de Gop in the district of Nasir, where they defeated the soldiers and captured fourteen rifles, including two machine guns, and a considerable amount of ammunition.[65] Such skirmishes and ambushes were widespread throughout Southern Sudan and added greatly to the rebel supply of arms and ammunition.

THE ANYA-NYA CONTACT THE ISRAELIS

The African countries south of the Sahara were only privately sympathetic to the liberation struggle. Between 1955 and 1965, the Anya-Nya acquired most of their weapons within Sudan and along the Congo-Sudan border. Oliver Batali Albino became a major gun runner for the Anya-Nya movement, and between 1963 and 1965 he made contact with foreign embassies in Kampala and Nairobi.[66]

In 1965, Albino was introduced to Israeli General Moshe Dayan, who was present in Nairobi on a diplomatic mission. Dayan assured Albino that Israel would be sympathetic to the Southern Sudanese if the latter "could convince him." Albino later recounted that he "brought Joseph Lagu, who, after seeing [Dayan], gave me a list [things the Israelis wanted to supply to them] to type all night." Thus the Anya-Nya owed their first contacts with the Israelis to Albino's diplomatic efforts in East Africa.[67]

Initial Israeli relations with the Southern Sudanese were based primarily on strategic considerations. The Israelis showed no interest in the Southern cause's "moral and ideological grounds," but supported the Anya-Nya in order to establish a second front against the Sudanese Arabs. Israeli military support might allow the Southerners to tie down a sizeable number of Sudanese troops and "to neutralize effectively the possibility of Sudanese military involvement in the Middle East Zone."[68]

When in 1967, after the Six-Day War, Lagu wrote to Israeli prime minister Levi Eshkol to congratulate him, he added that he "was also fighting the same Arabs, and that if he would strengthen me, I would do one thing . . . I would tie the Sudan army down . . . it would not go to join the Egyptians in the Canal Zone to fight them." Eshkol's successor, Golda Meir, followed up on these plans, urging Israeli military officers to fly General Lagu to Israel for "further discussions" on possible military and financial assistance to the Anya-Nya.[69]

In November of that year, Aggrey Jaden went to Kinshasa in search of foreign support. While there he met Francis Mayar Akol, a lawyer and Dinka from Aweil, who helped facilitate Jaden's contacts with a number of foreign diplomats. These included the Israelis, who promised military and financial assistance but asked him to return to Anya-Nya headquarters at Bungu (thirty miles west of Juba) for further consultations with the movement's political and military leaders.[70]

A few weeks before Jaden's return to Bungu, Lagu also returned to headquarters, where he told the Southern Sudan Provisional Government (SSPG) cabinet that he had made contact with Israeli diplomats in the Congo; these, in turn, had told him of their talks with Jaden and said that he should "unify or coordinate his contacts" with him. The Israelis wanted the SSPG leadership to officially introduce Lagu to Israeli embassy officials. After discussing the matter through the night, the cabinet resolved that Lagu should be officially accredited to the Israeli embassy in

Nairobi, but first they wanted him to formally accept the position of chief of staff of the Anya-Nya National Armed Forces (ANAF). Despite his reservations about working under Amadeo Taffeng (see Chapter 6), Lagu finally consented. The SSPG cabinet then wrote an official letter introducing Lagu as chief of staff of the ANAF to the Israeli embassy in Nairobi and authorizing him "to talk about the help needed for the armed struggle." Gordon Muortat, foreign minister of the SSPG, accompanied Lagu to Nairobi in December 1967 to meet the Israeli ambassador, then left to return to SSPG headquarters at Bungu.[71]

When Jaden then appeared at Bungu a month later, Muortat and Vice President Khamilo Dhol briefed him about the diplomatic and military contacts they had made with the Israelis. Although Lagu was supposed to report to Anya-Nya headquarters to take up his duties as chief of staff under Taffeng and to brief the leadership and general staff about his mission in Nairobi, he refused to appear. When contacted by letter, he gave the excuse that "he was still occupied with the contacts."[72]

Between January and June 1968, Muortat spent much time at the Israeli embassy in Nairobi. Israeli officials there, realizing there was a rift between Lagu and the leaders of the SSPG, told Muortat in June 1968 to convey a message to Jaden that "the time [was] ripe for the Southern Sudan Provisional Government and their government to meet and negotiate." Muortat returned to ANAF headquarters and a strong SSPG delegation was formed that included Jaden, Muortat, Lagu, and Sarafino Wani Swaka, an SSPG representative in East Africa.[73]

By June 1968, talks between the Israelis and the SSPG delegation produced results in an agreement that the Israelis would provide the Anya-Nya with military assistance. The only uncertainty was over whether Uganda, Kenya, Ethiopia, and Zaire (formerly the Congo) would allow weapons and other supplies to be shipped through their territories. President Obote of Uganda was hostile to the Anya-Nya and President Mobutu Sese Seko of Zaire was uncooperative, though Kenya was privately sympathetic. Israeli officials reassured the SSPG that they would "do it in their own way."[74]

Although the SSPG delegation in Nairobi achieved remarkable results, Lagu had his own plans. Instead of returning with the delegation to ANAF headquarters at Bungu, he transferred his own headquarters to Eastern Equatoria, where he had previously established his military organization. When Jaden then abdicated his position as SSPG president in August 1968 and the Nile Provisional Government (NPG) and its splinter groups, the Anyidi Revolutionary Government and Sue River Republic, struggled to fill the vacuum,[75] Lagu remained preoccupied with military organization and training in Eastern Equatoria and therefore "never paid attention to them."[76]

Thus, while the politicians faced leadership crises in Southern Sudan, Lagu remained aloof. He continued his secret contacts with the Israelis, who were losing confidence in the Southern political leaders. The Israelis "thought that these politicians were really awful and that the best way [was] to start a leadership which [was] military only, and isolate" it from the politicians. They were therefore more interested in supporting an Anya-Nya officer like Lagu than the Southern politicians, who were unable to create a second front in Southern Sudan against the Arabs.[77] Lagu was the only military officer who could be groomed to cooperate with them and enable Israeli arms shipments to the Anya-Nya in Southern Sudan. It was for this reason that Israeli Prime Minister Golda Meir ordered Israeli officials in East Africa and Zaire to facilitate Lagu's visit to Tel Aviv. Consequently, in late 1969 Lagu traveled to Kinshasa, where Francis Akol "helped him to obtain the UN travel document," and from there he flew to Italy and Israel.[78]

THE ISRAELI GOVERNMENT BEGINS SUPPLYING THE ANYA-NYA WITH WEAPONS

In Israel, Lagu received fourteen days of intensive training. The Israelis had a well-founded fear that the countries neighboring Southern Sudan might not allow arms delivery to the Anya-Nya through their territories. Lagu assured them that Tshombe had supplied weapons to the Anya-Nya through the Congo, and Congolese military forces had even dropped weapons for Lagu's Anya-Nya in Garamba Park. Lagu recounted how he had personally used a hand-generated radio to signal Kinshasa and Congolese aircraft to drop military supplies to him.[79] The Israeli military, of course, had more sophisticated means than the Congolese had used in 1965. Israeli planes could fly over Ethiopia, which was sympathetic to the Southern cause, and could also refuel in Uganda and Kenya en route.[80]

An Israeli military delegation was sent to Southern Sudan to confirm Lagu's earlier promise. The delegation was impressed and reported that Lagu had done an excellent job in marking a drop zone. "Massive airdrops" of Israeli weaponry ensued. News of this spread rapidly to all the Anya-Nya, who began to travel to Lagu's headquarters to acquire arms and ammunition. Lagu "gave them brief training and sent them to their [respective] places to go and get further training there."[81]

By the time Lagu contacted the Israelis, they had already established diplomatic ties with Kenya, Uganda, Ethiopia, and the Congo, but although diplomacy was one thing, arms shipments were another. The Israelis wanted permission to use the airspace of these countries. Emperor Haile Selassie of Ethiopia had remarkably good relations with Israel, whose pilots were training his air force. John Lueth later recounted that when traveling to Israel via Ethiopia in 1971, he met a few Israeli air force colonels who were training Ethiopian fighter pilots. Selassie was sympathetic to the Southern liberation struggle because the Khartoum government was supporting Eritrean guerrilla forces fighting for independence from Ethiopia.[82]

After Lagu's return to Southern Sudan from Israel in 1969, he flew with Israeli officials to Uganda, Kenya, and Ethiopia, where he "organized support for Upper Nile province straight from Ethiopia." Only Bor, a town in the Dinka area of Upper Nile 120 miles north of Juba, was receiving military supplies from Equatoria. Selassie allowed the Israelis to establish a training depot in Ethiopia, where Lagu sent Anya-Nya cadets to be trained as officers.

A few cadets were also sent to Israel for technical training and other aspects of military science.[83] Lueth was among the first batch of Anya-Nya officers sent to Israel for training in 1971. Some were instructed in communications, some in administration, and some in medical treatment. Officers destined to become unit commanders had more rigorous training in intelligence, demolition, and battlefield tactics.[84]

Within the South, Lagu established a military academy with the assistance of four Israeli officers at Anya-Nya headquarters at Owiny-ki-Bul. These officers returned to Israel every year during the dry seasons when the Sudanese army was on the offensive, since Lagu did "not want them to be hurt."[85] Rolf Steiner later identified four Israeli military advisers at Lagu's command post at Owiny-ki-Bul: a colonel who presumably led the team, a doctor, a radio specialist, and an infantry instructor. All came from the Israeli embassy in Kampala five or six weeks at a time.[86] The Israeli officers used aliases for security reasons, and they did not like the Anya-Nya names associated with Nazi Germany: one Anya-Nya officer called "Hitler" was asked to change his name because the Israeli officers disliked it.[87] Such names were usually chosen out of naïveté without regard to their religious or political implications.

Israeli relations with Uganda under President Obote, however, were not as cordial as those with Ethiopia and Kenya. Although the Israelis had an embassy in Kampala, relations were based primarily on military cooperation. Israeli air force pilots and technicians trained Ugandan personnel to man Israeli-made Fouga fighter planes.[88] For a while, Obote allowed the Israelis to use Ugandan airspace to ferry weapons to the Anya-Nya,[89] but in late 1969, after General Numayri came to power in Khartoum, Obote[90] "indicated that he wished to make peace with Khartoum and would no longer support the Israelis in Southern Sudan."[91]

Consequently, when General Zamir, the Israeli intelligence chief, visited Kampala in late 1969 to ask for "refueling rights in Uganda for their arms ferry to the guerrillas" in Southern Sudan, "he received a blunt refusal." Obote could not prevent General Idi Amin, the commander in chief of the Ugandan army, from cooperating with the Israelis. Amin had ethnic ties with the Southern Sudanese[92] and had given them "secret support."[93]

Then on January 25, 1971, Amin overthrew Obote in a bloody coup. He now continued his support for the Anya-Nya movement. According to Lagu, Amin, accompanied by Israeli officers, visited him twice by light plane at his headquarters at Owiny-ki-Bul in Acholiland in Eastern Equatoria. To demonstrate his full support, Amin permitted military supplies to be transported by road instead of by air.[94] Lueth later confirmed Lagu's story, "Idi Amin had a very good relationship with the Israelis," and he visited Owiny-ki-Bul a number of times before the war ended in March 1972.[95]

Despite cordial relations between Amin and the Israelis on the one hand, and between him and the Anya-Nya on the other, events in Uganda and Sudan in 1971 to 1972 dramatically altered the atmosphere. Numayri had begun to explore the possibility of a peaceful resolution to the war, and he now tried to involve Uganda, Kenya, and Ethiopia in a peace process. Although Amin showed interest, the Israelis were suspicious of any deal that might hamper their objectives in Sudan.[96]

In early 1972, Amin fell out with the Israelis, and he now undertook to repair Uganda's relations with the Arab countries. The Israelis had reportedly injected money into the ailing Ugandan economy, loans that Amin "could not repay even in part." When Amin visited President Muammar al-Gaddafi of Libya in February 1972, they "issued a joint communiqué condemning Israel" and declared their unswerving support of the Palestine Liberation Organization.[97] Amin consequently ordered the closing of the Israeli embassy in Kampala on March 30, 1972.[98]

The departure of the Israelis from Uganda had a profound and far-reaching impact on the Anya-Nya movement and its leadership. Its main source of financial and military assistance had dried up, which no doubt affected the morale of the officers and men of the movement, as well as reducing their military strength—prior to this, the Anya-Nya forces had become a formidable force that the Sudanese army had to reckon with. At the time of the Addis Ababa peace agreement of March 3, 1972, the Anya-Nya numbered about eighteen thousand.[99] A greater portion of their weapons had been supplied by the Israeli military forces. According to Steiner, the Anya-Nya were armed with weapons "captured from the Arabs" during the Six-Day War of 1967, Russian grenades, 120mm mortars, land mines, and 303 World War II rifles.[100] The Israelis also supplied antiaircraft guns.[101] According to Lueth, these weapons "were not sophisticated" enough for conventional warfare, but they were better than nothing.[102] Lagu complained that the "Israelis gave [the] Anya-Nya obsolete arms that never matched" the government's firepower, and this influenced his decision to talk peace with the Numayri regime in 1971 to 1972.[103]

ADDITIONAL SOURCES OF ANYA-NYA SUPPORT

Between 1963 and 1972, President Jomo Kenyatta of Kenya was sympathetic to the Southern Sudanese cause. Kenyatta himself had been a freedom fighter, and he understood the reasons for which the Anya-Nya were fighting Khartoum. Kenya for a time also had very cordial relations with the Israelis and had provided them facilities to ship arms to Southern Sudan.[104] Kenya permitted Israeli planes to refuel in Nairobi after dropping arms at Anya-Nya bases in the South.[105] Lagu also states that "on one occasion, the plane went to Kenya, got loaded with maize [corn] and came and dropped it for us. . . . Kenyatta even went further to render [a] little financial assistance to the Anya-Nya movement."[106]

Lueth has confirmed Lagu's view that although the Kenyan government did not openly support the Southern guerrilla movement, privately Kenyatta was always "behind the Southern Sudanese." The Kenya government facilitated transportation of the first batch of Anya-Nya officers to Israel, and Kenyatta even met them while they were at Nairobi airport. The Israelis' excellent relations with Kenya continued after the Addis Ababa Agreement of 1972.[107]

While the Zairean (formerly Congolese) government of President Mobutu was openly hostile to the Sudanese Arabs, he did not supply weapons to the Anya-Nya. Mobutu did, however, facilitate transportation of Israeli military supplies to the Anya-Nya. Zairean troops received weapons from the Israelis and delivered them to the depot at Angundri, whence the Anya-Nya in Bahr al-Ghazal received their arms.[108] This arrangement was particularly important for those units located far from the major routes of military supplies along the Uganda-Sudan and Ethiopia-Sudan borders.

Aside from the assistance the Anya-Nya received from the Simba, Congolese mercenaries, Israelis, and African heads of state, specific individuals also lent support. In 1963, Henerick Rossi was the first European to provide military training to the Anya-Nya.[109] Although he did not spend much time in the South, he laid the foundations for a more organized Anya-Nya military operation. Other soldiers of fortune also made contributions, particularly during 1969 to 1970 when the Biafran war was coming to an end. The first mercenary from Biafra was a Frenchman called Armo. He was recruited by politicians of the NPG in 1969 who believed that the appearance of a "white man" would assist in acquiring weapons for the Anya-Nya. But while Armo introduced rudimentary commando training for a few Anya-Nya officers and men, he had no means of providing weapons, and at the end of 1969 he mysteriously disappeared.[110]

Rolf Steiner had also fought as a mercenary in the Biafran war. In 1969, he left Nigeria for Uganda to give a "helping hand" to the Anya-Nya, disguising his motive as humanitarian. He wanted Obote's government to grant permission to transport blankets, agricultural implements, and medical supplies to Southern Sudan. Arms and ammunition could easily be concealed in these consignments to escape detection by Ugandan security forces.[111] Obote did not want any assistance passing through his country lest it jeopardize relations with Khartoum. His successor Idi Amin, on the other hand, ordered the army "to turn a blind eye to Steiner's harmless smuggling service."[112]

It was with Amin's help that Steiner was able to cross the border and reach Anya-Nya headquarters at Morta in Central Equatoria in 1969. While at Morta, he and a handful of Anya-Nya "made a daring attack on Kajo-Kaji," which ended in disaster when the Anya-Nya were driven off by the superior firepower of the Sudanese garrison. Following this ill-fated attack, Steiner crossed the Nile to seek arms and ammunition for his military adventures inside Southern Sudan.[113]

Steiner arrived in Eastern Equatoria just when Taffeng had renounced his position as commander in chief of the Anya-Nya and refused to cooperate with Muortat's new NPG. Taffeng was glad to have assistance from the European countries, but although Steiner promised him arms, he had no money to purchase them.[114] To demonstrate his commitment, Steiner went to Germany to solicit support from missionary groups and other benevolent organizations. With Steiner's help, Taffeng contacted the Biafran-Sudan Action Committee, an organization that had helped the Ibo during the Biafran war. The founders were "ready to mobilize public opinion about the troubles in the Southern Sudan," which could strengthen Taffeng's position in his Anyidi Revolutionary Government.[115]

Taffeng had such confidence in Steiner's activities that he provided eight hundred Anya-Nya to protect him. Steiner was given the title "commander of the regular army of the Anyedi [Anyidi]," but he soon realized that tension existed between Lagu and Taffeng.[116] When he discovered that the Israelis were supplying Lagu with weapons, "he crossed over" to him and pledged his allegiance, abandoning Taffeng.[117]

When the Israelis learned about Steiner's presence in Lagu's military headquarters at Owiny-ki-Bul, they objected because Steiner "was a Nazi." Thereupon Lagu told Steiner to "go back to your country and raise funds for us" there.[118] According to Lueth, the Israelis told Steiner that the Southerners needed arms, ammunition, medicine, and other essential supplies, not mercenaries.[119]

Steiner returned to Morta, but before he could enter Uganda on his way to Europe, Obote learned he was in Southern Sudan and hoped to implicate Amin in this breach of national security so that he could arrest him. Amin quickly dispatched officers to arrest Steiner before Obote's men could intercept him.[120] Steiner was stripped of all papers that might implicate Amin, and then handed over to Obote.[121] The Ugandan authorities declared this "a major African victory which should mark the beginning of the end of white mercenary activities in Africa."[122] They then extradited him to Khartoum as a demonstration of Obote's goodwill.[123] He was tried for illegal entry and sentenced to twenty years in prison,[124] though he was later released after the Addis Ababa Agreement.[125]

FRENCH INVOLVEMENT IN SOUTHERN SUDAN

While serving as president of the SSPG between April 1967 and August 1968, Jaden and his foreign minister Muortat met French officials in Kinshasa to discuss French military and economic assistance to the Anya-Nya. The SSPG raised important issues, "We offered them a permanent military base in Southern Sudan. . . . We also offered them to be the first nation to organize or to plan our economic development." [126] French officials pledged their readiness to support the Anya-Nya in achieving complete independence rather than in negotiating a peace treaty between the North and South, agreeing that the Southern problem could be resolved only by force.[127]

After Jaden's abdication of the SSPG in August 1968 and Muortat's election as president of the NPG in April 1969, the French promised military assistance to the Anya-Nya and accepted three Anya-Nya officers for joint training with some Biafrans. In February 1970 they were flown to France, where they were given military training.[128]

French authorities now learned the Israelis were already shipping weapons to Lagu, and they feared that if they supplied the NPG, those

Anya-Nya loyal to the NPG would clash with those whose allegiance was to Lagu. Meanwhile, since the French were trying to demonstrate "good relations with many Arab states," it seemed unwise to openly supply arms to the Anya-Nya "to fight an Arab government." [129] The only solution was for the NPG to unite with Lagu and his supporters. In this way the French could channel military assistance "through the Israelis" so that no Arab country could detect it.[130]

When the three Anya-Nya officers returned to Southern Sudan, they briefed the NPG leadership about the French offer of arms and the need for the Southerners to unite under a single political leadership. As Colonel Stephen Madut asserted to the politicians, "Our national liberation is not to be tribal . . . the best thing for us is to unite . . . we are not here to protect individual politicians." It was under such foreign pressure from the French and the Israelis that Anya-Nya officers ultimately decided to overthrow the NPG in April 1969 and give their allegiance to Lagu.[131]

The French, however, never provided any real military assistance to the Anya-Nya. From the Central African Republic, where French help could have been significant, the Anya-Nya received nothing.[132] By the end of the first civil war in 1972, the French were seen by Southern Sudanese as the "friends of their enemies."

U.S., BRITISH, AND WEST GERMAN SUPPORT FOR KHARTOUM

While the Anya-Nya were receiving supplies from abroad, the Sudanese government was acquiring its own foreign support. During his time in power between 1958 and 1964, General Abboud established close relations with the United States, which provided Sudan financial and technical assistance.[133] Between 1958 and 1967, the United States channeled about $2.2 million, $101.7 million of which was earmarked for military assistance.[134] In December 1963, the United States provided four helicopters and one light airplane for mapping and surveying work in Sudan;[135] on December 19, a government newspaper reported that two Sudanese generals were to use the helicopters for survey purposes in flooded parts of Southern Sudan. But "it was learned the helicopters were flown to hunt Southerners in those disturbed and less accessible areas instead of carrying out any survey work."[136] Although the United States had not intended to get involved directly in the war, Khartoum was not concerned about any impact on U.S.-Sudanese relations. In addition to this technical assistance, the U.S. army provided military training from 1958 to 1967.[137]

Prior to 1965, the Sudanese government got more than half its military hardware from the West German government. In fact, much of the $2.2 million the United States gave Sudan was used to purchase weapons from West Germany. They acquired German-made rifles, other sophisticated weapons, Mercedes-Benz cars, and military trucks.[138] Before 1965, the West Germans had very good diplomatic relations with Khartoum, providing "a half million [Sudanese] pounds a year" and half the military equipment and supplies of the Sudanese army.[139]

In 1965, economic and military aid dried up when the West German government broke diplomatic relations with the government of al-Khalifa, which was viewed as being socialist and leaning toward the communist world.[140] By the end of the Sudanese war in 1972, most of Khartoum's economic and military assistance was coming from Britain, Egypt, Libya, Algeria, the Arab countries, China, and the USSR.

After the outbreak of civil war in Sudan in 1955, the British continued to provide financial and military support to successive Khartoum regimes. Whether the government in Khartoum was pro-West, civilian, military, socialist, or communist-oriented had no significant impact on the British. The British helped train Sudanese airmen in addition to supplying civil and combat aircraft. They also provided naval training to Sudanese navy officers, while Sudan purchased armored cars[141] and other light weapons from Britain.

On January 12, 1967, the Southern Sudan Information Service (SSIS) in London reported that the Sudanese government had planned as early as December 1966 to launch a campaign against the Anya-Nya with the help of British ground crews and airmen. The British were to man machine guns and rockets. The Royal Air Force had already been providing training to Sudanese pilots in night bombing.[142] Also in 1967, a special correspondent of the SSIS claimed that the British government had offered to train six Sudanese army officers in "chemical warfare techniques," which could be used by the Sudanese army to poison foodstuff and water.[143] This claim has never been corroborated.

SUDAN SOLICITS SUPPORT FROM ARAB NATIONS

Aside from receiving assistance from Western powers such as the United States, West Germany, and Britain, the Sudanese government also received help from Algeria, Libya, Egypt, and Saudi Arabia. The Egyptians had long religious and racial ties with Northern Sudan and had a vital interest in the Nile waters.[144] Since 1902, an Egyptian garrison had been stationed in Malakal to monitor the flow of the White Nile to Northern Sudan and Egypt.[145]

Although there was no direct involvement of Egyptian troops on the frontlines in Southern Sudan, some were stationed in garrisons in the North to relieve the Khartoum regime from maintaining large troop concentrations there. Northern troops could then be transported to the South to carry on the campaign against the Anya-Nya.[146] Egypt also provided military training for the Sudanese army. Relations between the two countries remained amicable until Numayri turned to the United States for support.[147]

During the seventeen-year civil war, successive Sudanese governments tried to obtain support from the Arab countries, especially Algeria, Libya, and Saudi Arabia, which provided Sudan economic and military support.[148] As early as 1966, King Faisal of Saudi Arabia visited Khartoum and "expressed his concern over the Southern problem." He declared to the Sudanese leaders his unwavering support and his country's determination to supply weapons to Khartoum,[149] though the amount of military assistance was never mentioned.

The Libyan government was also sympathetic to Khartoum. According to Lueth, Libyan troops were deployed in Southern Sudan,[150] while Allan Reed has asserted that two hundred Libyan paratroopers fought alongside the Sudanese troops when they attacked and captured the Anya-Nya stronghold at Morta in September-October 1970.[151]

THE SUDANESE ARMY ACQUIRES EQUIPMENT FROM THE USSR

The largest supplier of weapons for the Sudanese government, however, was the USSR. Sudan, like other Third World states, was caught up in the Soviet-U.S. rivalry in the decades of the Cold War. The Soviet Union had long regarded the Red Sea region as strategically important for consolidating its influence in the Middle East and Indian Ocean. The Soviets had naval bases at Aden (Yemen) and Socotra (Djibouti), and it coveted Port Sudan. They therefore offered Sudan economic and military assistance.[152]

In the late 1960s, when Khartoum realized that the war in the South was draining the resources of the country, the Soviet Union was ready to grant aid that would allow the government to continue to prosecute the war. Mahgoub's government thereby signed an arms deal with the Soviets in January 1968, under which they pledged $100 million, mostly for weapons. Sudan ordered MiG fighters and helicopters "purely for external defence" (in Mahgoub's words), but in fact to strengthen the Sudanese army against the Anya-Nya.[153]

This agreement was followed up by Numayri;[154] during his first two years in power (1969 through 1970) Soviet-Sudanese military cooperation increased. Numayri was confident that with Soviet weaponry he could destroy the Anya-Nya, and so he invited Soviet military advisors, pilots, and technicians to Sudan. According to U.S. intelligence sources, some one to two hundred Soviet advisors were "directly planning and participating in the counter-guerrilla operations of the Arab-led Sudan army against the Africans of Southern Sudan." It was believed that about one thousand Soviet personnel were providing support to the Sudanese army in the way of advisors, pilots, ground crew, and missile technicians.[155]

The biggest obstacle the Sudanese army faced in tracking down Anya-Nya forces was topography: thick bush, mountainous areas, swamplands, and sticky clay soil during the rainy season. These conditions made the army more vulnerable to Anya-Nya forces, who knew their territory well. Consequently, the Numayri government purchased Soviet aircraft to help destroy Anya-Nya bases. In October 1970, a special correspondent of London's *Daily Telegraph* reported that Numayri had requested twenty-seven Russian bombers to boost the army's air capability and that these were stationed at the Khartoum airport.[156]

In November, Tel Aviv's *Evening Standard* reported that the Soviets had supplied sixty MiG-21 fighter planes to Sudan, which were stationed in a newly built base at Juba.[157] Sudan also purchased Soviet MI-8 helicopters, Antonov twenty-four bombers, two squadrons of TU-16 medium bombers, and half a dozen AN-24s that could be equipped with rockets. Khartoum also received Soviet T-55 heavy tanks, light tanks, howitzers, ground rockets, and artillery pieces.[158] Lagu confirmed the Soviet military presence in the Sudan in a letter addressed to Pope Paul VI on May 25, 1970, "Even as we write to you, Soviet tanks are rumbling through the streets and Soviet MiG-21 jets are flying overhead in a parade to commemorate African Revolution Day. Yesterday these same tanks and planes were in action in Southern Sudan, killing and maiming our defenceless people, and tomorrow they will return to continue their mission of death and havoc. Our people have grown accustomed to the sight of Russian soldiers directing the Sudanese Arab soldiers in their war."[159]

Numayri's vision after coming to power was to end the war by dealing the Anya-Nya a devastating blow. Like his predecessor, Numayri accused the Israelis of extending military assistance to the Anya-Nya; it was largely because of the Israeli threat that Numayri sought massive Soviet military assistance.[160] The military assistance Sudan received from the USSR and its satellite states was the largest such influx in sub-Saharan Africa since the beginning of the Cold War.[161]

In 1972, the *Almanac of World Military Power* summarized the weaponry acquired by the Sudan government between 1955 and 1971 as follows:

> In 1956 Britain left sufficient weapons and equipment to outfit the small armed forces then planned. Small British army and air training missions continued in the Sudan through 1966. Naval training has been conducted in Britain and Yugoslavia, and West Germany. Aircraft have been obtained from Britain, the Netherlands, Switzerland, and Egypt. Military training has been received from Britain, the United States, Ethiopia, Pakistan, and India. Small arms, artillery, and vehicles have been purchased from West Germany and armored cars from Britain and the United States. From 1965 through 1967 the US has provided $700,000 worth of military aid.... With the 1967 change of policy toward Israel and the West, the Sudan is accepting large quantities of military aid from the Soviet Union, Czechoslovakia, and Yugoslavia. The Soviet program alone is said to have amounted to $100 to $150 million. Soviet and Czech contributions include tanks, armored personnel carriers, artillery, and jet aircraft, as well as training missions. Yugoslav aid involves sea and river patrol craft as well as air and ground equipment and training.[162]

The first civil war in the Sudan would not have lasted seventeen years had it not been sustained by foreign military and financial assistance to the belligerent parties, the Sudanese army, and the Anya-Nya armed forces. The Anya-Nya movement received moral and financial support from Southern refugees in the neighboring countries. The Israelis provided them with military hardware and combat training in guerrilla warfare, but little financial support. Meanwhile, the Simba and the Sudanese army indirectly armed the Anya-Nya forces when they acquired sophisticated weapons from these two parties in skirmishes with and ambushes of enemy troops or vehicles. On the other hand, the Sudanese government, which had greater financial resources than the Anya-Nya, acquired sophisticated weapons from the West as well as the East. In particular, the Sudanese army received massive Soviet military and financial assistance in the period 1968 to 1972. The Arab countries gave the Sudanese government political and moral support as well as financial and military assistance, but although the Sudanese army's firepower was superior to the Anya-Nya's, they failed to crush these mobile guerrilla forces who knew their territory well. Yet neither belligerent force could score a clear-cut victory. The only alternative left for the warring parties was to negotiate a peace settlement to the civil strife in the South.

CHAPTER 9

THE ROAD TO PEACE, 1969-72

THE START OF THE PEACE PROCESS AND THE subsequent negotiations between the Southern Sudan Liberation Movement (SSLM) and the military government of Major General Jaafar Mohammed Numayri that resulted in the signing of the Addis Ababa Agreement in February 1972 have been discussed already by Cecil Eprile, Edgar O' Ballance, Dunstan M. Wai, Abel Alier, and Douglas H. Johnson.[1] My intent is not to repeat what these scholars have presented, but rather to present a new analysis and interpretation of the peace agreement from a Southern Sudanese perspective, using information elicited primarily from interviews with leading Southerners who participated directly or indirectly in the peace process and subsequent settlement of the seventeen-year conflict in Sudan. It is my hope that this new and rare information will shed light on many unanswered questions pertaining to the peace agreement.

ECONOMIC AND POLITICAL CONDITIONS IN SUDAN PRIOR TO THE 1969 COUP

The collapse of the military regime of General Ibrahim Abboud paved the way for the emergence of the political platform of the right-wing parties once again in Sudan. The civilian administration of these parties (the Umma Party and the Democratic Unionist Party [DUP]) inherited the political, and especially the economic, problems of the Abboud regime. To try to address the economic crisis, the government introduced a Ten-Year-Plan that sought to reduce the role of the state in the private sector while at the same time encouraging private ownership and investment. In the period 1964 through 1969, Sudan secured foreign loans for nearly all its development projects. The parliament passed legislation favorable to foreign industrial investment and foreign trade. These policies were aimed at strengthening the private sector and generating revenue.[2]

In the meantime, the civil war in Southern Sudan was depleting the government treasury. Until 1967, the government was channeling £14 million sterling annually to sustain military operations in the South. In addition to this war effort, the government had to contribute human and financial resources in support of the Arab cause against Israel. As a result, its annual military expenditure was half its entire budget.[3]

In September 1967, Sudan had foreign exchange reserves of £19.6 million, but by June 1968, that amount had dwindled to £17 million.[4] And although the balance of payments was at its lowest point, living costs continued to rise. The poor were paying heavy indirect taxes to sustain the economy,[5] and high unemployment and corruption, especially in the public sector, compounded the problems.[6]

The government in Khartoum was incompetent and unable to resolve the "immediate or long term problems of poverty and underdevelopment."[7] Neither could it contain the increasing strength of the guerrilla forces in the South. Meanwhile in the North, the right-wing political parties were struggling to produce an Islamic constitution they intended would become the foundation for a religious politics in Sudan. This constitution would legitimize them as the guardians of an Islamic state while undermining the organized secular forces on the left, such as the Communist Party.[8]

THE FREE OFFICERS MOVEMENT AND NUMAYRI'S COUP

In 1957, a year after Sudan's independence, the Free Officers Movement was established in the military. Heavily influenced by a similar movement founded eight years earlier in Egypt, it comprised young Northern Sudanese officers, some of whom had been trained in the Military College in Khartoum and who had filled the ranks vacated by the British military officers during Sudanization.[9] Among its members was Colonel Jaafar Mohammed Numayri. Born in 1930 in Northern Sudan, he joined the Sudan Defense Force and became a second lieutenant in 1952. Numayri had an impressive military career. He had been trained in Sudan's Military College, the Sudan Staff College, and the United States Army Command College in Fort Leavenworth, Kansas, and he also commanded the infantry school in Northern Sudan. In Southern Sudan, Numayri had distinguished himself as a tough military officer, especially in Equatoria.[10]

In 1967, these officers, who had first-hand experience in the battlefields of the South, realized that neither of the belligerent forces would ever achieve a clear-cut victory over the other. They therefore urged the Sudanese government to adopt a new approach toward the Southern question.[11] According to General Ahmed el-Sheriff, the army commanding officer in the South, the army was capable of maintaining security in the Southern towns, but not in the countryside. He therefore advocated a political solution to the "Southern problem."[12]

Frustrated in their efforts to bring about reforms in the military, on May 25, 1969, Colonel Numayri and senior officers of the movement seized power from the civilian administration of Prime Minister Mohammed Mahgoub.[13] They now formed a national Revolutionary Command Council (RCC) comprising ten army officers and a single civilian.[14] Numayri took over as president, and by October had assumed the position of prime minister as well. Understanding that his government would be vulnerable to a military or civilian coup if he did not form a government with varied political ideologies, Numayri appointed to his twenty-four member cabinet a combination of socialists, communists, radical intellectuals, academics, people without particular political affiliations, and two Southerners, Joseph Garang and Abel Alier.[15]

On the day of the coup, Numayri spelled out why the RCC had taken power. With respect to Southern Sudan in particular, the RCC for the first time recognized the "Southern problem" that had plagued the civilian and military regimes prior to the coup, though they blamed the imperialists, neo-colonialists, and the traditional political and sectarian parties for the conflict and suffering in the South. The RCC also acknowledged the deterioration of the country's economy and the decline in living standards of the Sudanese people in general.[16] The new regime summed up its reasons for seizing power thus: "It is the result of the policies of British colonialism, which left the legacy of uneven development between the North and Southern parts of the country.... Our revolution is ... directed against imperialists, the reactionary circles and corrupt parties that destroyed the October Revolution [that overthrew General Abboud in 1964] and were aiming at finally liquidating any progressive movement and installing a Reactionary Dictatorship."[17]

To counter any threat to his military administration by right-wing politicians, political parties, or counter-revolutionaries, Numayri announced the day after the coup a number of drastic measures to suppress dissent. He ordered the dissolution of the political parties and suspended the constitution, getting rid of the National Assembly, the Supreme Court, and the Civil Service Commission.[18] On the military front, Numayri assumed the rank of major general and held the portfolio of the minister of defense. He also ordered the retirement of twenty-six senior officers, purged more than thirty officers, and promoted new officers to strategic positions in the military.[19]

NUMAYRI GRANTS REGIONAL AUTONOMY TO THE SOUTH

Numayri was waging psychological warfare on the civilian population and the military forces both to instill fear to stifle any opposition to his policies and to establish an absolute grip on his new administration. At this time, Numayri, the RCC, and the Council of Ministers saw no need for contact with the Anya-Nya nor even considered the possibility of engaging them in dialogue. By and large, the Numayri administration "still believed only in a military solution" to the conflict in Southern Sudan.[20]

Despite Numayri's determination to pursue a military solution, Abel Alier—a Dinka lawyer from Bor, a judge, and member of the Southern Front in Khartoum—proposed instead the idea of granting local autonomy to the South. He considered this new political framework a basis for solving the Southern problem and achieving permanent peace in the country. He also envisioned creating an Office for Southern Affairs that would address the political and economic problems facing the Southern region. Numayri and the Council of Ministers took this proposal seriously, and on June 9, 1969, Alier was appointed minister of housing. On the same day, Numayri broadcast a new policy statement proposing regional autonomy for the South that stated in part: "The Revolutionary Government is confident and determined enough to face existing realities. It recognizes the historical and cultural differences between the North and South and firmly believes that the unity of our country must be built upon these objective realities. The Southern people have the right to develop their respective cultures and traditions within a united socialist Sudan."[21]

Numayri was undoubtedly the first head of state since Sudan's independence in 1956 to recognize the magnitude of the Southern problem. However, Southern Sudanese living inside Sudan or in exile received his policy statement for local autonomy with mixed feelings. Those Southerners under the jurisdiction of the Sudanese army and police forces, or who had migrated to Northern Sudan, generally embraced the program of the RCC. Those living in exile in neighboring countries (numbering around 350,000) had little enthusiasm for the policy, while those who fended for themselves in areas controlled by the Anya-Nya felt "that it was better to wait and see."²² Despite government assurances of amnesty to the Southerners in refugee camps, the latter remained suspicious of these overtures. Only a few left their hideouts in Southern Sudan and sought protection in the military garrisons or peace camps in the South.²³

To demonstrate his commitment to the June 9 declaration of regional autonomy for the South, Numayri appointed Joseph Garang—a Dinka lawyer from Wau in Bahr al-Ghazal and a leading member of the central committee of the Communist Party—the new minister of state for Southern affairs.²⁴ Although Garang had supported Numayri's military junta and the policies of the RCC, his socialist ideas were "much further Left than Numayri's."²⁵ Nonetheless, he was given the enormous task of tackling the political, economic, and social issues pertaining to Southern Sudan.

While Numayri had essentially asked Garang to present a political framework for establishing a limited autonomous government in the South, Garang's plan was ideologically based—he first wanted to "build up a Communist base in the South before implementing any form of autonomy."²⁶ He steadily moved to realize his vision of spreading communist ideology and establishing communist institutions in the South, which he filled with non-Southern officials because he could find no Southern Sudanese who embraced the same political persuasion.²⁷ Unaware of Garang's political designs for Southern Sudan, Numayri trusted him, not knowing that Garang and his communist ideologues were working together to frustrate his agenda for the country at large, and for the South in particular.²⁸

Thus, a year and a half after the May 1969 coup, the Numayri administration had failed not only to define the local autonomy proposed for the South, but also to translate its policy into action. The result was that Southern officials working with the Numayri government were growing increasingly frustrated with the way local autonomy was being interpreted and implemented in the South.²⁹

Officials of the Southern resistance movement were not totally surprised by the slow pace of implementing local autonomy. They had been critical of and skeptical about Numayri's declaration of local autonomy from the beginning, but because of their genuine commitment to peace in Sudan, they decided to halt their guerrilla operations against Khartoum's military forces for one year.³⁰ The Khartoum regime, however, did not take this Southern commitment to a negotiated settlement of the conflict seriously.

Some Southern observers believed that Numayri's long-term goal was to pursue a program of "Arab expansionism" into the heartland of black

Africa. According to them, Numayri, the political leadership, and the Islamic community in Northern Sudan viewed the South as an obstacle to the penetration of Islam and Arab and Islamic cultures into Islam's southern frontier. Thus, the North regarded Arab expansionism as the ultimate solution to the Southern problem. These Southerners, in turn, regarded Numayri's recognition of the historical and cultural differences between the North and the South as lacking substance and "flowery."[31]

Garang for his part completely failed to implement his communist agenda in Southern Sudan because he did not have a political base, let alone the confidence and support of the Southerners in the region.[32] He and Numayri had also underestimated the political will of the Southern Sudanese, presumably because they believed the Southerners were resigned to their subjugated condition.

Although Numayri's political program in Southern Sudan was thus an embarrassment to his regime, this did not prevent him from launching a diplomatic offensive abroad to signal to the international community that he was still committed to his June 9, 1969, declaration of local autonomy. Both Numayri and Garang pledged to work together to implement an amnesty law, "In order that we may be able to carry out this program it is of utmost importance that peace and security should prevail in the South and that life returns to normal. It is primarily the responsibility of you all whether you are in the bush or at home to maintain peace and stability. The way is open for those abroad to return home and co-operate with us in building a prosperous Sudan united and democratic."[33]

Numayri and Garang appealed to the Southern Sudanese refugees abroad to consider reconciliation with the Khartoum administration and resolve the problems facing the country. They gave Southerners a "full programme of amnesty" and further promised employment opportunities, especially to former civil servants, as well as recruitment and training of Southern policemen and soldiers. The Khartoum regime also pledged to initiate new economic, social, and educational programs in the South that would help address the problems of poverty, health care, and illiteracy.[34] In May and June 1970, the Khartoum regime also sent Garang as a special envoy to London and New York to solicit funds for resettling Southern returnees. A portion of the money was to be earmarked for reconstructing the South.[35]

Numayri's political language, filled with promises for peace and political stability in Southern Sudan, apparently earned him sympathy and financial support from the international community, but on the domestic front, he failed to present a comprehensive program for peace to the Southern politicians in exile and the resistance movement waging war against his government. Instead, he simply presented a list of promises to Southern exiles upon their voluntary return to their homeland. Such "peace" overtures fell on the deaf ears of Southern exiles, who were fully aware of the manipulative tactics of the Khartoum regimes, past and present.[36]

Moreover, although Numayri attempted to use Southerners like Garang to bring about a peaceful settlement in the South, he did not abandon the military option. Upon seizing power, Numayri and the RCC had believed that if the army were equipped with more effective weapons and better "transport facilities," they could completely destroy the Southern resistance movement.[37] By the middle of 1970, General Joseph Lagu had succeeded in unifying all the guerrilla factions into the single, well-equipped, and well-trained fighting force of the Anya-Nya. Lagu was also able to obtain funds and weapons from foreign sympathizers. This military development in the South strengthened Numayri's resolve to acquire more sophisticated weapons for the Sudanese army. To that end, he solicited the military assistance of the Egyptians, Libyans, and Soviets.[38] In October, Numayri requested Soviet help to contain the ever-increasing strength of the Southern resistance movement and eventually crush the Southern rebellion.[39]

A German journalist working for the Munich *Suddeutsche Zeitung* accompanied the pilot and crew of a Soviet MI-8 helicopter gunship in one of its flights from Juba in Central Equatoria to Meridi in Western Equatoria. As he recounted, "Although the captain of the aircraft was a Sudanese, it was actually flown by a Russian pilot and an Egyptian navigator. . . . [T]hese helicopters are used for bombing and striking operations, and they are always under the effective command of Russians or Egyptians. . . . 24 bombers and 12 T4–16 bombers have been used for bombing and striking. . . . Soviet advisors are also joining in ground operations."[40] Soviet military advisors were also stationed in Juba, the administrative headquarters of Equatoria Province, to provide tactical and strategic advice to the Sudanese military forces and to escort them on patrol.[41]

Despite Numayri's solicitation of foreign military assistance to crush the resistance, his plans ultimately failed. The well-equipped Sudanese army was unable to easily locate or pin down the Anya-Nya, a mobile guerrilla force familiar with its home terrain, giving it leverage over the Sudanese army despite being poorly equipped. The Sudanese army was losing men in the rank and file, but above all the war continued to drain the nation's treasury. The only feasible solution to the conflict was a negotiated peace settlement. Although by the middle of 1971, two years after the coup that ended the reign of Mahgoub, neither Numayri nor

Lagu and his SSLM were prepared for a meaningful dialogue to end the civil war in Southern Sudan, this stalemate was about to change.

THE COMMUNIST COUP AGAINST NUMAYRI

When President Numayri came to power in a bloodless coup supported by communists, pan-Arabists, and secular political activists representing a wide political spectrum, it appeared his regime would be assured of political stability and peace. Over time, however, ideological differences gradually weakened the coalition. Although Numayri assumed power with a socialist agenda, his political views differed from those of the communists to the far left. Thus, it was not surprising that they split ranks with Numayri's regime a few months after his military takeover. Numayri acted swiftly by purging "orthodox communists" from his government, sparing only Garang.[42]

On July 19, 1971, Communist Party leaders staged their own coup against Numayri, charging that he "had led the country through corruption and was rapidly establishing himself as a Dictator. . . . He had failed to solve major economic and social problems. . . . He had proved unable to solve the Southern problem."[43] Within a few days, however, intervention by Egypt and Libya forced the communists from power and reinstated Numayri. The coup leaders were quickly arrested and executed, along with Joseph Garang.[44]

After being reinstated to power, Numayri clearly recognized the weaknesses of his administration in the North. He also lost confidence in the Soviet Union, regarding it now with suspicion. He solicited the support of "pragmatic men of some intellectual sophistication" and adopted a much more cautious approach to political situations. While continuing to embrace his ideology of pan-Arabism and Arab socialism, he turned to the West for moral and political support.[45] In 1972, Numayri also outlawed all the existing political parties, establishing in their place the Sudanese Socialist Union (SSU) as the country's sole legal political party.

NUMAYRI AND SOUTHERN LEADERS
DECIDE TO PURSUE PEACE

The failed communist coup also meant that Numayri needed to reconsider a peaceful negotiated settlement to the civil war, because he did not want to confront two foes simultaneously, the South and the North.[46] Other external and internal factors also prompted Numayri to seriously pursue the peace option. According to former Anya-Nya officer John

Lueth, by 1969 Israeli military assistance to Anya-Nya military operations had become significant and had strengthened the rebels against the Sudanese army. The Numayri regime was aware of this "symbiotic" relationship between the Israelis and the Anya-Nya.[47]

Dr. Pacifico Lolik further observed that when Lagu united all Anya-Nya forces under his command, guerrilla operations became more effective in the battlefields, leading to many setbacks for the Sudanese army. At this point, the general commanders of the Sudanese army recognized that despite their military superiority over the Anya-Nya forces, they would never win the conflict in the South. They now preferred a peaceful settlement to the crisis.[48] According to Barnaba Dumo Wani, Numayri himself acknowledged that the war was "an unnecessary loss of lives and resources at the expense of the country's development plans."[49] Lueth likewise stated that because the war in the South was continuously draining the national treasury, little money was being spent on developing infrastructure, social services, and education.[50]

Another critical factor on the domestic front that prompted Numayri to consider peace talks with the Southern resistance movement was his shaky power base. Having lost the support of the communists and knowing that the traditional political parties like the Umma and DUP neither recognized nor supported his military regime, he knew that his only hope for surviving in power was to talk peace with the South and secure its alliance.[51] As Wani summed up Numayri's desire for peace in Sudan, "He had a pretty good assessment that to concede autonomy to the South was a lesser evil than continuation of the war, which could end up in the total loss of the South."[52]

The Organization of African Unity (OAU), upholding its charter on noninterference in the internal affairs of a member country, showed no interest and exerted no effort in these matters, nor did it even pressure the North and South to stop the civil war. The United Nations extended only material and financial resources to Southern Sudanese refugees in neighboring countries—it did not intervene in the war and made no effort to bring a peaceful end to the crisis.[53] However, as the war continued, strong opposition to it grew, especially from human rights organizations, humanitarian organizations, and churches in the Western world, which were providing material support and financial assistance to Southern refugees. Thus, internationally the Sudanese government was losing its friends, especially in the West. When Numayri turned to the West after the abortive communist coup, he felt the time was opportune for his government to secure Western allies who could jump-start the peace process. Under these circumstances, the World Council of Churches (WCC) took the first initiative to gather support for a negotiated peace settlement from both the Southern rebel movement and the Sudanese government.[54]

As early as October 1970, Abel Alier, the architect of "regional autonomy" for the South, had presented a memorandum to the Council of Ministers, urging them to consider "dialogue with the Anya-Nya." As Alier explicitly stated, "The government should re-examine its stand on the question of dialogue with the rebels. Our proposed solution of regional autonomy is well known. Rebel leaders continue with rebellion. These leaders are known. We do not lose anything by probing into the rebels' attitudes to our proposed solutions. Those responsible for rebellion may wish to have regional autonomy specified in terms of powers, institutions and values and spelt out clearly in working out this framework already laid down."[55]

Now in light of the abortive communist coup and the other internal and external factors working against his regime, Numayri felt an urgent need to pursue a peaceful solution. To portray himself as a peacemaker and to convince the Southern Sudanese both at home and in exile that his government was committed to a negotiated peace settlement, he appointed Alier the new minister of state for Southern affairs as well as one of the three vice presidents of the republic. According to Dunstan Wai, Alier was given such important appointments because he was a prominent Southern politician in whom the Southerners had vested their confidence,[56] while Dr. Dominic Mohammed has stated that Alier's appointments were based on a number of considerations. Alier was a moderate member of the Southern Front, an important Southern Sudanese political organization based in Northern Sudan. As a politician and lawyer, it was judged he would be very influential in bringing Northerners and Southerners together for a negotiated peaceful settlement. Alier was also a strong advocate of the unity of Sudan. He had himself initiated the peace proposals, and he clearly understood the kind of "peace" that Numayri "would accept or reject." Alier also recognized that the civil strife in the South had been going on for a long time and that many Southerners had died. He thus considered it necessary to bring the war to an immediate end.[57]

Southern Sudanese politicians in exile, suspicious of Khartoum's political maneuvering, received the news of Alier's appointment to the two key positions with little enthusiasm. While they acknowledged Alier's credible qualities, they questioned Numayri's right to appoint a Southerner to an important position without consulting Southerners from a wide political spectrum, and they criticized Numayri for selecting leaders for them. Nevertheless, they also stated that "at any rate the struggle for the South is above individual personalities and we are going, therefore, to watch whether General Nimeiri will allow Mr. Alier to contribute creatively to the solution of the Southern problem or whether he would rather make use of him (and the other Southern Sudanese in his cabinet) as mere tokens of South Sudan participation in Government of the country and as his propaganda mouthpiece abroad."[58]

Although Southerners within and outside Sudan were skeptical toward Alier's appointment, the overwhelming opinion was that he should be given a chance to implement the peace proposal he had presented to Numayri and the Council of Ministers. Thus, Alier quickly restructured the ministry for Southern affairs and solicited the help of important Southern politicians in Khartoum to develop a blueprint for local autonomy in the South. He also successfully convinced Numayri to recognize that the Anya-Nya needed to be an integral part of any peace talks leading to the settlement of the Southern question.[59]

Leaders of the WCC and the All Africa Conference of Churches (AACC), which had been providing material and financial resources to the Southern Sudanese refugees in the neighboring countries, together with the Church World Service (CWS) of New York, now became instrumental in facilitating peace talks between the Numayri administration and the SSLM.[60] When the WCC/AACC delegation delivered Numayri's peace proposal to the SSLM leadership, the latter reacted cautiously,[61] replying:

> We call upon General Nimeiri to abandon his policy of seeking military allies and to show more concerns for the grave social and political issues in his own country. . . . As far as the Southern Sudanese are concerned, it is well recorded in history that our attitude has always been to find a peaceful solution to the Southern cause. Therefore, in conformity with this constant policy for a negotiated settlement that we have pursued during the reign of different and consecutive governments in Khartoum, we call upon General Nimeiri to meet the Southern Sudan Liberation Movement to determine conditions aimed at bringing a final end to war and atrocities in South Sudan.[62]

Lagu appeared enthusiastic about pursuing a peaceful strategy to end the civil war but was not convinced by Numayri's peace overtures, based on concerns that Numayri's efforts to secure foreign military allies might escalate the war rather than end it. Lagu also found himself facing a number of internal and external factors that prompted him to seriously consider peace talks with the Numayri regime. According to him, the war in the South had dragged on for a long time, yet still no decisive victory was in sight. The Anya-Nya armed forces were experiencing war fatigue, and as commander in chief, he wanted to give them a rest. Lagu also acknowledged the magnitude of suffering among the Southern Sudanese both inside and outside Sudan. And so he wanted peace for the South.[63] Furthermore, according to Lolik, by the time Numayri offered peace talks to the SSLM, the Anya-Nya guerrilla movement was riddled with problems. Some Anya-Nya fighters had abandoned the armed struggle, while other ambitious military officers had attempted to overthrow Lagu, prompting him to dismiss some of his senior Anya-Nya officers and political advisors. In the face of such political squabbles, Lagu opted for peace to save his own life as well as to preserve his military and political career.[64] Wani has further asserted that Lagu's success in uniting the Anya-Nya forces gave him the confidence and support that he needed to negotiate peace with Numayri's regime. This was a time when he enjoyed the overwhelming support of the Anya-Nya armed forces. There was, in any event, little resistance from the political leaders in the SSLM.[65]

According to Oliver Batali Albino, a former combatant in the Anya-Nya and a politician in the SSLM, Southern Sudanese intellectuals outside Sudan were also influenced by foreign Christian missionaries to talk peace. Southern Sudanese living in the North were also pressuring the intellectuals and politicians to end the war through peaceful means.[66]

In addition, Lagu, Lueth, Albino, and Mohammed have all stated that the Israelis, who were the principal suppliers of arms to the Anya-Nya, were not providing weapons sophisticated enough to win the civil war in the South. They only supplied weapons that could prove a nuisance to the Sudanese government.[67]

Lagu has further observed that the Israelis enjoyed a good relationship with Uganda during the presidencies of Milton Obote and Idi Amin from 1966 to 1972. After Amin overthrew Obote in January 1971, he continued to provide safe passage for the Israelis on their way to Southern Sudan, as his predecessor had done, but when Amin turned to North Africa and the Middle East for moral and financial support, his relationship with the Israelis quickly deteriorated and subsequently ended. The Israelis were literally forced out of Uganda by Amin. This political development ended Israeli military assistance to the Anya-Nya armed forces. Lagu thus had no other alternative but to seek a peaceful settlement to the civil war.[68]

Thus, on January 26, 1971, Mading de Garang (SSLM representative in London) delivered to the Sudanese government a letter of peace overture reflecting the viewpoint of the SSLM leadership. Garang's letter called for:

... cessation of hostilities which would include stopping construction of bridges and establishment of new military posts in the war zone ... appointment of an OAU member observer team to be stationed in Juba with freedom to move in the Southern Sudan in order to monitor the ceasefire arrangements ... the Sudan government to recognize the Anya-Nya as the sole and only body to represent the South in the talks ... the venue of preliminary talks to be outside the Sudan, under the chairmanship of the current Chairman of the OAU or any other African Head of State ... and the release of Clement Mboro, the veteran Southern politician, then in detention.[69]

This was followed in the summer of that year by a second official letter sent by Lagu to the Numayri government expressing his commitment to peace. These two letters to Numayri from powerful leaders of the SSLM convinced him that the Southern Sudanese rebel movement was committed to genuine peace. In Khartoum, Southern students and members of the Southern Front and of SANU-inside supported Alier's peace proposal.[70] According to Wani, the Sudan Council of Churches (SCC) in Khartoum also pledged its support for a peaceful settlement.[71] This overwhelming Southern support for the peace initiative was an opportunity that Numayri and his administration did not want to miss as a positive development that could help maintain him in power.

SUPPORT IS RALLIED FOR THE PROPOSED NEGOTIATIONS

The United Nations had declared 1971 the Year of Refugees, and the United Nations High Commissioner for Refugees (UNHCR) and nongovernmental organizations (NGOs) such as voluntary organizations now embarked on a comprehensive program to raise money in the West, especially for African refugees.[72] Southern Sudanese refugees in neighboring countries had been receiving humanitarian assistance or relief aid from the UN, the UNHCR, and other voluntary organizations for more than a decade and were bound to benefit from this financial campaign. It was therefore not surprising that the WCC, AACC, and CWS all showed keen interest in the Lagu-Numayri peace proposals. Above all, Numayri, himself a Muslim, recognized the importance of engaging such church organizations in the peace process.[73]

Not everyone was enthusiastic over the proposed negotiations. According to Gordon Muortat, former president of the Nile Provisional Government, in 1971 the Reverend Cannon Burgess Carr, a Liberian citizen who was general secretary of the AACC and spokesperson for the WCC, together with other officials of these church organizations, embarked on a tour of Southern Sudanese refugee camps in Zaire and Uganda to mobilize public opinion and support for the peace process. While in Kinshasa, capital of Zaire, Carr and his delegation met with Muortat, Francis Mayar, a Dinka lawyer in Kinshasa, and other Southern politicians, but they failed completely to persuade them to accept the Numayri-Lagu peace proposal. The Southern politicians in Zaire took a hard-line position against the negotiations because they were suspicious of Numayri's motives for talking peace following the abortive communist coup.[74]

Carr and the WCC/AACC delegation also visited Kampala in Uganda to "sell" the peace proposal to the Southern Sudanese refugees in that country, but received a mixed response to their campaign for peace. A core group of Southern politicians, including some members of the SSLM like Eliaba Surur who were staunch supporters of an independent Southern Sudanese government, refused to endorse the peace initiative. According to Surur, he quickly mobilized Southern politicians and intellectuals to write a document opposing the peace proposal.[75] Mohammed notes that other Southern political exiles in neighboring countries welcomed the peace initiative, motivated by the desire to "gain positions in any new regional government."[76]

Mohammed, who represented the SSLM in the United States, met with Carr, the WCC/AACC delegation, and Dr. Lawrence Wol Wol, the SSLM representative in Europe, in 1971 in New York. This peace group had traveled to the United States to drum up support from Southern Sudanese intellectuals for the peace process. Mohammed clearly recognized that Wol Wol and Mading de Garang represented the interests of the vast majority of the WCC but not of the vast majority of Southern Sudanese. He referred to these SSLM politicians as "puppets" of the three church organizations and said they "were told what to do." The primary goal of these "peacemakers" was to secure the endorsement of Alier's peace proposal by Southern intellectuals in the United States.[77]

Carr clearly understood that if he could persuade Mohammed to embrace the peace proposal, it would be a major diplomatic achievement for the AACC, the WCC, and the CWS in the United States. He assured Mohammed that if he endorsed the peace initiative, in the event of a meaningful peace agreement he would be given a ministerial position in the new regional government of Southern Sudan. Mohammed refused, declaring, "I am not for sale!"[78]

Meanwhile, the Southern Front in Khartoum was busy persuading Southern communities in Northern Sudan to rally behind the peace efforts. The Southern Front also recognized the importance of soliciting the support of Southern refugees in the neighboring countries of Zaire, Uganda, and Kenya. Alier headed a Southern Front delegation (which also included Hillary Paul Logali, a Bari lawyer, and Lubari Ramba, a Kakwa politician) that went to Uganda to urge Southern exiles to accept the peace initiative.[79]

According to Lawrence Tombe, Southern Sudanese students at Makerere University in Uganda were taken aback when SSLM politicians in Kampala informed them of the intent by the SSLM and the government of Sudan to negotiate a peaceful settlement to the civil war. This is particularly interesting because the SSLM representatives had been discussing prospects for peace with the Numayri regime in secret. The vast majority of Southern refugees in neighboring countries were equally surprised by this new political development. Because of this, the students wanted to know "how prepared were we as Southern Sudanese or as a movement to go and face Northern Sudan?" The students were very suspicious of Khartoum's political maneuvers and manipulations in the South because they knew that Southerners had been cheated by successive Khartoum governments in past decades. Although they recognized the Southern Sudanese yearning for peace, the students were cautious about the kind of peace that would be acceptable to both the North and the South.[80]

Tombe has further asserted that Southern students at Makerere University played a significant role "in forming a political opinion on the Southern issue." The students urged the Southern politicians to delay any peace talks with the Numayri administration to allow them a chance to consult with Southern exiles in the refugee camps of neighboring countries. This would also give Southern politicians a chance to discuss the peace proposals with student organizations in Uganda, Kenya, Tanzania, and other neighboring countries. The primary aim was to elicit ideas or suggestions from the refugee population that would strengthen the Southern position at the peace talks. It was also important to have the indirect participation of the Southern refugee population in the talks.[81]

According to Dunstan Wai, Southern students in exile recognized that the various Southern Sudanese political factions needed foremost to iron out their differences and rally behind the SSLM. Achieving unity would enable the Southern politicians in exile to begin contacting their Southern counterparts inside Sudan like Alier, the architect of regional autonomy and the peace proposal. The Southern students in exile also wanted Southern politicians, whether inside or outside, to request the Numayri regime to organize "a conference of representatives from both the North and the South to discuss the fundamental principles and details of the policy of Regional Autonomy."[82] Because the students at Makerere were committed to cultivating friendly relations between Southerners inside and outside Sudan, they dispatched a delegation to Khartoum to establish communication between Southerners inside Sudan and those in exile, and to assess the general opinion of Southerners inside on the question of regional autonomy.[83] It was also a bold move on their part to visit Khartoum when the civil war was still ongoing.

According to Colonel Stephen Madut, a former Anya-Nya officer, the peace process also took the Anya-Nya rank and file by surprise. Their main suppliers of arms, the Israelis, were equally taken aback and disappointed. It is Madut's belief that the WCC put tremendous pressure on Numayri to end the civil war.[84]

Prelude to the Addis Ababa Peace Talks

In August 1971, Lagu sent his own special envoys, including Wol Wol and Mading de Garang, to meet with Southern Sudanese politicians and refugees in Zaire, Uganda, and other neighboring countries in order to seek approval of the impending negotiations with the Sudanese government. The Southern politicians in Kinshasa, comprising Gordon Muortat, Francis Mayar, and others, declared to the delegation that they would not oppose the negotiations with the Numayri regime because the military option was not the ultimate solution to any conflict, and that they would accept peace talks with the Sudanese government based on a number of important considerations. Muortat later recounted that they asked, "First of all, tell the World Council of Churches to postpone rushing the negotiations and allow the Southern Sudanese to hold a conference in East Africa on this issue; all the political organizations outside, including the Anya-Nya, must be represented—even the parties inside, the representatives of SANU, [the] Southern Front . . . so that the Southerners [can] brainstorm and come up with concrete ideas about their demands during the negotiations—is it federation, local autonomy or otherwise?"[85]

During the night-long discussions between the two parties, it was agreed that if the Southerners reached a consensus in their demands from Numayri's administration, the delegates in the conference would appoint Southern representatives to negotiate with the Khartoum government. Meanwhile, it was important that the Southerners seriously assess the military strength of the Anya-Nya forces. They considered it essential that the military commanders brief the delegation about the status of the military forces in terms of manpower and equipment so that they could negotiate from a position of strength.[86]

The Southern Sudanese politicians in Kinshasa asked the SSLM envoys to convey the principal points they had raised to the WCC and to inform the council that if it embraced these ideas, the Southerners would be ready to attend the peace negotiations. Surprisingly, Wol Wol "was adamant and downplayed the demands of the exiles in Kinshasa."[87] He argued that most of the Southerners in the diaspora had already accepted peace negotiations with the Numayri regime, and he wondered why the Southern politicians did not follow suit. He displayed an arrogant attitude, and almost fought with Francis Mayar.[88]

Meanwhile, Southern Sudanese in Bahr al-Ghazal, Upper Nile, and Equatoria were putting tremendous pressure on Lagu in the few months preceding the actual peace talks in Addis Ababa. The people of Equatoria were particularly "skeptical about the peace process." Lagu was thus obliged to consult with the Southern Sudanese about the type of peace agreement that might be acceptable to them. To that end, Southerners in neighboring Kampala set up a committee that drafted a "compromise proposal." This document stipulated that "all powers must be given to the region, except Foreign Affairs, Defense, and Currency." Lagu was given the mandate to present this document to the Khartoum delegation, and in the event the proposal was turned down, he was to return home and report to the committee. Joseph Oduho, who was from Equatoria Province and who was skeptical of the peace process, was chosen to accompany Lagu to Addis Ababa. Oduho was strongly advised that if Lagu did not "follow up the demands," he should come back to Kampala and report to the committee.[89]

When it came time to choose delegates to represent the Southern region at the negotiations, disagreements arose. Lagu has stated that he thought the representation should be even, and so he selected nine delegates, three from each province, to ensure equal representation. He maintains this was a fair representation, and that no one complained afterwards about being underrepresented, although some delegates did not show up.[90]

Not everyone thought this was fair. Daniel Tongun felt that the Addis Ababa peace process would have produced a comprehensive and just peace for Southern Sudan if the intellectuals or politicians, the Anya-Nya military forces, and the public at large had all been fairly represented. All these groups should have been drawn from the three Southern provinces: twelve politicians, with four delegates from each province; two military commanders; some soldiers representing the Anya-Nya forces in each province; and representatives from the general population. These groups should have been an integral part of the SSLM delegation to Addis Ababa in 1971. Politicians like Aggrey Jaden, the former president of the Southern Sudan Provisional Government, and Francis Mayar, the Dinka lawyer who lived in Kinshasa, Zaire, should have headed the peace delegation to Addis Ababa. In Tongun's view, it was unfair for Lagu, the head of the SSLM, to solely determine who among the Southern Sudanese people should represent the interests, needs, and political aspirations of the Southern region.[91]

According to Surur, Lagu was advised to wait for the various Southern political groups and Anya-Nya military commanders and soldiers to assemble so that they could travel together to Addis Ababa as a formidable body. This delegation would then have been able to negotiate with the Khartoum delegation from a position of strength. The Southerners also wanted diplomats from foreign countries, whether inside Africa or outside the continent, to attend the peace talks as observers. Such a representation was necessary to ensure fair and amicable negotiations between the two belligerent parties. Despite these concerted efforts by Southerners, Lagu ignored their demands and unilaterally decided to pick a few delegates of his own choice and go to Addis Ababa for the talks.[92]

Southerners were meanwhile disappointed to learn that the Northern Sudanese delegation was being led by Abel Alier, especially because the Southern politicians in exile had expected Alier to lead the Southern Sudanese delegation within Sudan at the talks. These two groups (external and internal) would have been a formidable force to reckon with at the negotiating table, but to the surprise and dismay of the Southern Sudanese, Alier headed the Khartoum delegation representing the views and interests of Numayri and his party, the SSU, and the Sudanese government.[93]

Lolik and Tongun were dismayed not only that Alier led the Khartoum delegation, but also that he participated in the peace talks on behalf of Numayri's government and the SSU. In their view, both Lagu and Alier should have been on the same delegation (SSLM), which would have strengthened the Southern position. Lolik in particular contended that when Alier sat on the side of the Northern delegation, "he made it easier for the North to get more from the South and more difficult for the South to get more from the North." [94]

Clement Mboro has stated that although Alier was a Dinka from Southern Sudan, in his capacity as vice president of Sudan and minister of state for Southern affairs, he was essentially representing the Sudanese government and the SSU.[95] In Mboro's view, Southerners should not be naive in thinking that Alier was a puppet of Numayri's regime. It should be noted that Mboro was sympathetic to Alier's role in the Addis Ababa peace agreement. Both men had worked together in the Southern Front in Khartoum and had also served the Khartoum governments in various capacities in the North and South. Above all, they were astute politicians who clearly understood the "political game" between Northerners and Southerners within the country.

Daniel Tongun, however, was very critical of Alier's role in the Addis Ababa peace process and talks. At the time, he was highly suspicious and skeptical of any political cooperation between the Southern and Northern politicians, and he wondered how foes and friends could work together for a common cause. As he put it, the Southerners considered Lagu and Alier as "brothers—people from the same region upholding the same aims, objectives, and a common destiny."[96]

START OF THE PEACE TALKS AND SIGNING OF THE PEACE AGREEMENT

The peace talks between the SSLM and the representatives of Numayri's administration commenced in Addis Ababa, Ethiopia, in October 1971,[97] but the Southern politicians and refugees in the diaspora were not well prepared. The SSLM leadership was under tremendous pressure from the WCC, the AACC, and Emperor Haile Selassie of Ethiopia, whom the WCC had persuaded to broker the agreement.[98]

The SSLM delegation in Addis Ababa included Esbon Mondiri Gwonza as leader as well as Lawrence Wol Wol, Mading de Garang, Colonel Frederick Brian Maggot as special military representative, and Oliver Batali Albino, among others,[99] while the Khartoum delegation included Alier, Dr. Mansour Khalid (foreign affairs minister), Mohammed El Baghir Ahmed (interior minister), as well as other cabinet members and military representatives.[100] Non-Sudanese officials and observers who initiated the peace negotiations included Nabiyelul Kifle as representative of the emperor of Ethiopia, Leopoldo J. Niilus and Kodwo E. Ankrah of the WCC, and Burgess Carr, general secretary of the AACC. Within Sudan, Samuel Athi Bwogo represented the Sudan Council of Churches.[101]

Critical examination of the composition of the SSLM and Sudanese government delegates to the peace talks clearly shows that the members of the Khartoum delegation were better educated, more highly politicized, and more sophisticated than their Southern counterparts. Alier and Khalid were lawyers by training who understood the importance of writing laws that would preserve the sovereignty of Sudan but at the same time provide a measure of local autonomy to the people of the South. In contrast, the Southern delegation members were inexperienced in peace negotiations; they had never participated in writing the constitution of the country, let alone writing laws that would protect their rights and privileges as citizens of Sudan as stipulated in the June 9, 1969, declaration. It was therefore not surprising that in the ensuing talks, the Southern delegates felt manipulated, cheated, or coerced into accepting certain conditions that were detrimental to the interests, needs, and political aspirations of their people.

It is Madut's belief that the WCC officials and Carr of the AACC did not present themselves as impartial peace brokers; instead, they intimidated the SSLM delegates to the extent that the latter became submissive to the Northern delegation.[102] Concurring with Madut, Mohammed observed that Wol Wol and Garang, as "puppets" of the WCC and AACC, succumbed to pressure from the WCC officials and Carr.[103]

Mohammed was also critical of the role played by Emperor Haile Selassie during the peace negotiations. According to him, the emperor pressured Lagu into accepting an agreement by telling him he would otherwise not be allowed to travel in any of the neighboring countries like Kenya, Uganda, Zaire, and Ethiopia.[104] Mboro observed that when the Southern Sudanese delegation demanded their own army in the South before they could accept any agreement, the Ethiopian foreign minister presented this critical issue to the emperor, who, in turn, presented a compromise that the troops deployed to the South should be 50 percent from the South and the North alike.[105]

During the peace talks, the Khartoum delegation granted Southern Sudan regional self-government consisting of a Regional Assembly with legislative powers and a High Executive Council (HEC) with executive powers.[106] The people of Southern Sudan were thus for the first time given the right to exercise their democratic values and principles in their own legislative assembly. Article 11 stipulated that "the People's Regional Assembly shall legislate for the preservation of public order, internal security, efficient administration and the development of the Southern Region in culture [and the] economic and social fields."[107] Article 7, on the other hand, excluded the following charges: national defense, external affairs, currency and coinage, air and interregional river transport, communications and telecommunications, customs and foreign trade (with some exceptions), nationality and immigration, planning for economic and social development, educational planning, and public audit.[108]

Reaction to the Addis Ababa Agreement

When the Addis Ababa Agreement was finally signed on March 12, 1972, various political circles at the national and international levels reacted either positively or negatively. For his part, Numayri, speaking to the nation following the signing, praised the efforts of both Southern and Northern intellectuals that had brought peace and tranquility to the nation. He acknowledged that the agreement "did not provide new structure to the Sudan by altering international boundaries nor to divide its people in lines of racial, cultural, or religious creeds." He argued that the agreement was testimony to the fact that the diverse ethnic and racial groups in the country could co-exist harmoniously. Thus for the first time in modern Sudanese history, the people of Southern Sudan were granted the right to govern themselves and make laws that pertained to their political, economic, and social, and cultural aspirations.[109]

Numayri further observed that the accord provided "security guarantees" for Southerners at both the regional and national levels,[110] and he himself acknowledged for the first time the marked cultural and racial differences between Southerners and Northerners. He also went further to state that the people of the South were entitled to their freedom of mobility around the country.[111] Numayri summed up his satisfaction with the terms of the agreement thus, "The radiance of happiness and hope which I have witnessed in the South increased my belief in the wisdom of our revolutionary decision on the Agreement and the unity of the country."[112]

Southern intellectuals, on the other hand, were more cautious in their reactions. They believed that if the terms of the agreement were implemented honestly, the accord could help diffuse the tension between the North and South, which in turn could ultimately help restore confidence and trust between the peoples of the two regions. Thus, the intellectuals urged Numayri and Lagu, as well as Southerners at large, "to educate the Northern public about the terms of the agreement." This they could do by traveling to Northern cities and enlightening Northerners about the terms of the accord, which would help alleviate Northern fears about a possible separation of the South from the North.[113]

The Southern intellectuals also urged Numayri to seek assistance, financial or material, from the international community, because the South in particular lacked funds. They also feared that if some terms of the agreement were not implemented, Numayri's political opponents might exploit the inaction for personal ends, which might then derail the accord. They further demanded that Numayri appoint a provisional government for the Southern region, primarily to prevent any political squabbles among the Southerners.[114]

According to Madut, the Anya-Nya officers viewed the peace agreement as something they had not endorsed, "There was no consensus reached between the Anya-Nya forces and General Joseph Lagu. Nor was it an agreement between the Sudan government and Lagu . . . it was rather an agreement between the Sudan government and the World Council of Churches. The World Council of Churches intimidated the Anya-Nya (SSLM) and Numayri, citing the Israeli blackmail."[115]

In Lueth's view, the peace agreement was signed at the wrong time, because Anya-Nya military strength was growing steadily, and they were receiving more modern weapons from the Israelis such as anti-aircraft guns and mortars with "longer shelling capability."[116] And in Mboro's opinion, Numayri's primary aim in initiating the peace settlement was "to collect arms from the Anya-Nya."[117]

WEAKNESSES OF THE PEACE AGREEMENT

Oliver Albino, a member of the SSLM delegation to the peace talks, clearly recognized from the beginning that the subsequent agreement was bound to be weak. He thought its implementation would fail because the SSLM delegation had compromised Southern aspirations by subjecting the South to the Northern SSU. In his view, the diverse Southern cultural communities should not have agreed to be included in a single socialist movement, because this compromise "could not have worked without depriving the North of its theocratic concept of rule. As it was, they were not deprived, and the South had to suffer deprivation of its secularity instead."[118]

Madut believed as well that the Southern delegates made a mistake in compromising the interests and aspirations of the Southern peoples with SSU ideology and political aspirations. Numayri in fact believed in an Arab socialism diametrically opposed to Southern cultural diversity. According to Madut, the sophisticated Northern delegation exploited the weakness of the SSLM delegation, as a result of which "Southern Sudanese politicians in exile were . . . co-opted into [the] SSU."[119] This faulty decision of the SSLM delegation at the peace talks would subsequently haunt the leadership of the HEC, the cabinet ministers, and the members of the Regional Assembly throughout the period the agreement lasted, from 1972 to 1983.

Other Southern intellectuals have concurred with Albino's and Madut's views on this compromise at the talks. According to Lolik, the members of the Regional Assembly simply accepted integration and absorption into the SSU "even before the end of the transitional period of five years [1972 to 1977]." Thus, the complete absence of the SSLM as a political party in the South meant that its politicians, who were co-opted into the SSU, failed to transform a political platform that could guard against corruption and tribalism.[120]

Moreover, although the Addis Ababa accord granted regional autonomy to Southern Sudan, it failed to clarify the position of the North in terms of central authority. For instance, although the South possessed mineral resources, the North, as the central authority, controlled these resources while enjoying revenue from other resources around the country as well. The North also neglected to provide financially for the regional government, which would have enabled it to operate more effectively and efficiently. The agreement moreover failed to clarify the financial needs of the regional government, and the South depended primarily on the national treasury in Khartoum.[121] This meant that the latter could strangle the former's economy out of political motives. This is clearly evident in the deterioration of social services throughout the South. Agricultural production also declined, rendering the region dependent on food from the North. Because health services in the South were insufficiently funded, the NGOs became instrumental in providing medicine and medical equipment. Most of these health services were concentrated in Juba, the capital of Equatoria. The towns of Wau in Bahr al-Ghazal and Malakal in Upper Nile were neglected entirely.[122]

During the period of the agreement, fifteen secondary schools and the University of Juba were opened in the South to revive the educational system, which had been virtually destroyed during the war, but the dire lack of funds in the regional government undermined any efforts to revive or improve the system. Schools lacked educational equipment and textbooks. This was further compounded by a serious shortage of qualified teachers and lack of funds to pay their salaries on a regular basis. All these factors contributed to further deterioration of the standard of education throughout the South, leading to an increase in school dropouts,[123] while the number of qualified students admitted to various levels of education continuously declined.[124]

Moreover, Southern politicians and civil servants grew corrupt and "tribalistic" and actively engaged in nepotism. They embezzled government funds for personal enrichment or to "buy the loyalty of their constituencies."[125] Thus, instead of equitably distributing public resources to the people in the South, a certain few individuals in positions of power and influence benefited from these resources.[126]

In addition, although the Addis Ababa Agreement was written with the help of trained lawyers like Alier and Khalid, it made no provision for judiciary organs. There was no mechanism for keeping records of legislation. Instead, any legislation passed by the Regional Assembly was simply recorded on paper. The agreement "lacked the mechanisms for enforcing these laws."[127] This was a serious structural problem for the regional government—lawmakers could not enforce the laws, nor would they refer to laws passed in preceding legislation. Moreover, most members of the Regional Assembly had no training in law and therefore lacked the necessary competence and confidence to handle legislative issues pertaining to Southern Sudan in particular and to the nation at large. Thus, the absence of a judiciary organ for the most part rendered the assembly a mere forum for freedom of speech and expression.[128]

Yet despite all these weaknesses, the South did enjoy a measure of democracy through its Regional Assembly that the North did not have, let alone the other regions of the country. And so, after an estimated 1.3 million deaths and the displacement of over five million others as refugees in neighboring countries, Southern Sudan had finally achieved, if not independence, then at least local autonomy. Indeed, the price of peace and autonomy had come to the people of Southern Sudan at a high cost, but as the South now set about the arduous task of learning to run its own affairs, Northern politicians, jealous of Southern democratic rights and local autonomy, would work to gradually dismantle the peace agreement.[129] Aided by growing tensions and jealousies among the Southerners themselves, they would finally succeed with General Numayri's abrogation of the agreement in June 1983.

Conclusion

SUDAN, THE LARGEST COUNTRY IN AFRICA, was the first nation on the continent to gain its independence from the British colonial administration amidst a civil war. The root causes of the war can be traced to both foreign and internal political, economic, and social forces, which favored the North but adversely affected the South. It is therefore no surprise that these policies would sow the seeds of discord and hostility among the people of Southern Sudan, who were suspicious of and hostile towards the Muslim and Arabized people of the North. At the same time, Northerners, who had little knowledge of the South, viewed its inhabitants as backward in terms of civilization, culture, and religion. They felt they had a duty to spread the Islamic faith and bring the superior "Arab" civilization and culture to the region. It is this dichotomy between the North and South that brought so much devastation, death, and suffering to the South for seventeen years in the first civil war and another twenty-two years in the second.

When the British granted Sudan its independence on January 1, 1956, the educated, sophisticated, and highly politicized elite in Khartoum inherited the reins of power and enjoyed a firm grip on the country's economy as well. Instead of presenting a new road map for the political, economic, and social development of the new republic, reorganizing the richness of its African, Arab, and European civilizations, and creating a unique African-Arab civilization, they chose to create a small "Arab" ruling clique at the expense of the vast majority of the African peoples in Sudan. At the national level, they dictated political, economic, and social policies detrimental to the people in the periphery. While infrastructure in the center, north, and east was developed, the western region (Darfur and Kordofan), Southern Blue Nile, and Southern Sudan remained backward.

In addition, the Northern elite, viewing the South as backward in every way, believed that Southern opinions did not matter in the decision-making process pertaining to Sudan's future. Thus, in the 1950s when Northern politicians were discussing Sudan's road to independence, Southern views were not consulted. During the Sudanization Program, Southerners felt openly cheated when only six junior administrative posts were allocated to them. Meanwhile, their consistent demand for federal status was frustrated by the various civilian and military administrations of the North.

The new Sudanese civilian government and the departing British administration were taken aback when the soldiers of the Equatoria Corps mutinied in Torit. This incident was not only an embarrassment to the Northern and British officials in Khartoum, but also a threat to the national security and unity of the country. That was why they opted to brutally suppress the mutiny in Torit and other Southern towns. To the Southern Sudanese, however, the incident in Torit was not simply a mutiny, but rather a rebellion by Southern patriots against all forms of injustice imposed on the South by the North. It was the first attempt by the African people in Southern Sudan to express their political aspirations, their strong belief in African nationalism, and above all, their assertion of Africanism over Arabism.

In response, a resistance movement that became known as Anya-Nya arose determined to seek independence for the South. Soon the struggle became internationalized, caught up in the Cold War tensions between East and West and the contest between Israel and the Arab powers. The military aid provided for the Southern Sudanese resistance movement by Israel enhanced Anya-Nya firepower in the battlefield against the Soviet-equipped Sudanese army. With neither side able to score a decisive victory, eventually outside church organizations and certain African governments stepped in to broker a peace agreement that finally ended the war by granting the South a form of local autonomy. Because of serious structural weaknesses in the agreement, it would last only ten years before collapsing, thereby paving the way for the outbreak of Sudan's second civil war in 1983.

It is fair to say that the Arab-dominated governments in Khartoum, whether civilian or military, bear much of the responsibility for the outbreak and sustenance of the first civil war. A small, but powerful, ruling elite stubbornly refused to recognize the multiplicities of race, ethnicity, culture, language, and religion. With respect to the South, it refused to acknowledge the "Southern problem" and provide a solution to it. Instead, the government in Khartoum strove to transform Sudan's image into an "Arab" and "Islamic" nation. This image was only superficial, for Sudan is characterized by historical racial, ethnic, cultural, religious, and linguistic diversity.

At the same time, the people of Southern Sudan were partly responsible for creating adverse political and social conditions that brought death and suffering to the region during the first civil war. The historical ethnic conflicts in the South were on display in the various political organizations and liberation movements formed in this period, compounded by personality clashes and personal ambitions. The lack of political education and the failure of Southern Sudanese to recognize the importance of peaceful coexistence and cooperation between the various ethnic groups rendered the South vulnerable to Khartoum's political and military maneuverings in the region. Had the Southern Sudanese been able to bury their ethnic differences and personal ambitions, they might have founded a single liberation movement, consolidated it, and directed it with the determination necessary to contain the firepower of the Sudanese government. This in turn might have ended the civil war sooner rather than later, while preventing the outbreak of the second.

Today, the future of the Sudanese will depend on their recognizing their commonalities and national identity, emphasizing political education, and pursuing freedom, justice, democracy, peace, and prosperity in a historically diverse country. Only if all the various racial and ethnic groups acknowledge that the country faces many problems and that a collective effort is needed to provide permanent solutions will Sudan have a bright future, but if the ruling elite in Khartoum continues to refuse to share political and economic power with the marginalized peoples occupying the country's periphery, Sudan's future will be bleak indeed.

NOTES

INTRODUCTION

1. Beshir, *The Southern Sudan: Background to Conflict* (New York: Praeger, 1968); Albino, *The Sudan: A Southern Viewpoint* (London: Oxford University Press, 1970); Wai, *The African-Arab Conflict in the Sudan 1955–1972* (New York: Africana, 1981); Ruay, *The Politics of Two Sudans: The North and the South 1821–1969* (Uppsala, Sweden: Nordiska Afrikainstitutet, 1994); Eprile, *World Realities: War and Peace in the Sudan, 1955–1972* (London: David and Charles, 1974); O'Ballance, *The Secret War in the Sudan* (London: Faber, 1977); Johnson, *The Root Causes of Sudan's Civil Wars* (Bloomington: Indiana University Press, 2003).
2. *Report of the Commission of Enquiry into the Disturbances in the Southern Sudan during August 1955* (Khartoum: McCorquadale, October 1956).
3. Sanderson and Sanderson, *Education, Religion, and Politics in Southern Sudan, 1899–1964* (London: Ithaca Press, 1981).
4. Alier, *Southern Sudan: Too Many Agreements Dishonoured*, 2nd ed. (Khartoum: A. Alier, 2003).

CHAPTER 1

1. Ruay, 11.
2. Mekki Abbas, *The Sudan Question: The Dispute over the Anglo-Egyptian Condominium 1884–1951* (London: Faber and Faber, 1952), 2; Muddathir Abd al-Rahim, *Imperialism and Nationalism in the Sudan: A Study in Constitutional and Political Development, 1899–1956* (Oxford: Clarendon, 1969), 3.
3. Abbas, 5–6; Abd al-Rahim, 3–4.
4. Stephanie Beswick, *Sudan's Blood Memory: The Legacy of War, Ethnicity, and Slavery in Early South Sudan* (Rochester, N.Y.: University of Rochester Press, 2004), 11; Abbas, 4.
5. Encyclopedia.com, "Sudan Political Geography," http://www.encyclopedia.com/category/Places/Africa/sdngeo.html.

6. Robert O. Collins, *Disaster in Darfur*, n.d., 1. Document available in the private collection of the author.
7. Ruay, 11.
8. Beshir, 1.
9. Dunstan M. Wai, ed., *The Southern Sudan: The Problem of National Integration* (London: Frank Cass, 1973), 9.
10. Human Rights Watch, *Sudan, Oil, and Human Rights. Part 1, Oil in Southern Sudan (New York*: Human Rights Watch, 2003), http://www.hrw.org/reports/2003/sudan1103/9.htm#_Toc54492563.
11. Wai, *Southern Sudan*, 9–10.
12. C. G. Seligman, *The Pagan Tribes of the Nilotic Sudan* (London: G. Routledge, 1932).
13. Mandour El-Mahdi, *A Short History of the Sudan* (London: Oxford University Press, 1965); Francis Mading Deng, *War of Visions: Conflict of Identities in the Sudan* (Washington, D.C.: Brookings Institution, 1995); Beshir, *Southern Sudan*.
14. Wai, *African-Arab Conflict*; Ruay, *Politics of Two Sudans*.
15. Edgar O'Ballance, *Sudan, Civil War, and Terrorism, 1956–1999* (London: Macmillan, 2000).
16. Kjell Hodnebo, "From Cattle to Corn: Economic Trends in Northeast Africa, Equatoria, Southern Sudan, and Northern Uganda, During the Last Three Centuries," Ph.D. Dissertation, University of Bergen, Norway, July 1997, p. 98; Severino Matti, "The Peopling of Eastern Equatoria," Paper presented at the University of London, December 4, 1980, 9.
17. Matti, 10.
18. P. T. W. Baxter and Audrey Butt, *The Azande and Related People of the Anglo-Egyptian Sudan and Belgian Congo* (London: International African Institute, 1953), 11.
19. Robert O. Collins, ed., *Problems in African History* (Englewood Cliffs, N.J.: Prentice-Hall, 1968), 115.
20. C. W. B. Huntingford, "The Peopling of the Interior of East Africa by its Modern Inhabitants," in Collins, *Problems in African History*, 121.
21. Bethwal A. Ogot, "Kinship and Statelessness Among the Nilotes," in Collins, *Problems in African History*, 157–59.
22. Beswick, xiii–xiv.
23. E. E. Evans-Pritchard, *The Nuer: A Description of the Modes of Livelihood and Political Institutions of a Nilotic People* (New York: Oxford University Press, 1940), 3.
24. Ibid. See also John W. Burton, *A Nilotic World: The Atuot-Speaking Peoples of the Southern Sudan* (New York: Greenwood, 1987), 1.
25. Seligman, *Pagan Tribes*, 3–4.
26. Evans-Pritchard, 3–4.
27. Ibid, 3.
28. Seligman, *Pagan Tribes*, 37.
29. Ibid, 108–9.

30. Hodnebo, 95.
31. L. F. Nalder, ed., *Tribal Survey of Mongalla Province by Members of the Province Staff and Church Missionary Society* (New York: Negro University Press, 1970), 9.
32. Daniel Wani Tomilyan, *The Kuku Cultural Phenomenon* (Koboko, Uganda: 1999), 3.
33. Seligman, *Pagan Tribes*, 305.
34. Nalder, 9.
35. Beshir, 1.
36. Author's personal observations.
37. "Arabs versus Africans in the Sudan" in *The Memorandum Presented by the Sudan African National Union to the Commission of the Organization of African Unity for Refugees* (Kampala, Uganda: 1964), 1.
38. John Garang de Mabior, interview by Betty Hinds, Washington, D.C., 1996.
39. Nanne Op't Ende, "History of the Nuba" Nuba Mountains Homepage. http://home.planet.nl-ende0098/content/nuba/01History03.html.
40. Suleiman Musa Rahhal, "The Nuba—Who Are They?" www.nubasurvival.com, 2. See also Suleiman Musa Rahhal, *The Right to be Nuba: The Story of a Sudanese People's Struggle for Survival* (Lawrenceville, N.J.: Red Sea, 2001), 6–8.
41. Ibid., 1.
42. Collins, *Disaster in Darfur*, 1; Mahgoub el Tigani Mahmoud, "Inside Darfur: Ethnic Genocide by a Governance Crisis" *Comparative Studies of South Asia, Africa and the Middle East*, 24, no. 2 (2004): 1.
43. Collins, *Disaster in Darfur*, 1.
44. Beshir, 1.
45. Wikipedia contributors, "Aswan Dam," *Wikipedia, The Free Encyclopedia*, http://en.wikipedia.org/wiki/Aswan_High_Dam (accessed March 15, 2008).
46. El-Mahdi, 28–31.
47. P. M. Holt and M. W. Daly, *The History of the Sudan: From the Coming of Islam to the Present Day*, 3rd ed. (London: Weiden and Nicolson, 1979), 3–4.
48. Beshir, 1.
49. Holt and Daly, 7–8.
50. El-Mahdi, 3.
51. Ibid., 27–28.
52. Ibid., 3, 32–33; see also Holt and Daly, 4–5.
53. El-Mahdi, 33; see also Holt and Daly, 4–5.
54. El-Mahdi, 32–33.
55. Ibid., 32.
56. Ruay, 15.
57. Stephen Wondu, interview by Betty Hinds, Washington, D.C., 1996.
58. Deng, *War of Visions*, 2–3.
59. Ibid., vii.

60. Ibid., 3.
61. Wondu, interview.
62. Deng, *War of Visions*, 3.
63. Al-Baqir Al-Afif Mukhtar, "The Crisis of Identity in Northern Sudan: The Dilemma of a Black People with a White Culture," in Carolyn Fluehr-Lobban and Kharyssa Rhodes, eds., *Race and Identity in the Nile Valley* (Trenton, N.J.: Red Sea, 2004), 214–15.
64. Ibid., 213–14.
65. Ibid., 214–15.
66. Ruay, 15.
67. Deng, *War of Visions*, 3.
68. Ibid., 3–4.
69. El-Mahdi, 28.
70. Garang, interview.

Chapter 2

1. *Memorandum Presented*, 86.
2. Muddathir Abdel-Rahim, "Fourteen Documents on the Problem of the Southern Sudan," *Middle Eastern Journal* (April 1966): 1.
3. Ibid.
4. Robert O. Collins, "The Sudan: Link to the North," in *The Transformation of East Africa: Studies in Political Anthropology*, ed. Stanley Diamond and Fred G. Burke (New York: Basic Books, 1962), 374.
5. Ibid., 374, quoting *Proceedings of the Southern Governors Meeting*, March 1922, Civil Secretary, I/9/31, SGA.
6. Ibid., 374–75, quoting from "Notes regarding Chiefs Courts and Native Administration in Mongalla Province," December 1, 1924, by A. W. Skrine, Mongalla I/1/2, SGA.
7. Ibid., 377.
8. Robert O. Collins, *The Southern Sudan in Historical Perspective* (Tel Aviv: University of Tel Aviv Student Association, 1975), 62.
9. Robert O. Collins, interview by Scopas Poggo, Santa Barbara, California, 2002.
10. Ibid.
11. Clement Mboro, interview by Nathan Wojia Pitia, Nairobi, Kenya, 2004.
12. Barnaba Dumo Wani, interview by Evans Sokiri Kijore, Khartoum, Sudan, 2005.
13. Mboro, interview.
14. Ibid.
15. Wani, interview.
16. *Report of the Commission*, 81.
17. Robert O. Collins, *Shadows in the Grass: Britain in the Southern Sudan 1918–1956* (New Haven, CT: Yale University Press, 1983), 172–78, 222–23, 261–73. See also Muddathir Abdel-Rahim, "The Development of British

Policy in the Southern Sudan: 1899–1947," University of Khartoum, 1965, 6. [Conference Paper]
18. John Tosh, "The Economy of the Southern Sudan under the British, 1898–1955," *Journal of Imperial and Commonwealth History*, 9, no. 3 (1981), 277.
19. Ibid.
20. Ibid. Though according to Clement Mboro (interview), the Nuer resistance continued into the 1930s, and he cites the British recruitment of men in his area of the Bahr al-Ghazal to fight the Nuer.
21. Ibid., 277–78.
22. Douglas H. Johnson, interview by Scopas Poggo, Washington, D.C., August 2003.
23. Abdel-Rahim, "Development of British Policy," 6.
24. Ibid, 3.
25. Joseph Oduho and William Deng, *The Problem of the Southern Sudan* (London: Oxford University Press, 1963), 45.
26. M. W. Daly, *Imperial Sudan: The Anglo-Egyptian Condominium, 1934–1956* (Cambridge: Cambridge University Press, 1991), 104–14.
27. Collins, *Shadows in the Grass*, 65–67.
28. Daly, 104–14.
29. Collins, *Shadows in the Grass*, 198.
30. Ibid.
31. Ibid.
32. Ibid.
33. Theresa Scherf, "The Sudan Conflict: Its History and Development" (n.d.), 4. Unpublished document available in the private collection of the author of this book.
34. Collins, *Shadows in the Grass*, 199.
35. Ibid., 199–200, quoting Stefano Santandrea, "The History of Our Missions," *The Messenger* (October 1933).
36. Ibid., 203–4.
37. Abdel-Rahim, "Development of British Policy," 238.
38. Ibid., quoting from *Annual Report of 1926* (Sudan, no. 2, 1927), Cmd. 2991/8.
39. Ibid.; Collins, *Shadows in the Grass*, 203–4.
40. Collins, *Shadows in the Grass*, 203–4.
41. Ibid.
42. J. Girodot, "Sudan: The Revolutionary Task," (n.d.), 67. Document available in the private collection of the author.
43. C. H. Stigand, *Equatoria: The Lado Enclave* (London: Frank Cass, 1968), 201.
44. Ibid., 201–2.
45. Collins, *Shadows in the Grass*, 169.
46. Kenneth David Druitt Henderson, *Sudan Republic* (London: Ernest Benn, 1965), 161.

47. Pacifico Lado Lolik, interview by Scopas Poggo, Dallas, Texas, 2005.
48. Ibid.
49. Robert O. Collins, *Land Beyond the Rivers: The Southern Sudan, 1898–1918* (New Haven, CT: Yale University Press, 1971), 225–26.
50. Lolik, interview.
51. Ibid.
52. Wani, interview.
53. Ibid.
54. Collins, interview.
55. "Shaping of Politics in the Nile Valley," *The Times*, November 15, 1948.
56. Ibid.
57. Frank Burdette Jackson, "Condominium Rule in the Anglo-Egyptian Sudan," (Ph.D. Dissertation, Ohio State University, 1982), 299.
58. *Memorandum Presented*, 3.
59. Jackson, 306.
60. Collins, *Shadows in the Grass*, 438.
61. *Memorandum Presented*, 3.
62. Ibid.
63. "Sudanese Place in Nile Valley: View of Egyptian Demands," *The Times*, November 27, 1950.
64. Ibid.
65. Ibid.
66. *Petition to the United Nations by Sudan African Closed Districts National Union (SACDNU), South Sudan, On Behalf of the People of Southern Sudan* (April 29, 1963): 20–21.
67. Mboro, interview.
68. Ibid.
69. *Petition to the United Nations*, 20–21.
70. Ibid.
71. "Cairo Agreement on Sudan: Home Rule Proposed by End of the Year," *The Times*, October 30, 1952.
72. *Petition to the United Nations*, 20–21.
73. Ibid.
74. "The Sudan's Future," *The Times*, December 1, 1953.
75. "Intentions of Sudan Government," *The Times*, January 18, 1954.
76. Mboro, interview.
77. "Sudan Officials' Dilemma: Uncertainty of Posts," *The Times*, December 28, 1954.
78. Collins, *Shadows in the Grass*, 454–55.
79. Ibid.
80. *Memorandum Presented*, 3.
81. *Report of the Commission*, 114.
82. Luigi Adwok Bong, "The Period 1956–1958," (n.d.), 1–2.
83. Wani, interview.
84. Mboro, interview.

85. Joseph Lagu, "Beginning of the Revolt," *Anya-Nya: What We Fight For* (Anya-Nya Armed Forces: South Sudan Liberation Movement, January 1972), 2 [Pamphlet].
86. *Memorandum Presented*, 4. See also *Petition to the United Nations*, 22.
87. *Memorandum Presented*, 4.
88. Wani, interview.
89. Ibid.
90. Mboro, interview.
91. "Assassin at Sudan Tea Party: Incident in Premier's Southern Tour," *The Times*, October 27, 1954.
92. *Memorandum Presented*, 4, quoting from Ronald Segal, *Political Africa: A Who's Who of Personalities and Parties* (New York: Praeger, 1961), 448.
93. Ibid, 4.
94. "Assassin at Sudan Tea Party," 6.
95. *Memorandum Presented*, 4.
96. Daniel Jumi Tongun, interview by Nathan Wojia Pitia, Yei, Southern Sudan, 2004.
97. Ibid.
98. Ibid.
99. *Report of the Commission*, 87.
100. Bong, "The Period," 4.
101. Bona M. M. Ring, "The Causes of the Southern Dissensions," Khartoum (September 24, 1964): 6. Document available in the private collection of the author.
102. *Memorandum Presented*, 4.
103. *Report of the Commission*, 87.
104. Wani, interview.
105. Ibid.
106. *Report of the Commission*, 82.
107. Ibid., 83.
108. Ibid.
109. Ibid., 105.
110. Ibid., 106.
111. Ibid.
112. Ibid.
113. "Unanimous Vote in Khartoum: Self-Determination Process Begun," *The Times*, August 16, 1955.
114. Wani, interview.
115. Tongun, interview.
116. Ibid.
117. *Report of the Commission*, 80.
118. Ibid., 26–28.
119. Lolik, interview.
120. *Report of the Commission*, 44.
121. Tongun, interview.

122. *Report of the Commission*, 80.
123. Ibid.
124. Ibid., 44.
125. Ibid., 45.
126. "Confidential from Khartoum to Foreign Office," Governor General's Office, No. 212, August 19, 1955. Robert O. Collins Collection. Sudan Archives. Durham University, Durham, UK.
127. *Report of the Commission*, 42.
128. Ibid., 37.
129. Ibid., 38–39.
130. Joseph Lagu, interview by Scopas Poggo, London, March 25, 1997.
131. Dunstan M. Wai, "The Afro-Arab Conflict in the Sudan," (Ph.D. Dissertation, Harvard University, 1973), 114.
132. *Memorandum Presented*, 5.
133. Ibid., 41–42.
134. *Petition to the United Nations*, 22.
135. Ring, "Causes of the Southern Disturbances," 7.
136. Lagu, interview.
137. Ibid.
138. Mboro, interview.
139. Tongun, interview.
140. Wani, interview.
141. Lolik, interview.
142. *Memorandum Presented*, 5.
143. Lagu, interview.

Chapter 3

1. Oduho and Deng, 37.
2. Mama Anna Poni Wani-Buluk, interview by Benjamin Lou Poggo, Nairobi, Kenya, June 15, 1997.
3. Ibid.
4. Ibid.
5. Paul Urpac, interview by John Ukech Lueth, Juba, Southern Sudan, January 28, 1980, Interview No. 84.
6. Mboro, interview.
7. Tongun, interview.
8. Ibid.
9. Ibid.
10. Ibid.
11. Ibid.
12. Ibid.
13. Oduho and Deng, 41.
14. Ibid., 33.
15. Ibid.

16. Mboro, interview.
17. Simon Makwac, interview by John Ukech Lueth, Malakal, Southern Sudan, May 25, 1980, Interview No. 24.
18. Gabriel Gang, interview by John Ukech Lueth, Bor, Southern Sudan, April 6, 1980, Interview No. 103.
19. Ibid.
20. Oduho and Deng, 41.
21. Ibid.
22. "A Sudan Amnesty: Some Southerners Excluded," *The Times*, December 31, 1955.
23. Ibid.
24. *Petition to the United Nations*, 5.
25. Ibid.
26. Girodot, 69.
27. Ibid., 68.
28. Ibid.
29. Ibid., 68–69.
30. Ibid., 67–68.
31. Johnson, interview.
32. *Memorandum Presented*, 5.
33. Ibid.
34. Ibid.
35. Oduho and Deng, 33.
36. *Memorandum Presented*, 5.
37. Bong, "The Period," 4.
38. Ibid.
39. Ibid.
40. Ibid., 5.
41. Ring, 6.
42. *Memorandum Presented*, 6.
43. Ibid.
44. Ibid.
45. Albino, 40–41.
46. Oduho and Deng, 38.
47. *Memorandum Presented*, 6.
48. Ibid., 6.
49. Ibid.
50. Ibid.
51. Albino, 42–43.
52. Ibid., 43.
53. Ibid.
54. Ibid., 41–44.
55. Bong, "The Period," 7. See also Albino, 43.
56. Albino, 43.

57. Gordon Muortat Mayen, interview by Scopas Poggo, London, March 27, 1997.
58. Wai, *African-Arab Conflict*, 142.
59. Ibid., 141.
60. *Memorandum Presented*, 6.
61. Ibid.
62. Ibid.
63. "Mr. G. A. Kwanai, SANU Secretary of Information, Reports on the Addis Ababa Conference—May 1963—and on the Refugees in Ethiopia," in *Voice of Southern Sudan* (1963), 16.
64. Ibid.
65. Lance Corporal Vincensio Heworu Lajok, interview by John Ukech Lueth, November 24, 1979, Interview No. 1.
66. Ibid.
67. Lagu, interview.
68. John Ukech Lueth, *A Manuscript of the Rise of the Anya-Nya Movement* (Juba, 1980), 46.
69. Wojia Masiri and Enoka Digga Amen, Anya-Nya Veterans, interview by James Duku Janka, Kajo-Kaji, Southern Sudan, August 12, 1997.
70. Wani-Buluk, interview.
71. Masiri and Amen, interview.
72. Lueth, 46–47.
73. Ibid.
74. Ibid.
75. Ibid., 57–58.
76. Ibid.
77. Muortat, interview.
78. Lueth, 37–38.
79. Albino Mathiang Thiep, interview by John Ukech Lueth, (n.d), Interview 112.
80. Lueth, 37–38.
81. Ibid.
82. Wani-Buluk, interview.
83. Lajok, interview.
84. Ibid.
85. Lueth, 39.
86. Ibid.
87. Lagu, interview.
88. Ibid.
89. Lueth, 48.
90. Ibid.
91. Ibid., 47. Inyanya is "a snake poison extracted by old women from a river snake which they baited by pouring beer up to the river. They then kill the drunken snakes and remove the poison, dry it and use it for poisoning anybody

they wanted to die." It could be put in food or beer or be spread airborne in the direction of the person targeted.
92. Ibid.
93. Ibid., 47–48. This is "a tiny and dangerous insect usually moving in [an] organized column. They attack their enemies by spreading all over the body and cause the death of their victims." This insect can inflict death on elephants, other wild animals, and even humans.
94. Ibid.
95. Lueth, 47–48.
96. Lagu, interview.
97. Colonel Stephen Madut, interview by Scopas Poggo, London, April 2, 1997.
98. Ibid.
99. Scopas S. Poggo, "The Pattern of Azande Resistance to British Rule in the Southern Sudan, 1898–1914" (Master's Thesis, Memphis State University, TN, 1992), 100–15.
100. Lueth, 61.
101. Ibid., 62.
102. Brigadier General John Ukech Lueth, interview by Scopas Poggo, Santa Barbara, California, April 12, 1997.
103. Lueth, 56.
104. Francis Gume Ulane, interview by John Ukech Lueth, Rumbek, February 7, 1980, Interview No. 83, n. 1.
105. Paul Urac Udo, interview by John Ukech Lueth, Wau, November 28, 1980, Interview No. 84, n. 2.
106. Luis Mongo Boolo, interview by John Ukech Lueth, Rumbek, February 5, 1980, Interview No. 88.
107. Lueth, 50.
108. Ibid.
109. Ibid., 58.
110. Ibid.
111. Madut, interview.
112. Lueth, 59.
113. Ibid.
114. Ibid.
115. Ibid., 60.
116. Lueth, interview.
117. Lueth, 50.
118. Lueth, interview.
119. Lueth, 52.
120. Ibid., 53.
121. Ibid., 57–58.
122. Ibid., 57–58.
123. Ibid.
124. Ibid.
125. Ibid.

Chapter 4

1. *Report of the Commission*, 87.
2. *Memorandum Presented*, 19.
3. Oduho and Deng, 41. See also *Memorandum Presented*, 19.
4. *Memorandum Presented*, 19.
5. Ibid., 19–20.
6. Ibid., 17.
7. Ibid., 18.
8. Ibid., 18–19.
9. "Case No. 10: Destruction of Pachalla Villages," in *Memorandum Presented*, 25.
10. Ibid., 26.
11. Joseph Oduho, "F— Report From SANU Central Office: Bahr El Ghazal Province," *Voice of Southern* Sudan, 1, no. 3 (1963): 21, reproduced in *Sudan Informazioni* (Milan, Italy: Agenzia di notizie e documenti, March 25, 1969), 83.
12. *Memorandum Presented*, 24. The information on the Sudanese army attack on the Southern refugees in the Congo was relayed by the Congolese National Army (CNA) unit in Bunia to Lieutenant Colonel Leornard Mulumba, commander of the Stanleyville-based Third Army Group of the CNA.
13. Allan Reed, "The Anya-Nya: Ten Months' Travel with Its Forces inside the Southern Sudan," *Munger Africana Library Notes*, no. 2 (February 1972): 12.
14. "Former Political Prisoners Restricted," *Voice of Southern Sudan*, 1, no. 2 (1963): 17.
15. Ibid., 18.
16. Ibid.
17. *Petition to the United Nations*, 9.
18. Ibid., 29.
19. "Alfonse Arop, Amosa Aburi, Tito Wani: Victims of False Accusations," in *Petition to the United Nations*, 31.
20. "Duku Bojo: A Victim of Arbitrary Arrest," in *Petition to the United Nations*, 31.
21. "Micah Luwate, John Baden: Victims of Arbitrary Charges," in *Petition to the United Nations*, 32.
22. Ibid.
23. Ibid.
24. Ibid., 13.
25. Ibid., 23.
26. Ibid., 18–19.
27. Ibid., 19.
28. Ibid.
29. Oduho, "F— Report: Bahr El Ghazal," 83.

30. Ibid.
31. "Testimony of Sister Sandralisa Campedelli and Sister Albertina Modenese," in *Genocide in the Southern Sudan: Human Rights Violated, Arabs vs. Africans* (Milan: Sudan Informazioni News Agency Documents, 10/83/88573), 45–46.
32. Ibid., 46.
33. "Testimony by Brother Francesco Mariotti," in *Genocide in the Southern Sudan*, 45. This information was provided to Brother Mariotti by a clerk in Wau who was imprisoned, tortured, and released from Grinti military prison.
34. Ibid.
35. "Testimony of Father Agrati Antonio," in *Genocide in the Southern Sudan*, 47.
36. "Testimony of Father Santino Locatelli," in *Genocide in the Southern Sudan*, 41. Father Locatelli had been a missionary in Southern Sudan for eleven years.
37. "Statement of Valentino Saoncella," Wau, February 1–2, 1964, in *Memorandum Presented*, 51.
38. "Testimony by Father Parlemo Pasquale of Bussere and Kpaile Seminaries," in *Genocide in the Southern Sudan*, 47–48.
39. Ibid., 48.
40. "Statement of Colussi Giacomo," Wau, February 2, 1964, in *Memorandum Presented*, 50.
41. "Bahr al-Ghazal," in *Memorandum Presented*, 24.
42. "Sudan African National Union: Famine in the Bor District, Southern Sudan," *Voice of Southern Sudan*, 2, no. 1 (April 1964): 14.
43. Ibid., 14–15.
44. "Petition by Delegation for Bor Citizens: Cry for Flood Destruction," in *Memorandum Presented*, 13.
45. "Famine in Bor District," 15.
46. "Petition by Delegation for Bor Citizens," 13.
47. Joseph Oduho, "F— Report from SANU Central Office: Upper Nile Province," *Voice of Southern* Sudan, 1, no. 3 (1963): 21, reproduced in *Sudan Informazioni* (Agenzia di notizie e documenti, Milan, Italy, March 25, 1969), 83.
48. "Situation in the Southern Sudan," *Voice of Southern Sudan*, 1, no. 2 (1963): 16.
49. See *Voice of Southern Sudan*, 2, no. 1 (April 1964): 11.
50. "Report From SANU Central Office: Upper Nile," *Voice of Southern Sudan*, 2, no. 1 (1964): 11–12.
51. "Upper Nile: School Girl as Hostage," *Voice of Southern Sudan*, 2, no. 1 (1964): 12.
52. "Upper Nile: Beaten to Abortion," *Voice of Southern Sudan*, 2, no. 1 (1964): 12.
53. "Destruction of Pachalla Villages," in *Memorandum Presented*, 25–26.
54. "Upper Nile," in *Genocide in the Southern Sudan*, 52.

55. "Ethiopian Villages Burnt Down by the Sudanese Armed Forces While Pursuing Refugees," in *Memorandum Presented*, 25–26.
56. "Upper Nile," in *Genocide in the Southern Sudan*, 51.
57. Ibid., 52.
58. "Al Ayam Condemns Juba Massacre," *The Vigilant*, July 13, 1965, 2.
59. Eliaba James Surur, interview by James Duku Janka, Kampala, Uganda, 2004.
60. Lueth, interview.
61. Surur, interview; "Juba Death Toll Rises to Over 1400: Massacre, a Deliberate Army Plan," *The Vigilant*, July 13, 1965, 44.
62. "Juba Death Toll," 44.
63. Surur, interview. See also Tongun interview.
64. Surur, interview.
65. Ibid.
66. "S.F. [Southern Front] Condemns and Deplores Juba Massacre: President Flies to the Scene," *The Vigilant*, July 13, 1965, 43.
67. Lueth, interview.
68. Mboro, interview.
69. "The Juba Martyrs of Freedom," *The Vigilant*, July 13, 1965, 45. See also "S.F. Condemns and Deplores," 43.
70. Dominic Akec Mohammed, interview by Scopas Poggo, Miami, Fla., September 18, 1998.
71. "76 Southerners Slaughtered in Wau: Plan to Kill Educated Southerners Started," *The Vigilant*, July 14, 1965, 49.
72. Ibid.
73. Mohammed, interview, September 18, 1998.
74. "76 Southerners Slaughtered," 49.
75. Vakindi Unvu, telephone interview by Scopas Poggo, Denver, Colo./Santa Barbara, Calif., September 29, 1998.
76. Dr. Dominic Akec Mohammed, interview, September 18, 1998. Dr. Mohammed is a Dinka from Turale in Gogrial District of Northern Bahr al-Ghazal who avoided the massacre in Wau because his uncle convinced him not to take the train from Khartoum to Wau to attend the wedding.
77. Mboro, interview.
78. Ibid.
79. "Juba Death Toll Rises," 44.
80. "S.F. Condemns and Deplores," 43.
81. Ibid.
82. Muortat, interview.
83. Ibid.
84. "F.S. [S.F.] Appeal to African Observers, Intervention of OAU, Human Rights & International Jurists Commissions Sought," *The Vigilant*, July 14, 1965, 1.
85. Ibid.
86. "Army Raids Kayango Village," *The Vigilant*, March 29, 1966, 29.

87. Ibid.
88. Lueth, interview.
89. Ibid.
90. "Army Raids Kayango Village," 29.
91. Ibid.
92. Ibid.
93. "Equatoria," in *Documents in the Collection of Robert O. Collins*, 1–2.
94. Ibid.
95. Ibid., 2–3.
96. Reed, 16.
97. Ibid.
98. Ibid.
99. "The Cholera Outbreak in the Southern Sudan," *Grass Curtain*, 2, no. 1 (July 1971): 2, 6.
100. Ibid., 2, 6–7.
101. Ibid.
102. Ibid.
103. Ibid.
104. Ibid.
105. "An Appeal to the Afro-Asian Peoples Solidarity Organization in Tripoli," *Grass Curtain*, 2, no. 1 (July 1971): 22.

Chapter 5

1. "Mr. G. A. Kwanai Reports," 31–34.
2. Ring, 9.
3. Wani, interview.
4. Mboro, interview.
5. "Missionary Expulsion: Is It a Solution?" *Voice of Southern Sudan* 1, no. 1 (April 1, 1964): 1.
6. Ibid., 2. See also the *Report of the Commission*, 94.
7. *Report of the Commission*, 94.
8. "Missionary Expulsion," 2.
9. "Editorial Comment," *Voice of Southern Sudan* 1, no. 2 (1963): 9.
10. Ibid.
11. "Missionary Expulsion," 2.
12. *Memorandum Presented*, 7.
13. Sanderson and Sanderson, 357.
14. *Memorandum Presented*, 7.
15. "Missionary Expulsion," 2.
16. "Sudan Africans Die: Long Live African Unity," *Voice of Southern Sudan*, 1, no. 1 (April 1, 1964): 4.
17. Ibid.
18. *Memorandum Presented*, 43.
19. Ibid.

20. "Editorial Comment," *Voice of Southern Sudan*, 1, no. 2 (1963): 12.
21. Ibid.
22. Ibid., 2.
23. *Memorandum Presented*, 7.
24. Sanderson and Sanderson, 368.
25. "The Problem of the Sudan: Violent Racial Action Involving Genocide in the Southern Sudan," n.d., 6.
26. "Missionary Expulsion," 2.
27. Wai, "Afro-Arab Conflict," 47.
28. Ring, 9.
29. "Missionary Expulsion," 2.
30. Lawrence Modi Tombe, interview by Scopas Poggo, London, March 25, 1997.
31. Ibid.
32. Ibid.
33. Ibid.
34. "Problem of the Sudan," 7–8.
35. "Editorial Comment," *Voice of Southern Sudan*, 1, no. 2 (1963): 5.
36. Ibid.
37. Ibid.
38. Tombe, interview.
39. Madut, interview.
40. Lueth, interview.
41. Tombe, interview.
42. Madut, interview.
43. Hilary T. Elonai, interview by Scopas Poggo, Los Angeles, California, December 2007.
44. Ibid.
45. "Mr. G. A. Kwanai Reports," 31–34.
46. "Missionary Expulsion," 2.
47. Ibid., 107.
48. A Letter from S. M. Ahmed, for Governor of Equatoria to Assistant Governor, Yambio, D.C. Kapoeta, Torit, Juba, Yei, Maridi, Tembura, February 24, 1959, EP/SCR/46.C.1.10., XR/SCR/46.A.2.
49. Letter from Osman Gad EL RAB [for Governor of Equatoria] to Assistant Governor, Juba District, EP/SCR/46C.2/8, XR/SCR/46A.1.
50. A strictly confidential letter from Acting Governor Osman Gad el Rab to Assistant Governor, Juba, D.C.'s Torit, Kapoeta, Maridi, Yei, Yambio, and Assistant District Commissioner Tembura, E/SCR/46.A.1, EP/SCR/46.2. The "trek" program was an action plan that the assistant governor and district commissioners had to execute in Equatoria. As these high-ranking officials traversed the province, they were expected to implement government policies laid out by the governor of Equatoria.

51. Luigi Adwok Bong, "Christian Missionaries in the South: How and Why Religion Has Become an Issue in the Southern Problem," (Khartoum, September 20, 1965), 3, quoting from *Al-Rai Al-Amm*, September 9, 1959.
52. *The Black Book of the Sudan on the Expulsion of the Christian Missionaries from Southern Sudan: An Answer* (Milano: Instituto Artigiannelli, 1964), 100–101.
53. A Letter from Hassan Ali Abdulla, Permanent Under Secretary, Ministry of Interior to President of the Supreme Council and H.E. the Minister of Interior, Khartoum, December 29, 1959, MI/SCR/46.A.20.
54. A Letter from Dominic Ferrara, Prefect Apostolic of Mupoi, Catholic Mission, Yambio, Western Equatoria to H.E. Hassan Ali Abdulla, Permanent Under Secretary, Ministry of Interior, Khartoum, January 17, 1960, PA/G-GJ/1/60.
55. *Black Book*, 98–99, note, March 5, 1960.
56. Ibid., 101.
57. Ibid.
58. *Black Book*, 67.
59. Bong, "Christian Missionaries," 3, quoting from *Al-Rai Al-Amm*, May 7, 1960.
60. A Letter from A. Baroni, Vicar Apostolic, Khartoum to the Permanent Under Secretary, Ministry of Interior, Khartoum, June 22, 1960.
61. A Letter from Hassan Ali Abdulla, Permanent Under Secretary, Ministry of the Interior, Khartoum to His Lordship, Bishop Baroni, Vicar Apostolic, Khartoum, June 28, 1960, MI/SCR/46.A.16.
62. A Letter from A. Baroni, Vicar Apostolic, the Catholic Church, Khartoum to the Permanent Under Secretary, Ministry of the Interior, Khartoum, July 4, 1960.
63. A Strictly Confidential Letter from Ali Baldo, Governor, Equatoria Province Headquarters, Juba to all missions, August 30, 1960, EP/SCR/46.A.1, XR/SRC/46.A.1/2.
64. Ibid.
65. A Strictly Confidential Letter from Ali Baldo, Governor of Equatoria, Juba, to Procurator, R. Catholic Mission, Juba, Secretary CMS, Juba, Field Secretary African Inland Mission, Torit, Procurator, RCM Mupoi, May 11, 1960, EP/SCR/46.A.1.1., XR/SCR/46.C.1/4.
66. A Strictly Confidential Letter from Ali Baldo, Governor, Equatoria, Juba to Procurator, Catholic Mission, Secretary, CMS Juba, Field Secretary, Africa Inland Mission, Torit, Procurator RCM Mupoi, January 31, 1960, EP/SCR/46.A.1/1.
67. "Editorial Comment," *Voice of Southern Sudan*, 1, no. 2 (1963): 12.
68. *Black Book*, 208–9.
69. "The Southern Sudan Today: A Test Case in Afro-Arab Co-operation," *Voice of Southern Sudan*, 1, no. 3 (1963): 18.
70. "On Persecution in the Sudan," *Catholic Telegraph* (US), January 11, 1962.
71. "Southern Sudan Today," 18.
72. *Black Book*, 112.
73. "Sudan Expels Missionaries," *Christian Century* (January 2, 1963): 19.

74. "Southern Sudan Today," 18.
75. S. A. M. Salih, Letter, *Catholic News* (New York), January 24, 1963.
76. Ibid.
77. "Expelled Priest Confirms Policy Is Clear: Stifle the Church," *Catholic News*, February 7, 1963.
78. Ibid., 3.
79. Bishop Ireneo Dud was a Dinka from Bahr al-Ghazal and the only Southern Sudanese Catholic bishop. A member of the Verona Fathers order in Southern Sudan, he remained in service as archbishop until his death in Sudan in 1997.
80. "On Persecution," 3.
81. "Sudan Wages Cold War: To Exterminate Christians," *Catholic News*, January 17, 1963.
82. Ibid., 6.
83. Leo Kurk, "The Problem of the Southern Sudan: Origin of Sudan Government Violent Attack on Great Britain and the Institute of Race Relations," *Voice of Southern Sudan*, 1, no. 3 (1963): 6.
84. Ibid.
85. "Memorandum on Reasons that Led to the Expulsion of Foreign Missionaries and Priests from the Southern Provinces," in *Expulsion of Foreign Missionaries and Priests from the Southern Provinces* (Republic of the Sudan: Ministry of the Interior, March 1964), 16.
86. Ibid.
87. Ibid., 17–18.
88. *Black Book*, 38.
89. "The Missionary Societies in the Sudan," in *Expulsion of Foreign Missionaries and Priests*, 2.
90. "Memorandum on Reasons," 19.
91. Ibid., 18–19.
92. *Black Book*, 199–200.
93. Ibid., 200–204.
94. "Editorial Comment," *Voice of Southern Sudan*, 1, no. 4 (1964): 16.
95. *Times* (London), March 13/14, 1964, excerpts published in *Voice of Southern Sudan*, 2, no. 1 (April 1964): 7.
96. Ibid., 7–8.
97. "Revenge for Rome," *Der Spiegel*, March 19, 1964, translated excerpt published in *Voice of Southern Sudan*, 2, no. 1 (April 1964): 8–9.
98. Ibid.

Chapter 6

1. Elias Nyamlell Wakoson, "The Origin and Development of the Anya-Nya Movement 1955–1972," in *Southern Sudan: Regionalism and Religion Selected Essays*, ed., Mohamed Omer Beshir (Khartoum, Sudan: University of Khartoum, Graduate College Publications, 1984), 184.

2. Lueth, 38–39.
3. "The Creation of SANU," 34. Robert O. Collins Collection. Sudan Archives. Durham University, Durham, UK.
4. Ibid.
5. Lagu, interview.
6. Ibid.
7. Muortat, interview.
8. Ibid., 34.
9. Oliver B. Albino, interview by Laura N. Beny, Cambridge, MA, June 30, 1997.
10. Ibid.
11. Wakoson, 185.
12. Ibid.
13. Lagu, interview.
14. Wakoson, 185.
15. Ibid.
16. Lagu, interview.
17. Wakoson, 186.
18. "Creation of SANU," 35–36. Robert O. Collins Collection. Sudan Archives. Durham University, Durham, UK.
19. Lagu, interview.
20. Ibid.
21. "Creation of SANU," 35–36. Robert O. Collins Collection. Sudan Archives. Durham University, Durham, UK.
22. Ibid., 37.
23. Wakoson, 186–87, quoting from "SANU File of Records and Correspondences," n.d.
24. "Creation of SANU," 38. Robert O. Collins Collection. Sudan Archives. Durham University, Durham, UK.
25. Ibid.
26. Ibid.
27. Muortat, interview.
28. Lagu, interview.
29. Wakoson, 187, quoting from "SANU File of Records and Correspondences," February 25, 1965.
30. Joseph Lagu, *Sudan: Odyssey Through a State: From Ruin to Hope* (Omdurman: MOB Center for Sudan Studies, 2006), 129.
31. Wakoson, 188.
32. Lagu, interview.
33. Ibid.
34. Lagu, *Sudan: Odyssey*, 130.
35. Wakoson, 188, quoting from "SANU File of Records and Correspondences."
36. Ibid.
37. Ibid. See also Albino interview.
38. Wakoson, 189.

39. Muortat, interview.
40. Lagu, interview.
41. Lagu, *Sudan: Odyssey*, 130.
42. Albino, interview.
43. Ibid.
44. Lagu, interview.
45. Muortat, interview.
46. Wakoson, 189–90.
47. Lagu, interview.
48. Muortat, interview; Mboro, interview.
49. Mboro, interview.
50. Muortat, interview.
51. Tombe, interview.
52. Muortat, interview.
53. Ibid.
54. Ibid., and Tongun interview.
55. Muortat interview.
56. Lagu, interview.
57. Wakoson, 190–91.
58. Ibid.
59. Lagu, interview.
60. "SANU and the Anya-Nya Liberation Front," 2–3. Robert O. Collins Collection. Sudan Archives. Durham University, Durham, UK.
61. Ibid., 4–7.
62. Lagu, interview.
63. Muortat, interview.
64. Lagu, interview.
65. Ibid.
66. Ibid.
67. Ibid.
68. Muortat, interview.
69. Wakoson, 194.
70. "Southern Sudan Provisional Government," 1–2. Robert O. Collins Collection. Sudan Archives. Durham University, Durham, UK.
71. Muortat, interview.
72. "Southern Sudan Provisional Government," 3–4. Robert O. Collins Collection. Sudan Archives. Durham University, Durham, UK.
73. Ibid.
74. Ibid.
75. Wakoson, 194.
76. "The Southern Sudan Provisional Government," (1968), 3–4. Robert O. Collins Collection. Sudan Archives. Durham University, Durham, UK.
77. Wakoson, 195.
78. "Southern Sudan Provisional Government," 7. Robert O. Collins Collection. Sudan Archives. Durham University, Durham, UK.

79. Ibid., 1.
80. Ibid., 3–4.
81. Muortat, interview.
82. Ibid.
83. Ibid.
84. Ibid.
85. Ibid.
86. Wai, *African-Arab Conflict*, 200.
87. "Southern Sudan Provisional Government," 20–21. Robert O. Collins Collection. Sudan Archives. Durham University, Durham, UK.
88. Ibid.
89. Ibid., 21–22.
90. Ibid., 20.
91. "The Nile Provisional Government: Statement on the Balgo-Bindi Convention," *Voice of Southern Sudan* (May 15, 1969): 2.
92. Ibid.
93. Muortat, interview.
94. "Nile Provisional Government: Statement," 3.
95. Ibid.
96. Ibid.
97. Ibid., 4.
98. Ibid., 1–2.
99. Lagu, interview.
100. Muortat, interview.
101. Ibid.
102. Ibid.
103. Ibid.
104. Ibid.
105. Ibid.
106. Ibid.
107. Ibid.
108. Ibid.
109. Ibid.
110. Lueth, interview.
111. Lagu, interview.
112. Ibid.
113. Muortat, interview.

Chapter 7

1. Lagu, interview.
2. Lueth, interview.
3. Ibid.
4. Lagu, interview.
5. Ibid.

6. Ibid.
7. Ibid.
8. Ibid.
9. Muortat, interview.
10. Ibid.
11. Ibid.
12. Ibid.
13. Lueth, 50.
14. Ibid.
15. Ibid.
16. Ibid.
17. Ibid.
18. Lagu, interview.
19. Ibid.
20. Ibid.
21. Ibid.
22. Ibid.
23. "SANU and the Anya-Nya Liberation Front," 4–7. Robert O. Collins Collection. Sudan Archives. Durham University, Durham, UK.
24. Lagu, interview.
25. Ibid.
26. Muortat, interview.
27. Ibid.
28. Ibid.
29. Lagu, interview.
30. Ibid.
31. Ibid.
32. Madut, interview.
33. Muortat, interview; Lagu, interview.
34. Lagu, interview.
35. Muortat, interview.
36. Madut, interview.
37. Ibid.
38. Muortat, interview.
39. Madut, interview.
40. Lueth, interview.
41. Ibid.
42. Madut, interview.
43. Lueth, interview.
44. Madut, interview.
45. Lagu, interview.
46. Muortat, interview.
47. Wakoson, 201.
48. Muortat, interview.
49. Wakoson, 201.

50. Lagu, interview.
51. Ibid.
52. Lueth, interview.
53. Ibid.
54. Ibid.
55. Ibid.
56. Ibid.
57. Ibid.
58. Lueth, interview; Muortat, interview.
59. Lueth, interview.
60. Ibid.
61. Reed, 20.
62. Lueth, interview.
63. Lagu, interview.
64. Ibid.
65. Ibid.
66. Reed, 20.
67. Lagu, interview.
68. Ibid.
69. European-Sudanese Public Affairs Council (ESPAC), *The Search for Peace in the Sudan: A Chronology of the Sudanese Peace Process 1989–2001* (London: ESPAC, 2002), 31, http://www.espac.org/pdf/search_for_peace.pdf.
70. Lagu, interview.
71. Ibid.
72. Lueth, interview.
73. Ibid.
74. Lagu, interview.
75. ESPAC, 35.
76. "From South Sudan Liberation Movement," *Grass Curtain*, 2, no. 2 (October 1971): 4.
77. Lueth, interview.
78. Ibid.
79. Ibid.
80. Lagu, interview.
81. Ibid.
82. Ibid.
83. Ibid.
84. Lueth, interview.

Chapter 8

1. Wakoson, 137.
2. Mama Anna Poni Wani-Buluk, interview by Benjamin Lou Poggo, Nairobi, Kenya, June 15, 1997.
3. Lueth, 49.

4. Wakoson, 139.
5. Masiri and Amen, interview.
6. Wakoson, 138.
7. Ibid.
8. Ibid.
9. Lueth, 52.
10. Ibid.
11. Masiri and Amen, interview.
12. Wakoson, 138.
13. Ibid., 138–39.
14. Ibid., 139.
15. Lagu, interview. See also Wakoson, 139.
16. Muortat, interview.
17. Lagu, interview.
18. Lueth, 60.
19. Lueth, interview.
20. Ibid.
21. Lueth, 60.
22. Lueth, interview.
23. Colonel Habakuk Kefu Soro, interview by John Ukech Lueth, Wau, January 28, 1980, Interview No. 19.
24. Lagu, interview.
25. Muortat, interview.
26. Lagu, interview.
27. Masiri and Amen, interview.
28. Wani-Buluk, interview by Benjamin Lou Poggo.
29. Dr. Dominic Akec Mohammed, interview by Scopas Poggo, Miami, Florida, November 9, 1997; September 18, 1998.
30. "The Arrest of Southern Sudan Refugees in Uganda," *Voice of Southern Sudan*, 1, no. 4 (1963): 3.
31. Ibid.
32. Ibid.
33. Kenneth W. Grundy, *Guerrilla Struggle in Africa: An Analysis and Preview* (New York: Grossman, 1971), 122–23.
34. David Martin, *General Amin* (London: Faber and Faber, 1974), 158.
35. Muortat, interview.
36. "Rev. Fr. Saturnino is Confirmed Dead," *The Vigilant* (February 6, 1967): 121.
37. "Kampala Archbishop Hits at Expulsions," *The Vigilant* (January 30, 1967): 1.
38. Ibid.
39. "Refugees Harassed," *The Vigilant* (February 6, 1967): 121.
40. Lueth, interview.
41. Since achieving its independence from Belgium in 1960, the Congo (also known as Congo-Kinshasa) has undergone several name changes. From

1960 to 1964 it was known as the Republic of the Congo; from 1964 to 1971, it was the Democratic Republic of the Congo; from 1971 to 1997 it was called the Republic of Zaire; and in 1997, it reverted to the Democratic Republic of the Congo. It is not to be confused with the separate state currently known as the Republic of the Congo, or Congo-Brazzaville, on its Western border.

42. Moise Tshombe, *My Fifteen Months in Government* (Plano, TX: University of Plano Press, 1967), 45–46.
43. Ian Colvin, *The Rise and Fall of Moise Tshombe: A Biography* (London: Leslie Frewin, 1968), 192–93.
44. Tshombe, 37–38.
45. Lagu, interview.
46. Ibid.
47. Lueth, interview.
48. Ibid.
49. Wai, *African-Arab Conflict*, 137.
50. John Ukech Lueth, telephone interview by Scopas Poggo, Santa Barbara, California—Ames, Iowa, December 18, 1997.
51. Grundy, 123.
52. Wakoson, 157–58.
53. Reed, 25.
54. Wakoson, 157–58.
55. Ibid.
56. Lagu, interview.
57. Ibid.
58. Ibid.
59. Ibid.
60. Wai, *African-Arab Conflict*, 134–36.
61. Reed, 25.
62. Lueth, 51.
63. Lagu, interview.
64. Masiri and Amen, interview.
65. Philip Pedak Leith, "The War Scene," *Grass Curtain*, 1, no. 2 (1970): 13.
66. Lagu, interview.
67. Albino, interview.
68. Martin, 158; see also Rolf Steiner, *The Last Adventurer* (Boston: Little Brown, 1976), 158, 203.
69. Lagu, interview.
70. Muortat, interview.
71. Ibid.
72. Ibid.
73. Ibid.
74. Ibid.
75. Ibid.
76. Lagu, interview.

77. Lueth, interview.
78. Lagu, interview.
79. Ibid.
80. Ibid.
81. Ibid.
82. Lueth, interview.
83. Lagu, interview.
84. Lueth, interview.
85. Lagu, interview.
86. Steiner, 204.
87. Lueth, interview.
88. As a young refugee living at Gulu, Uganda, the author witnessed Israeli-made fighter planes take off and land at Gulu Airforce Base during training missions in 1968 through 1969. He also saw Israeli Fouga pilots and technicians at Gulu.
89. Henry Kyemba, *A State of Blood: The Inside Story of Idi Amin* (New York: Grosset and Dunlap, 1977), 239.
90. Martin, 158.
91. Kyemba, 239.
92. Martin, 158
93. Kyemba, 239.
94. Lagu, interview.
95. Lueth, interview.
96. Judith Listowel, *Amin* (Dublin: IUP Books, 1973), 131–33.
97. Ibid.
98. Ibid., 137.
99. Lagu, interview.
100. Wai, *African-Arab Conflict*, 139. See also Lueth, interview.
101. Lueth, interview.
102. Ibid.
103. Lagu, interview.
104. Ibid.
105. Eprile, 140.
106. Lagu, interview.
107. Lueth, interview.
108. Ibid.
109. Lueth, 49–50.
110. Lueth, interview.
111. Steiner, 186.
112. Ibid.
113. Lagu, interview.
114. Steiner, 187–88.
115. Ibid.
116. Ibid., 190, 201.
117. Lagu, interview.

118. Ibid.
119. Lueth, interview.
120. Lagu, interview.
121. Ibid.
122. "Excerpts, What the Anya-Nya Says," *Grass Curtain*, 2, no. 1 (July, 1971): 8.
123. Lagu, interview.
124. Lueth, interview.
125. Lagu, interview.
126. Muortat, interview.
127. Ibid.
128. Madut, interview.
129. Ibid.
130. Ibid.
131. Ibid.
132. Lueth, interview.
133. Ibid.
134. Wai, *African-Arab Conflict*, 135.
135. "U.S. Aid in Use to Suppress the South," *Voice of Southern Sudan* 2, no. 1 (April 1964): 6.
136. Ibid.
137. Wai, *African-Arab Conflict*, 135.
138. Lueth, interview.
139. "Report from the Sudan: Relations with West Germany," *Southern Sudan Information Service*, 16 (n.d.).
140. Lueth, interview.
141. Wai, *African-Arab Conflict*, 136.
142. *Southern Sudan Information Service* (January 12, 1967): 2.
143. Special Correspondent, "Military Training for Sudanese Officers in U.K." *Southern Sudan Information Service* (1967): 16.
144. Mohammed, interview, November 9, 1977.
145. Lueth, interview.
146. Ibid.
147. Ibid.
148. Wai, *African-Arab Conflict*, 136.
149. "Saudi Arms to Sudan," *The Vigilant* (March 15, 1966): 22.
150. Lueth, interview.
151. Reed, 25.
152. Eprile, 115–18.
153. Ibid., 103.
154. Lagu, interview.
155. David Robinson, "Sudan May be Soviet Version of Vietnam," (n.d.). Document available in the private collection of the author of this book.
156. Special Correspondent, "Russian Bombers for Sudan," *Daily Telegraph* (London), October 17, 1970: SID 82–70.

157. Standard Reporter, "MiG Build-up as China Joins Africa 'Grab'," *Evening Standard* (Tel Aviv), November 3, 1970: SID 93–70.
158. Eprile, 104.
159. Ibid., 110, quoting Lagu's letter to the pope.
160. Ian Colvin, "South Sudanese Rebels 'Step up' Activity," *Daily Telegraph* (Cairo), June 21, 1970: SID 77–70.
161. *The Almanac of World Military Power* (Dunn Loring, VA: T. N. Dupuy, 1972), 244.
162. Ibid.

Chapter 9

1. Eprile, *World Realities: War and Peace in the Sudan 1955–1972*; O'Ballance, *The Secret War in the Sudan 1955–1972*; Wai, *The African-Arab Conflict in the Sudan 1955–1972*; Alier, *The Southern Sudan: Too Many Agreements Dishonored*; Johnson, *The Root Causes of Sudan's Two Civil Wars*.
2. Girodot, 72.
3. "Editorial: New Regime Grants 'Regional Autonomy' to the South," *Voice of the Nile Republic of the Southern Sudan*, n.s., 1–3/13–3, no. 6 (n.d.): 2.
4. Ibid.
5. Girodot, 73.
6. "Editorial: New Regime Grants 'Regional Autonomy,'" 2.
7. Girodot, 73.
8. Ibid.
9. O'Ballance, *Sudan, Civil War, and Terrorism*, 56.
10. Ibid.
11. Girodot, 73.
12. "Editorial: New Regime Grants 'Regional Autonomy,'" 2.
13. Ibid., 74.
14. Ibid.
15. Girodot, 74. See also Alier, 43–45.
16. *The Democratic Republic of the Sudan: Policy Statement on the Southern Question* (Ministry of National Guidance, Khartoum: June, 1969), 1–2.
17. Ibid.
18. O'Ballance, *Sudan, Civil War, and Terrorism*, 57.
19. Ibid.
20. Alier, 55.
21. *Democratic Republic: Policy Statement*, 2.
22. Ibid.
23. "Refugees and Returnees," *Grass Curtain* 1, no. 4 (April 1971): 17.
24. Alier, 45, 50.
25. "Refugees and Returnees," 17.
26. Wani, interview.
27. Ibid.; see also Lolik interview.
28. Lolik, interview.

29. "June 9 Declaration not Implemented after 1¹/₂ Years," *Grass Curtain* 1, no. 4 (April 1971): 7.
30. Ibid., 8.
31. Ibid.
32. "Recolonization of Southern Sudan," *Neue Zürcher Zeitung*, Zurich, February 28, 1971, 73.
33. *Democratic Republic: Policy Statzement*, 3.
34. "How Nimeiri Lost the Chance of Peace," *Grass Curtain* 1, no. 4 (April 1971): 17.
35. "How Nimeiri Fails to Bring Peace," *Grass Curtain* 1, no. 4 (April 1971): 8.
36. *Democratic Republic: Policy Statement*, 3.
37. Alier, 46.
38. "Contradictions, Retractions and Deviations," *Grass Curtain* 1, no. 4 (April 1971):1–2.
39. "Russia Helps the Sudan to Suppress Africans," *Swiss Press Review and News Report*, April 26, 1971, 1–2.
40. Ibid., 2.
41. Ibid.
42. Wai, *African-Arab Conflict*, 148.
43. "Changing Guards in Khartoum," *Grass Curtain* 2, no. 2 (October 19, 1971): 1.
44. Ibid.
45. Wai, *African-Arab Conflict*, 148.
46. Ibid.
47. Lueth, interview.
48. Lolik, interview.
49. Wani, interview.
50. Lueth, interview.
51. Wani, interview.
52. Ibid.
53. Ibid.
54. Lolik, interview.
55. Alier, 51–52.
56. Wai, *African-Arab Conflict*, 148.
57. Mohammed, interview.
58. "South Sudanese Reaction to Mr. Abel Alier's Appointment as Minister for Southern Affairs," Grass Curtain 2, no. 2 (October 19, 1971): 31.
59. Ibid., 149.
60. Lueth, interview; also Mohammed, Wani, and Muortat interviews.
61. Muortat, interview.
62. "Policy Statement—Southern Sudanese Liberation Movement," *Grass Curtain* 2, no. 2 (October 19, 1971): 3.
63. Lagu, interview; also Wani and Lolik interviews.
64. Lolik, interview.

65. Wani, interview.
66. Albino, interview.
67. Lagu, Lueth, Albino, and Mohammed interviews.
68. Lagu, interview; also Lolik, interview.
69. Alier, 54.
70. Lolik, interview; also Wani, interview.
71. Wani, interview.
72. Alier, 55.
73. Lueth, interview.
74. Muortat, interview.
75. Surur, interview.
76. Mohammed, interview.
77. Ibid.
78. Ibid.
79. Tombe, interview.
80. Ibid.
81. Ibid.
82. Wai, "*Afro-Arab Conflict*," 256.
83. Ibid.
84. Madut, interview.
85. Muortat, interview.
86. Ibid.
87. Ibid.
88. Ibid.
89. Ibid.
90. Lagu, interview.
91. Tongun, interview.
92. Surur, interview.
93. Tongun, interview.
94. Lolik, interview; Tongun, interview.
95. Mboro, interview.
96. Tongun, interview.
97. Madut, interview.
98. Tombe, interview.
99. Wani, interview; Mohammed, interview.
100. *The Addis Ababa Agreement on the Problem of South Sudan* (Juba: Educational and Cultural Department, 1973), 37.
101. Ibid., 36.
102. Madut, interview.
103. Mohammed, interview.
104. Ibid.
105. Mboro, interview.
106. *The Southern Provinces Regional Self-Government Act*, 1972 (Khartoum, Democratic Republic of the Sudan), 12–18.
107. *Addis Ababa Agreement*, 1–3.

108. Ibid., 5.
109. *Speech Delivered by President Gaafar Nimeiri in Omdurman, Friday 3rd March 1972* (Omdurman, Sudan), 2, 4.
110. *Addis Ababa Agreement*, 4.
111. *Peace, Unity and Progress—President Nimeiri's Speech* (Khartoum, Sudan: Ministry of Culture and Information, March 1972), 9.
112. Ibid.
113. Ibid.
114. Jeanne Langi, "Principles of Peace," *Grass Curtain* 2, no. 3 (May 1972): 15.
115. Madut, interview.
116. Lueth, interview.
117. Mboro, interview.
118. Albino, interview.
119. Madut, interview.
120. Lolik, interview. See also *A Space for Preserving the Unity and the Diversity of the South Sudan* (House of Nationalities, 2001), 16.
121. *Addis Ababa Agreement*, 3. See also *Space for Preserving*, 16.
122. *Addis Ababa Agreement*, 9–11; *Space for Preserving*, 16.
123. *Space for Preserving*, 16.
124. Ibid., 16–17; also author's observations. He was employed as a teacher in Buluk Intermediate School in Juba in 1980 by the Office of the Commissioner of Education, Equatoria Province.
125. *Space for Preserving*, 16.
126. Ibid.
127. Wani, interview.
128. Ibid.
129. *Space for Preserving*, 16.

BIBLIOGRAPHY

INTERVIEWS

Albino, Oliver B. Interview by Laura N. Beny. Cambridge, MA, June 30, 1997.
Boolo, Luis Mongo. Interview by John Ukech Lueth. Rumbek, Southern Sudan, February 5, 1980.
Collins, Robert O. Interview by Scopas Poggo. Santa Barbara, CA, May 8, 2002.
Elonai, Hilary T. Interview by Scopas Poggo. Los Angeles, CA, December 2007.
Gang, Gabriel. Interview by John Ukech Lueth. Bor, Southern Sudan, April 6, 1980.
Garang de Mabior, John. Interview by Betty Hinds. Washington, DC, 1996.
Igga, James Wani. Interview by Nathan Wojia Pitia. Yei, Southern Sudan, February 2004.
Johnson, Douglas H. Interview by Scopas Poggo. Washington, DC, August 1, 2003.
Lagu Yakobo, Joseph. Interview by Scopas Poggo. London, March 25, 1997.
Lajok, Vincensio Heworu. Interview by John Ukech Lueth. Southern Sudan, November 24, 1979.
Lolik, Pacifico Lado. Interview by Scopas Poggo. Dallas, TX, September 2005.
Lueth, John Ukech. Interview by Scopas Poggo. Santa Barbara, CA, April 12, 1997.
———. Telephone interview by Scopas Poggo. Santa Barbara, CA/Ames, IA, December 18, 1997.
Madut, Stephen. Interview by Scopas Poggo. London, March 25, 1997.
Makwac, Simon. Interview by John Ukech Lueth. Malakal, Southern Sudan, May 25, 1980.
Masiri, Wojia, and Enoka Digga Amen (Anya-Nya Veterans). Interview by James Duku Janka. Kajo-Kaji, Southern Sudan, August 12, 1997.
Mboro, Clement. Interview by Nathan Wojia Pitia. Nairobi, Kenya. 2004.
Mohammed, Dominic Akec. Interview by Scopas Poggo. Miami, FL, November 9, 1997.
———. Interview by Scopas Poggo. Miami, FL, September 18, 1998.
Muortat Mayen, Gordon. Interview by Scopas Poggo. London, March 27, 1997.

Soro, Habakuk Kefu. Interview by John Ukech Lueth. Wau, Southern Sudan, January 28, 1980.
Surur, Eliaba James. Interview by James Duku Janka. Kampala, Uganda, 2004.
Thiep, Albino Mathiang. Interview by John Ukech. Lueth, Southern Sudan, n.d.
Tombe, Lawrence Modi. Interview by Scopas Poggo. London, March 25, 1997.
Tongun, Daniel Jumi. Interview by Nathan Wojia Pitia. Yei, Southern Sudan, 2004.
Udo, Paul Urac. Interview by John Ukech Lueth. Southern Sudan, November 28, 1980.
Ulane, Francis Gume. Interview by John Ukech Lueth. Rumbek. Southern Sudan, February 7, 1980.
Unvu, Vakindi. Telephone interview by Scopas Poggo. Denver, CO/Santa Barbara, CA. September 29, 1998.
Urpac, Paul. Interview by John Ukech Lueth. Juba, Southern Sudan, January 28, 1980.
Wani, Barnaba Dumo. Interview by Evans Sokiri Kijore. Khartoum, Sudan, 2005.
Wani-Buluk, Mama Anna Poni. Interview by Scopas Poggo. Moyo, Madi District, Uganda, August 18, 1996.
———. Interview by Benjamin Lou Poggo. Nairobi, Kenya, June 15, 1997.
Wondu, Stephen. Interview by Betty Hinds. Washington, DC, 1996.

Secondary Sources

"76 Southerners Slaughtered in Wau: Plan to Kill Educated Southerners Started." *Vigilant*, July 14, 1965.
Abbas, Mekki. *The Sudan Question: The Dispute over the Anglo-Egyptian Condominium 1884–1951*. London: Faber and Faber, 1952.
Abd al-Rahim, Muddathir. *Imperialism and Nationalism in the Sudan: A Study in Constitutional and Political Development, 1899–1956*. Oxford: Clarendon, 1969.
Abdel-Rahim, Muddathir. "The Development of British Policy in the Southern Sudan: 1899–1947." Paper presented at the University of Khartoum, Khartoum, Sudan, 1965.
———. "Fourteen Documents on the Problem of the Southern Sudan." *Middle Eastern Journal* (April 1966): 1.
The Addis Ababa Agreement on the Problem of South Sudan. Juba: Educational and Cultural Department, 1973.
Adefuye, Ade. "The Kakwa of Uganda and the Sudan: The Ethnic Factor in National and International Politics." n.d. Document available in the private collection of the author of this book.
"Al Ayam Condemns Juba Massacre." *Vigilant*, July 13, 1965.
Albino, B. Oliver. *The Sudan: A Southern Viewpoint*. London: Oxford University Press, 1970.

Alier, Abel. *Southern Sudan: Too Many Agreements Dishonoured.* 2nd ed. Khartoum: A. Alier, 2003.
The Almanac of World Military Power. Dunn Loring, VA: T. N. Dupuy, 1972.
"An Appeal to the Afro-Asian Peoples Solidarity Organization in Tripoli." *Grass Curtain* 2, no. 1 (July 1971): 22.
"Army Raids Kayango Village." *Vigilant,* March 29, 1966.
"The Arrest of Southern Sudan Refugees in Uganda." *Voice of Southern Sudan* 1, no. 4 (1963): 3.
"Assassin at Sudan Tea Party: Incident in Premier's Southern Tour." *Times,* October 27, 1954.
Baxter, P. T. W., and Audrey Butt. *The Azande and Related People of the Anglo-Egyptian Sudan and Belgian Congo.* London: International African Institute, 1953.
Beshir, Mohamed Omer. *The Southern Sudan: Background to Conflict.* New York: Praeger, 1968.
Beswick, Stephanie. *Sudan's Blood Memory: The Legacy of War, Ethnicity, and Slavery in Early South Sudan.* Rochester, NY: University of Rochester Press, 2004.
The Black Book of the Sudan on the Expulsion of the Christian Missionaries from Southern Sudan: An Answer. Milan: Instituto Artigianelli, 1964.
Bong, Luigi Adwok. "Christian Missionaries in the South: How and Why Religion Has Become an Issue in the Southern Problem." *Khartoum,* September 20, 1965.
———. "The Period 1955–1958." n.d. Document available in the private collection of the author of this book.
Burton, John W. A. *Nilotic World: The Atuot-Speaking Peoples of the Southern Sudan.* New York: Greenwood, 1987.
"Cairo Agreement on Sudan: Home Rule Proposed by End of the Year." *Times,* October 30, 1952.
"Changing Guards in Khartoum." *Grass Curtain* 2, no. 2 (October 1971): 1.
"The Cholera Outbreak in the Southern Sudan." *Grass Curtain* 2, no. 1 (July 1971): 2, 6.
Collins, Robert O. Disaster in Darfur. n.d. Document available in the private collection of the author of this book.
———. *Land Beyond the Rivers: The Southern Sudan, 1898–1918.* New Haven: Yale University Press, 1971.
———, ed. *Problems in African History.* Englewood Cliffs, NJ: Prentice-Hall, 1968.
———. *Shadows in the Grass: Britain in the Southern Sudan 1918–1956.* New Haven: Yale University Press, 1983.
———. *The Southern Sudan in Historical Perspective.* Tel Aviv: University of Tel Aviv Student Association, 1975.
———. "The Sudan: Link to the North." In The Transformation of East Africa: Studies in Political Anthropology, edited by Stanley Diamond and Fred G. Burke. New York: Basic Books, 1962.

Colvin, Ian. *The Rise and Fall of Moise Tshombe: A Biography.* London: Leslie Frewin, 1968.

———. "South Sudanese Rebels 'Step Up' Activities." *Daily Telegraph, Cairo*, July 21, 1970.

"Contradictions, Retractions and Deviations." *Grass Curtain* 1, no. 4 (April 1971): 1–2.

Crazzolara, J. P. "Lwoo Migration." In *Collins, Problems in African History.*

Daly, M. W. *Imperial Sudan: The Anglo-Egyptian Condominium, 1934–1956.* Cambridge: Cambridge University Press, 1991.

The Democratic Republic of the Sudan: Policy Statement on the Southern Question. Cultural Section of the Ministry of National Guidance, Khartoum: Government Printing: 1969.

Deng, Francis Mading. *Africans of Two Worlds: The Dinka in Afro-Arab Sudan.* New Haven: Yale University Press, 1978.

———. *War of Visions: Conflict of Identities in the Sudan.* Washington, DC: Brookings Institution, 1995.

"Editorial Comment." *Voice of Southern Sudan* 1, no. 2 (1963): 9.

"Editorial Comment." *Voice of Southern Sudan* 1, no. 4 (1964): 16.

"Editorial: New Regime Grants 'Regional Autonomy' to the South." *Voices of the Nile Republic of the Southern Sudan* n.s., 1–3/13–3, no. 6 (n.d.): 2.

Ende, Nanne Op 't. "History of the Nuba." Nuba Mountains Homepage. n.d. http://home.planet.nl/~ende0098/content/nuba/01History03.html.El-Mahdi, Mandour. *A Short History of the Sudan.* London: Oxford University Press, 1965.

Eprile, Cecil. *World Realities: War and Peace in the Sudan 1955–1972.* London: David and Charles, 1974.

European-Sudanese Public Affairs Council (ESPAC). *The Search for Peace in the Sudan: A Chronology of the Sudanese Peace Process 1989–2001.* London: ESPAC, 2002. http://www.espac.org/pdf/search_for_peace.pdf.

Evans-Pritchard, E. E. *The Nuer: A Description of the Modes of Livelihood and Political Institutions of a Nilotic People.* New York: Oxford University Press, 1940.

"Excerpts, What the Anya-Nya Says." *Grass Curtain* 2, no. 1 (July 1971): 8.

"Expelled Priest Confirms Policy Is Clear: Stifle the Church." *Catholic News*, New York, February 7, 1963.

"Former Political Prisoners Restricted." *Voice of Southern Sudan* 1, no. 2 (1963): 17.

"From South Sudan Liberation Movement." *Grass Curtain* 2, no. 2 (October 1971): 4.

"F. S. [S. F.] Appeals to African Observers, Intervention of OAU, Human Rights & International Jurists Commissions Sought." *Vigilant*, July 14, 1965.

Girodot, J. "Sudan: The Revolutionary Task." n.d. Document available from the private collection of the author of this book.

Grundy, Kenneth W. *Guerrilla Struggle in Africa: An Analysis and Preview.* New York: Grossman, 1971.

Henderson, Kenneth David Druitt. *Sudan Republic*. London: Ernest Benn, 1965.
Hodnebo, Kjell. "From Cattle to Corn: Economic Trends in Northeast Africa, Equatoria, Southern Sudan, and Northern Uganda, During the Last Three Centuries." PhD diss., University of Bergen, 1997.
Holt, P. M., and M. W. Daly. *The History of the Sudan: From the Coming of Islam to the Present Day*. 3rd ed. London: Weidenfeld and Nicolson, 1979.
"How Nimeiri Fails to Bring Peace." *Grass Curtain* 1, no. 4 (April 1971): 8.
"How Nimeiri Lost the Chance of Peace." *Grass Curtain* 1, no. 4 (April 1971): 17.
Human Rights Watch. *Sudan, Oil, and Human Rights. Part 1, Oil in Southern Sudan*. New York: Human Rights Watch, 2003. http://www.hrw.org/reports/2003/sudan1103/9.htm#_Toc54492563.
Huntingford, C. W. B. "The Peopling of the Interior of East Africa by its Modern Inhabitants." In Collins, *Problems in African History*, 1968.
"Intentions of Sudan Government." *Times*, January 18, 1954.
Jackson, Frank Burdette. "Condominium Rule in the Anglo-Egyptian Sudan." PhD diss., Ohio State University, 1972.
Johnson, Douglas H. *The Root Causes of Sudan's Civil Wars*. Bloomington: Indiana University Press, 2003.
"Juba Death Toll Rises to Over 1400: Massacre, a Deliberate Army Plan." *Vigilant*, July 13, 1965.
"The Juba Martyrs of Freedom." *Vigilant*, July 13, 1965.
"June 9 Declaration not Implemented after 1 1/2 Years." *Grass Curtain* 1, no. 4 (April 1971): 7.
"Kampala Archbishop Hits at Expulsions." *Vigilant*, January 30, 1967.
Kurk, Leo. "The Problem of the Southern Sudan: Origin of Sudan Government Violent Attack on Great Britain and the Institute of Race Relations." *Voice of Southern Sudan* 1, no. 3 (1963): 6.
Kyemba, Henry. *A State of Blood: The Inside Story of Idi Amin*. New York: Grosset and Dunlap, 1977.
Lagu, Joseph. *Sudan: Odyssey Through a State: From Ruin to Hope*. Omdurman: MOB Center for Sudan Studies, 2006.
Langi, Jeanne. "Principles of Peace." *Grass Curtain* 2, no. 3 (May 1972): 15.
Leith, Philip Pedak. "The War Scene." Grass Curtain 1, no. 2 (1970).
Listowel, Judith. *Amin*. Dublin: IUP Books, 1973.
Lueth, John Ukech. *A Manuscript of the Rise of the Anya-Nya Movement*. Juba, 1980.
Mahmoud, Mahgoub el Tigani. "Inside Darfur: Ethnic Genocide by a Governance Crisis." *Comparative Studies of South Asia, Africa and the Middle East* 24, no. 2 (2004): 5–33.
Martin, David. *General Amin*. London: Faber and Faber, 1974.
Matti, Severino. "The Peopling of Eastern Equatoria." Paper presented at the University of London, London, UK, December 4, 1980.

"Missionary Expulsion: Is It a Solution?" *Voice of Southern Sudan* 1, no. 1 (April 1964): 1.

"Mr. G. A. Kwanai, SANU Secretary of Information, Reports on the Addis Ababa Conference—May 1963—and on the Refugees in Ethiopia." *Voice of Southern Sudan* (1963).

Mukhtar, Al-Baqir Al-Afif. "The Crisis of Identity in Northern Sudan: The Dilemma of a Black People with a White Culture." In *Race and Identity in the Nile Valley: Ancient and Modern Perspectives*, edited by Carolyhn Fluehr-Lobban and Kharyssa Rhodes, 207–40. Trenton, NJ: Red Sea, 2004.

Nalder, L. F., ed. *Tribal Survey of Mongalla Province by Members of the Province Staff and Church Missionary Society*. New York: Negro University Press, 1970.

O'Ballance, Edgar. *The Secret War in the Sudan*. London: Faber, 1977.

———. *Sudan, Civil War, and Terrorism, 1956–99*. London: Macmillan, 2000.

Oduho, Joseph. "F— Report from SANU Central Office: Bahr El Ghazal Province." *Voice of Southern Sudan* 1, no. 3 (1963): 21. Reproduced in *Sudan Informazioni*. Milan, Italy: Agenzia di notizie e documenti, March 25, 1969.

———. "F— Report From SANU Central Office: Upper Nile Province." *Voice of Southern Sudan* 1, no. 3 (1963): 83. Reproduced in *Sudan Informazioni*. Milan, Italy: Agenzia di notizie e documenti, March 25, 1969.

Oduho, Joseph, and William Deng. *The Problem of the Southern Sudan*. London: Oxford University Press, 1963.

Ogot, Bethwal A. "Kinship and Statelessness Among the Nilotes." In *Collins, Problems in African History*.

"On Persecution in the Sudan." *Catholic Telegraph*, USA, January 11, 1962.

Peace, Unity and Progress—President Nimeiri's Speech. Khartoum: Ministry of Culture and Information, 1972.

Poggo, Scopas S. "The Pattern of Azande Resistance to the British Rule in the Southern Sudan, 1898–1914." Master's Thesis, Memphis State University, 1992.

"Policy Statement—Southern Sudanese Liberation Movement." *Grass Curtain* 2, no. 2 (October 1971): 3.

Rahhal, Suleiman Musa. "The Nuba—Who Are They?" www.nubasurvival.com.

———. *The Right to be Nuba: The Story of a Sudanese People's Struggle for Survival*. Lawrenceville, NJ: Red Sea, 2001.

"Recolonization of Southern Sudan." Neue Zürcher Zeitung, February 28, 1971.

Reed, Allan. "The Anya-Nya: Ten Months' Travel with Its Forces Inside the Southern Sudan." *Munger Africana Library Notes*, no. 2 (February 1972): 12.

"Refugees and Returnees." *Grass Curtain* 1, no. 4 (April 1971): 17–18.

"Refugees Harassed." *Vigilant*, February 6, 1967.

"Revenge for Rome." *Voice of Southern Sudan* 2, no. 1 (April 1964). Translated excerpt from Der Spiegel, March 19, 1964.

"Rev. Fr. Saturnino is Confirmed Dead." *Vigilant*, February 6, 1967.

Ruay, Deng D. Akol. *The Politics of Two Sudans: The South and the North 1821–1969*. Uppsala, Sweden: Nordiska Afrikainstitutet, 1994.

"Russia Helps the Sudan to Suppress Africans." *Swiss Press Review and News Report*, April 26, 1971.
Sanderson, Lilian Passmore, and Neville Sanderson. *Education, Religion and Politics in Southern Sudan, 1899–1964*. London: Ithaca, 1981.
Santandrea, Stefano. "The History of Our Missions." *Messenger*, October 1933.
"Saudi Arms to Sudan." *Vigilant*, March 15, 1966.
Scherf, Theresa. "The Sudan Conflict: Its History and Development." n.d. Unpublished document available in the private collection of the author of this book.
Segal, Roland. *Political Africa: A Who's Who of Personalities and Parties*. New York: Praeger, 1961.
Seligman, C. G. *The Pagan Tribes of the Nilotic Sudan*. London: G. Routledge, 1932.
———. *Races of Africa*. 4th ed. London: Oxford University Press, 1966.
"S.F. Condemns and Deplores Juba Massacre: President Flies to the Scene." *Vigilant*, July 13, 1965.
"Shaping of Politics in the Nile Valley." *Times*, November 15, 1948.
"Situation in the Southern Sudan." *Voice of Southern Sudan* 1, no. 2 (1963): 16.
"South Sudanese Reaction to Mr. Abel Alier's appointment as Minister for Southern Affairs." *Grass Curtain* 2, no. 2 (October 1971): 31.
"The Southern Sudan Today: A Test Case in Afro-Arab Co-operation." *Voice of Southern Sudan* 1, no. 3 (1963): 18.
A Space for Preserving the Unity and the Diversity of the South Sudan. [Nairobi?]: The House of Nationalities, 2001.
Special Correspondent. "Military Training for Sudanese Officers." Southern Sudan Information Service 16, 1967.
Special Correspondent. "Russian Bombers for Sudan." *Daily Telegraph*, October 17, 1970.
Steiner, Rolf. *The Last Adventurer*. Boston: Little Brown, 1976.
Stigand, C. H. *Equatoria: The Lado Enclave*. London: Frank Cass, 1968.
"Sudan African National Union: Famine in the Bor District, Southern Sudan." *Voice of Southern Sudan* 2, no. 1 (April 1964): 14–15.
"Sudan Africans Die: Long Live African Unity." *Voice of Southern Sudan* 1, no. 1 (April 1964): 4.
"A Sudan Amnesty: Some Southerners Excluded." *Times*, December 31, 1955.
"Sudan Crisis: Was There a Coup?" *Grass Curtain* 2, no. 2 (October 1971).
"Sudanese Place in Nile Valley: View of Egyptian Demands." *Times*, November 27, 1950.
"Sudan Expels Missionaries." *Christian Century*, January 2, 1963.
"Sudan Officials' Dilemma: Uncertainty of Posts." *Times*, December 28, 1954.
"The Sudan's Future." *Times*, December 1, 1953.
"Sudan Wages Cold War: To Exterminate Christians." *Catholic News*, New York, January 17, 1963.
The Times. London, March 13–14, 1964. In Voice of Southern Sudan 2, no. 1 (April 1964).

Tomilyan, Daniel Wani. *The Kuku Cultural Phenomenon.* Koboko, Uganda: 1999.
Tosh, John. "The Economy of the Southern Sudan under the British, 1898–1955." *Journal of Imperial and Commonwealth History* 9, no. 3 (1981): 277.
Tshombe, Moise. *My Fifteen Months in Government.* Plano, TX: University of Plano Press, 1967.
"Unanimous Vote in Khartoum: Self-Determination Process Begun." *Times,* August 16, 1955.
"Upper Nile: Beaten to Abortion." *Voice of Southern Sudan* 2, no. 1 (April 1964): 12.
"Upper Nile: School Girl as Hostage." *Voice of Southern Sudan* 2, no. 1 (April 1964): 12.
"U.S. Aid in Use to Suppress the South." *Voice of Southern Sudan* 2, no. 1 (April 1964): 6.
Wai, Dunstan M. *The African-Arab Conflict in the Sudan, 1955–1972.* New York: Africana Publishing Company, 1981.
―――. "The Afro-Arab Conflict in the Sudan, 1955–1972." PhD diss., Harvard University, 1973.
―――, ed. *The Southern Sudan: The Problem of National Integration.* London: Frank Cass, 1973.
Wakoson, Elias Nyamlell. "The Origin and Development of the Anya-Nya Movement 1955–1972." In *Southern Sudan: Regionalism and Religion Selected Essays,* edited by Mohamed Omer Beshir, 138–201. Khartoum: University of Khartoum, Graduate College Publications, 1984.

Published Primary Sources

"Alfonse, Arop, Amosa, Aburi, Tito Wani: Victims of False Accusations." In *Petition to the United Nations by Sudan African Closed Districts National Union.*
"Annual Report of 1926." *Sudan,* no. 2 (1927): Cmd. 2991/8.
"Arabs Versus Africans in the Sudan." In *Memorandum Presented by the Sudan African National Union.*
"Bahr al-Ghazal." In *Memorandum Presented by the Sudan African National Union.*
"Case No. 10: Destruction of Pachalla Villages." In *Memorandum Presented by the Sudan African National Union.*
"Duku Bojo: A Victim of Arbitrary Arrest." In *Petition to the United Nations by Sudan African Closed Districts National Union.*
"Ethiopian Villages Burnt Down by the Sudanese Armed Forces While Pursuing Refugees." In *Memorandum Presented by the Sudan African National Union.*
Expulsion of Foreign Missionaries and Priests from the Southern Provinces. Republic of the Sudan: Ministry of the Interior, March 1964.
Genocide in the Southern Sudan: Human Rights Violated, Arabs vs. Africans. Milan: Sudan Informazioni News Agency Documents. 10/83/88573.

Lagu, Joseph. "Beginning of the Revolt." In *Anya-Nya: What We Fight For. Anya-Nya Armed Forces: South Sudan Liberation Movement*, January 1972. [Pamphlet].

"Memorandum on Reasons that Led to the Expulsion of Foreign Missionaries and Priests from the Southern Provinces of the Sudan." In *Expulsion of Foreign Missionaries and Priests.*

The Memorandum Presented by the Sudan African National Union to the Commission of the Organization of African Unity for Refugees. Kampala, Uganda: November 1964.

"Micah Luwate, John Baden: Victims of Arbitrary Charges." In *Petition to the United Nations by Sudan African Closed Districts National Union.*

"The Missionary Societies in the Sudan." In *Expulsion of Foreign Missionaries and Priests.*

"The Nile Provisional Government: Statement on the Balgo-Bindi Convention." *Voice of Southern Sudan*, May 15, 1969.

"Petition by Delegation for Bor Citizens: Cry for Flood Destruction." In *Memorandum Presented by the Sudan African National Union.*

Petition to the United Nations by Sudan African Closed Districts National Union (SACDNU), South Sudan, On Behalf of the People of Southern Sudan. April 29, 1963.

"The Problem of the Sudan: Violent Racial Action Involving Genocide in the Southern Sudan." n.d. Copies of this document are available from the private collection of the author of this book and the Sudan Archive at Durham University, UK.

"Report from SANU Central Office: Upper Nile." *Voice of Southern Sudan* 2, no. 1 (April 1964): 11–12.

"Report from the Sudan: Relations with West Germany." *Southern Sudan Information Service (SSIS)* 16, (n.d.).

Report of the Commission of Enquiry into the Disturbances in the Southern Sudan during August 1955. Khartoum: McCorquadale, 1956.

Robinson, David. "Sudan May be Soviet Version of Vietnam." n.d. Document available in the private collection of the author of this book.

Salih, S. A. M. "Letter." *Catholic Press News*. New York, January 24, 1963.

The Southern Provinces Regional Self-Government Act, 1972. Khartoum: Democratic Republic of the Sudan, 1972.

Speech Delivered by President Gaafar Nimeiri in Omdurman, March 3, 1972. Omdurman: Democratic Republic of the Sudan, 1972.

"Statement of Colussi Giacomo." In *Memorandum Presented by the Sudan African National Union.*

"Statement of Valentino Saoncella." In *Memorandum Presented by the Sudan African National Union.*

"Testimony by Brother Francesco Mariotti." In *Genocide in the Southern Sudan.*

"Testimony by Father Parlemo Pasquale of Bussere and Kpaile Seminaries." In *Genocide in the Southern Sudan.*

"Testimony of Father Agrati Antonio." In *Genocide in the Southern Sudan.*

"Testimony of Father Santino Locatelli." In *Genocide in the Southern Sudan.*

"Testimony of Sister Sandralisa Campadelli and Sister Albertina Modenese." In *Genocide in the Southern Sudan.*
"Upper Nile." In *Genocide in the Southern Sudan.*

ARCHIVAL MATERIAL

"Confidential From Khartoum to Foreign Office." Governor General's Office, No. 212, August 19, 1955. Robert O. Collins Collection. Sudan Archives. Durham University, Durham, UK.
"Equatoria." n.d. Robert O. Collins Collection, Sudan Archives. Durham University, Durham, UK.
Letter from A. Baroni, Vicar Apostolic, Khartoum, to the Permanent Under Secretary, Ministry of Interior, Khartoum, June 22, 1960.
Letter from A. Baroni, Vicar Apostolic, the Catholic Church, Khartoum, to the Permanent Under Secretary, Ministry of the Interior, July 4, 1960.
Letter from Dominic Ferrara, Prefect Apostolic of Mupoi, Catholic Mission, Yambio, Western Equatoria to H.E. Hassan Ali Abdulla, Permanent Under Secretary, Ministry of Interior, Khartoum, January 17, 1960. PA/G-GJ/1/60.
Letter from Hassan Ali Abdulla, Permanent Under Secretary, Ministry of the Interior, Khartoum, to His Lordship, Bishop Baroni, Vicar Apostolic, Khartoum, June 28, 1960. MI/SCR/46.A.16.
Letter from Hassan Ali Abdulla, Permanent Under Secretary, Ministry of Interior, to President of the Supreme Council and H.E. the Minister of Interior, Khartoum, December 29, 1959.
Letter from Osman Gad El RAB [for Governor of Equatoria] to Assistant Governor, Juba District. EP/SCR/46 C.2/8, XR/SCR/46A.1.
Letter from S. M. Ahmed, for Governor of Equatoria, to Assistant Governor, Yambio, D.C. Kapoeta, Torit, Juba, Yei, Maridi, Tembura, February 24, 1959. EP/SCR/46.C.1.10., XR/SCR/46.A.2.
Proceedings of the Southern Governors Meeting, March 1922. Civil Secretary, I/9/31, SGA. Robert O. Collins Collection. Sudan Archives. Durham University, Durham, UK.
Ring, Bona M. M. "The Causes of the Southern Dissensions." Khartoum, September 24, 1964. Document available in the private collection of the author of this book.
"SANU and the Anya-Nya Liberation Front." *n.d.* Robert O. Collins Collection. Sudan Archives. Durham University, Durham, UK.
"SANU File of Record and Correspondences." n.d. Robert O. Collins Collection. Sudan Archives. Durham University, Durham, UK.
Skrine, A. W. "Notes regarding Chiefs Courts and Native Administration in Mongalla Province." December 1, 1924. Mongalla, I/1/2, SGA. Robert O. Collins Collection. Sudan Archives. Durham University, Durham, UK.
Southern Sudan 1, no. 3 (1963). Robert O. Collins Collection. Sudan Archives. Durham University, Durham, UK.

"The Southern Sudan Provisional Govt." (1968). Robert O. Collins Collection. Sudan Archives. Durham University, Durham, UK.

Strictly Confidential Letter from Acting Governor Osman Gad el Rab to Assistant Governor, Juba, D.C.'s Torit, Kapoeta, Maridi, Yei, Yambio and Assistant District Commissioner Tembura. EP/SCR/46.A.1, EP/SCR/46/2.

Strictly Confidential Letter from Ali Baldo, Governor, Equatoria, Juba to Procurator, Catholic Mission, Secretary C.M.S., Juba, Field Secretary African Inland Mission Torit, Procurator, R.C.M. Mupoi, January 31, 1960. EP/SCR/46.A.1/1.

Strictly Confidential Letter from Ali Baldo, Governor of Equatoria, Juba, to Procurator, R. Catholic Mission, Juba, Secretary C.M.S., Juba, Field Secretary African Inland Mission, Torit, Procurator, R.C.M. Mupoi, May 11, 1960. EP/SCR/46.A.1.1., XR/SCR/46.C.1/4.

Strictly Confidential Letter from Ali Baldo, Governor, Equatoria Province Headquarters, Juba, to all missions, August 30, 1960. EP/SCR/46.A.1, XR/SCR/46.A.1/2.

Index

AACC. See All Africa Conference of Churches
Abba (Ibba), 125
Abboud, Gen. Ibrahim, 6, 58–60, 64, 75–76, 80, 91–111, 113, 118, 119, 150, 154, 164, 169, 171
Abboud's Intermediate School, 95
Abdalla, Hassan Ali, 102
Abdalla, Mohammed Ahmed Ibn, 121
abid (abeed), 18, 36, 53
aboriginal, 12
Abot, Edward Nyil, 66
abrogation, 192
Abujohn, Samuel, 137, 141–42, 143
  See also Kabashi, Samuel
Abur, Col. Emmanuel (Abur, Emmanuel), 127, 128, 137, 142, 143
Aburi, Amosa, 76
Acholi (Acholiland), 13, 31, 61, 65, 131, 154, 160
ADCs. *See* Assistant District Commissioners
Addis Ababa Agreement, 7, 139, 161, 169, 184–92
Aden, 166
Adung, Paul, 71
Adwok, Luigi, 86
African nationalism, 194

African Revolution Day, 167
African-Arab civilization, 193
Africanism, 194
Africanization, 23
Afro-Asiatic, 13
Afro-Asian Peoples Solidarity Organization, 89
Agar (Dinka), 13
  Dinka, 11, 14, 23, 31, 62, 67, 69, 70, 80, 118, 120, 137, 141, 147, 148
Agu Camp, 61, 146
Agwat, 87
Ahmed, Mohammed El Baghir, 187
Akeo, 42
Akobo, 13, 71, 81
Akoc, Isaiah Majok, 62
Akodho (Chief of Objale Village), 81
Akol, Francis Mayar, 156, 158
Akol, Valentino, 78
Akumbek, George, 64
Akuon, Brig. Joseph O., 143
Albino, Oliver Batali (Albino, Oliver), xvi, 4, 5, 58, 62, 117, 119, 156, 180, 187, 190
ALF. *See* Azania Liberation Front
Aliab (Dinka), 13
Alier, Abel, 7, 119, 169, 171, 172, 178–79, 183, 186–87, 192

All Africa Conference of Churches
  (AACC), 179, 181–82, 187–88
All African Peoples Congress, 114
All South Camp, 66
Almanac of World Military Power, 168
Al-Rai Al-Amm (Khartoum
  newspaper), 100, 102
Amena, Enoka Digga, 149
Amin, Gen. Idi (Amin), 160, 162,
  163, 180
Amun, Joseph Kuol, 69
ANAF. *See* Anya-Nya National
  Armed Forces
Anba el Sudan (Khartoum
  newspaper), 102
Andrago, Jovani, 63
Anglo-Egyptian
  administration, 22, 25–27, 33
  Agreement of 1953, 44
  Condominium, 22, 42
  forces, 22
Angu, Nilo (chief), 75
Angundri (W. Equatoria), 122–24,
  138, 140, 143, 161
Anjelika, 77
Ankrah, Kodwo E., 187
Annual Report of 1925, 28
Ansar sect, 54–55
  See also Umma Party
Anti-Demolition Battalion, 138
Anya-Nya, 123, 131–44
  Amin visits Owing-ki-Bul, 160
  High Command Council, 142
  Israeli military and, 2, 124,
    127–29, 139, 141, 142, 144,
    155, 157–61, 163–64, 167, 180,
    190
  Jaden reorganizes military command,
    137
  laying foundation for, 62
  leadership, 131–44
  meeting to plan, 64
  naming of, 64
  Upper Nile and Bahr al-Ghazal,
    138–40

Anya-Nya National Armed Forces
  (ANAF), 123, 126, 127, 128,
  129, 130, 137, 139–41, 143–44,
  157
Anyidi Revolutionary Government,
  127, 129, 142, 157, 162
Anyuak, 65, 70, 71, 81, 146
  See also Lwo
Apalemba, 68
Arab, 18–19
Arab Armies, 85, 86
Arab expansionism, 173–74
Arab Muslim Armies, 17, 19
Arab Muslim Conquest of Egypt, 16
Arab Provinces, 29
Arab Socialism, 2, 176, 190
Arabia, 9
Arabian Peninsula, 9, 17, 18, 19
Arabic (language), xii, 15, 16, 19
  Bilad al Sudan from, 9
  imposition of Islam via, 97, 110
  imposition on southerners, 92, 96
  legitimizing of social position via, 18
  medium of instruction, 96
  military promotion of, 95
  official language of government,
    56, 93
  "one country, one language, one
    religion," 95
  requirement for admission to
    schools, 95
Arabization, iv, vii, 16
  Abboud's policy of, 78, 91, 92, 96,
    97, 99, 100, 110
arbitrary arrests, 52, 68, 75–82, 89
Armo (French Mercenary), 162
Arop, Alfonse, 76
Arrow Incident of 1955, 40
Aru (Congo), 116, 132–33
ASA. *See* Azania Secret Army
Aswan High Dam, 16
Atar Intermediate School, 29
Atem, Akout (Mayen, Akout Atem),
  68, 124, 137, 142
Atout. *See* Atwot

Atwot, 13
Avukaya (Avokaya), 13, 31, 135
Aweil (District), 87
Aweil (town), 69, 138, 148
Aweil, Col. Paul (Aweil, Paul) 129, 138, 142
Awouda, Justice El Fatih, 76
Azande, xi, 13, 14, 23, 65, 66, 88, 123, 133, 135, 142
Azania Liberation Front (ALF), 120–22, 124, 135
Azania Secret Army (ASA), 64, 116–17
Azhari, Ismail el-, 5, 33, 34–36, 37, 38–40, 41, 44, 45, 47, 54, 56, 154

Babiti, Dr. (veterinarian), 84
Baden, John, 76
Baggara, 15, 17
Baggari village, 67
Baghir, Kamal, 100
Bago, Henry, 134
Bahr Al Gebel, 101
Bahr al-Ghazal, xix, xx, 4, 11, 13, 14, 16, 23, 25, 46, 66, 67, 68, 75, 78, 86, 87, 108, 146, 185, 191
  Anya-Nya in, 68, 69, 78, 138, 140, 141, 142
  attack on Wau, 69
  composition of soldiers in, 31
  education as manipulation in, 95
  education system in, 28
  effect of Torit Mutiny on, 50
  firearms for, 147
  internal discord, 140, 141
  Israeli weapons to, 161
  Mourtat's plans for, 135, 136
  refusal to transfer, 41
  security forces in, 79–80
  soldiers cheated in, 31
  student strikes in, 92–99
  taxation for, 148
  Torit Mutiny, 46
  underground movement in, 62, 147
  Wau, capital of, 49
  Wau, Massacre in, 84–85
Baka, 31, 65, 135
Baldo, Ali, 92, 101–2, 103
Balgo-Bindi, 126, 141
Banak, Joseph, 127
Bangidi, 146
Bantu, 13
Barabra, 16
Baro, 13
Baroni (bishop), 103
Bashir, Darius. *See* Beshir
Bashir, Gen. Omar Hassan al-, 10
Beja, 10, 16, 17
Beja Red Sea Hills, 20
  See also Red Sea hills
Belanda, 67
Belgium, 152
Belgian Congo, 52, 66
Beny, Laura N., xvi, 4
Berti, 15
Beshir, Darius, 62, 119, 120
Beshir, Mohamed Omer, 5, 12
Biafra, Biafrans, 162, 163
Biafran War, 162
Biafran-Sudan Action Committee, 162
Bilad al-Sudan (land of the blacks), 9, 11
Biringi, Gaetano, 78
Biseglie, 80
Bisquimbi (Zandeland), 66
Black Bloc, 32
Blake, Eugene, 105
Bojo, Duku, 76
Bokassa (President Jean Bodel), 75
Bol, Victor, 84
Bongomin, Geldino (chief), 75
Boolo, Luis Mongo, 67
Bor Balanda, 11
Bor, 13, 80, 141
Bor District, 80, 88
Bor (town), 159
Boya, 77, 100

British Army, 165, 168, 170
British in Condominium
 Assistant District Commissioners (ADC's), 4, 23, 24, 36, 37, 39, 50
 Civil Secretary, 25, 30
 Colonial Administration, 6, 11, 12, 14, 22–31, 33–37, 42, 43, 47, 54, 55, 171, 193, 194
 development of South, 46
 District Commissioners, 22, 23, 28, 37, 39, 73, 100
 Equatoria: Luce, 44
 Governors (provincial), 67
 Helm, 44, 45, 47
 Inspector of Southern Education, 28
 Legislative Assembly, 24, 32, 33
 Members of Parliament (MPs), 45
 Mongalla: Stigand, 29
 rule, xiii, 24, 29, 31, 46
 Symes, 25
 of Torit, 64
 Wingate, 27, 28, 30, 32
East African Territories: fear of influence on South, 44
 British rifles, 146, 155
 See also Sudanization policy
Bukhari, Idris, 73
'Bungit, Bismark, 97
Bungu, 124, 156, 157
Burun, 12, 70, 146, 147
Burundi, 152
Bussere, 79
Butana (river), 17
Bwogo, Samuel Athi, 187

cadre
 missionaries work to develop, 28
 others, 24, 26
Cairo Agreement, 34
Cam, Medho (chief), 81
Camel Corps, 60
 See also Haggana Corps
Cariolato, Sister Ermella, 82

Carr, Rev. Cannon Burgess (Carr, Burgess), 181–82, 187, 188
Catechist, 5, 38
 See also catechumenates
catechumenates, 101, 103
 See also catechist
Catholic and Protestant Missionary Society, 107, 108
census, 14–15
 Population Census of 1956, 14, 56
Central African Republic, 2, 9, 13, 14, 52, 65, 66, 68, 75, 89, 91, 111, 114, 118, 142, 148, 164
 See also French Equatorial Africa
Central Equatoria, 5, 12, 14, 31, 60, 61, 73, 122, 132, 133, 135, 140, 141, 142, 143, 149, 155, 162
Central Region, 10
Chad, Republic of, 9, 18
Chec, Lam, 119
Chief Akodho (of Objale Village). *See* Akodho (Chief of Objale Village)
Chief Courts Ordinance of 1931, 92
Chief Marcello. *See* Marcello (Chief)
chiefs. *See* chieftaincies
chiefs' courts, 23
chieftaincies, 22–23, 27, 37, 39, 74, 75, 76, 77, 80, 92, 93, 122
China, 1, 152, 153, 155, 165
Chukudum, 155
Church Missionary Society (CMS), 110, 199
Church World Service, 179, 181, 182
Ciec (Dinka), 13
Cier, Riang (chief), 84
Closed Districts Ordinance, 22
Cold War, xiv, 115, 166, 168, 194
colleges
 Police, Prisons, and Military, 24
 Military college, 144, 170
collectivization, 87
Collins, Robert O., xiii, xvi, 2, 31
Colussi, Giacomo, 80
Commission of Enquiry (Inquiry), 40

communist, 2, 153, 165, 171, 173, 174, 176
coup, 176, 177, 178, 182
compromise proposal, 185
Condominium. *See* British colonialism
conference in Cairo, 32
Congo
 Azande refugees in, 66
 British strategic interest, 30
 Catholic support for movement in, 131
 contact with Israeli officials in, 128, 156, 158
 flight of populations to, 52, 65, 66, 68, 69,75, 89, 92, 98, 100, 101
 geographic relationship to Sudan, 9
 guerilla and resistance activity in, 68, 69, 98, 114, 141, 142, 158,161
 Mobutu and Anya-Nya in, 161
 peoples of, 13, 14
 SANU in, 116, 118, 132
 Second National Convention in, 126
 Simba guerrillas' support to Anya-Nya, 151, 152, 153
 Sudanese Army activity in, 75, 91
 training camps in, 146, 148
 weapons to Anya-Nya by Congolese Government, 153, 154, 157, 158
Congo Basin, 12, 13
Congo-Brazzaville, 114, 152
Congolese government, 153, 154
Congolese National Army (CNA), 152
Constituent Assembly, 39, 47, 56, 108
Constitution, 1956 Interim, 59
Constitution, first Sudanese, 56
Constitution Amendment Commission, 32
cultural unification, 100
Czechoslovakia, Czech, 155, 168

Dabi, Dominic, 66
Daily Telegraph (London newspaper), 167
Daju, 15
Dajur (Kajo-Kaji), xi
Daym Zubayr, 79
Darfur, 10, 15, 16, 17, 20, 35, 54, 55, 193
 See also Fur
Daw, Capt. Santino Ajing, 69, 148
Dayan, Gen. Moshe, 156
decentralization program, 4
Democratic Party (Uganda), 122, 151
Democratic Republic of the Congo. *See* Congo
Democratic Republic of Sudan *See* Sudanese governments
Democratic Unionist Party (DUP), 169, 177
demonstration in Juba, 1955, 51–52
Deng, Francis M., 12, 18, 19
Deng, William (Secretary General of SACDNU), 63, 68, 113, 114, 115, 116, 117, 118, 119, 120, 121, 132, 134, 151
Denk, Georgia Kir, 36
DeVelder, Marion, 105
Dhaldhim, 71
Dhiew, Nyang, 67
Dhol, Capt. Thomas, 68
Dhol, Ferdinand, 78
Dhol, Kamilo. *See* Dhol, Khamilo
Dhol, Khamilo, 68, 122, 123, 125, 126, 127, 140, 142, 157
diaspora, 3, 185, 187
Didinga, 77
Didinga Ngalam, 77
Din, A. M. Sharaf El, 107
Dinka, 11, 14, 23, 65, 69, 70, 80, 118, 137
 as cattle raiders, 147
 composition of Eq. Corps, 31
 hostility between Zande and, 141
 relationship to Nuer, 13
 in Southern Front, 120
Dinka-Nuer, 13
Dito, 122, 124, 136
Dogale, Paulino (Father), 99

Dowds, Father W., 106
draft Constitution (Sudanese), 32, 125
Duach, Gaich, 81
Duang, Elia, 68
Dud, Ireno (bishop), 106
Dui, Buth. *See* Thung, Buth Dui
Duk-Fadiat, 80
Duk-Fadiet. *See* Duk-Fadiat
Duk-Faiwel, 80
Durham University, xiii, xvi, 2

East Africa, 9, 30, 42, 63, 97, 113, 114, 116, 120, 121, 149, 156, 157, 158, 184
East African Common Market, 123
East Germany (weapons supply), 1
Eastern Equatoria, 5, 13, 14, 31, 60, 61, 62, 63, 65, 68, 74, 75, 77, 88, 91, 116, 121, 124, 131, 132, 133, 135, 136, 137, 141, 142, 146, 149, 154, 155, 157
Eastern Europe, 153
Egypt, Upper Egypt, ix, xviii, 9, 16, 17, 21, 27, 32, 33, 34, 35, 37, 45, 47, 54, 55, 86, 152, 153, 155, 165, 166, 168, 170, 176
Egyptians, 22, 33, 34, 35, 36, 37, 45, 46, 139, 156, 165, 166, 175
See *also* Anglo-Egyptian; Turco-Egyptian
El Rai El Aam (Khartoum newspaper), 100, 102
electoral college, 33
electoral laws, 57
Eli (Kuku clergyman), xii
Elok, Tagiri, 74
Elok, Tugyala, 74
Elonai, Hilary T., 99
Endrizzi, Rev. Lawrence, 107
Eprile, Cecil, 5, 7, 169
Equatoria, Equatoria Province, xix, xx, 5, 11, 12, 23, 25, 29, 30, 41, 49, 50, 67, 71, 75, 77, 83, 87, 94, 95, 103, 107, 123, 125, 138, 140, 141, 159, 160, 170, 175, 185
Equatoria Corps, 5, 29–31, 37, 40, 43, 46, 47, 49–51, 53, 60, 62, 63, 64, 67, 70, 75, 76, 78, 117, 131, 145, 146, 147
 in Malakal, 31, 49, 50, 51, 53
 in Mongalla, 45
 in Torit, 30, 31, 41, 42, 46
 in Wau, 31, 50
Eritrea, 9, 18
Eshkol, Levi, 139, 156
Ethiopia, 2, 9, 14, 18, 30, 31, 53, 70, 75, 81, 82, 89, 92, 116, 118, 141, 142, 150, 152, 157, 158, 168, 188
 Addis Ababa, 187
 arms from, 146
 border with, 91, 161
 Israel and, 159
 Numayri and, 160
Evening Standard (Tel Aviv newspaper), 167

Fadul, Maj. Frederick, 142
Faisal (king of Saudi Arabia), 166
Fartak, Hassan (chief), 78
Father Vantini, xiii
federal status, 32, 33, 37, 39, 47, 49, 58, 120, 194
federal system, 11, 32, 37, 56
federation, 34, 37, 39, 56, 92, 118, 121, 184
Fellata, 15–16
Feroge, 67
Ferrara, Dominic (Apostolic Prefect), 101
Fertit, 11
Fertit Battalion, 138
Five-Year Plan, 26
Fort Leavenworth (Kansas). *See* United States Army Command College
Fouga Fighter Planes, 159
See also Israeli Defense Force (IDF)

INDEX

Free Officers Movement, 170
freedom fighters, 61, 64, 66, 70, 108, 132, 146, 147
French Equatorial Africa, 27–28, 66
  See also Central African Republic
Fuli, Severino, 64, 135, 150
Fur. *See* Darfur, 15, 16

Gaawar, 13
Gaddafi, Muammar al-, 160
Gambela, 70
Gambela, Albino, 82
Gang Laul, 81
Garamba Park (Congo), 154, 158
Garang, Joseph, 171, 173, 174, 175, 176
Garang, Mading de, 180, 182, 184, 187
Gbatalla, Ali, 137
Gederu (Kajo-Kaji), 76
general amnesty, 53, 54
Gezira, 16
Gezira cotton scheme, 10
Ghana, 86
Gogrial, Gogrial District, 36, 69, 75, 78, 84, 138
Goi, Ferdinand, 3, 4
Goi, Lt. Peter Utu, 68
Gordon Memorial College (Khartoum), 24, 26
  See also University of Khartoum
government security forces, xi, 51
Grinti military prison, 78, 79
Guardian (London newspaper), 88
Gulu (Uganda), xi, xii, 121, 149
Gulumbi (Yei), 77
Gur Mou ("revenge" in Jur), 69
Gwonza, Ezbon Mondiri, 62, 135, 187
  See also Mondiri, Ezbon

Habib, Mr., xi
Haforiere, 74, 77
Haggana Corps, 42, 43, 60
  See also Camel Corps

hardship post, 23
Helir, Corp. Latada (Helir, Latada; Latada), 60, 61, 74, 147
Helm, Sir Alexander Knox, 44, 47
High Court, Southern Provinces, 76
High Executive Council (HEC), 7, 188, 190
Hilal, George, 147
Hitler, 146, 163, 159
  See also Nazi-like
Hoover Institution, xiii, xvi, 2
House of the Mahdi, 54
Humr, 67
Hussey, E. R. J. (Chief Inspector of Schools), 28

Ifotu, 88
Ikotos, 78
Imehejez Elementary, 77
Imilai, 77
Immotong, 31
Imurok, 88
Ingessena Hills, 10
Intermediate Schools at Tonj, Kwajok, Bussere, 98
Inyanya. *See* Anya-Nya
Iro, Siricio, 58
ironstone plateau, 11, 80
irrigation schemes, 25
Irwa, Mohamed Ahmed, 150
Isaloro, Ofiriha, 77
Isiro (Congo), 66, 68
Islam, 10, 16–19, 21
  al-Mahdi, 21, 57, 58, 80
  constitution, 170, 174, 193, 194
  culture, 19
  faith, 16, 17, 19
  khalwas, 87, 100, 113
  as official religion, 56, 92, 93, 94, 95, 96, 99, 102, 107
  religious education, 94, 108
Islamic Centers (Centres), 100
Islamic Institutes (ma'ahad), Islamic Intermediate Schools, 94, 96, 107

Islamic kingdom, 58
Islamic laws, 93
Islamic nation, 194
Islamization, 16, 91, 92, 93, 96, 97, 99, 100, 106
Abboud's Arabic policy, 78, 102, 107, 110
Israel, Israeli, Israelis, xiii, xiv, 2, 6, 124, 127, 128, 129, 139, 141, 142, 144, 155–61, 163, 164, 167, 168, 170, 177, 180, 184, 190, 194
Israeli Defense Forces (IDF), 2, 15, 159
See also Fouga Fighter Planes
Istiwa, 43
Italian priests, 79, 80, 101
Itita, John, 60
Iwani (chief), 74

Ja'ali, 16
Jabal Marra, 10, 15
Jada, Simon, 142
Jaden, Aggrey, 118, 119, 120, 121, 122, 123, 124, 125, 126, 135, 136, 137–38, 139, 140, 141, 143, 154, 156, 157, 163, 186
Jale, Jeremiah, 61, 146
Jikany Nuer, 13
Jo Pap, 65
Joakino, Rocco T. (chief), 75
Joane, Capt. Peter, 134
Jodi, Ezbon, 136
John XXIII (pope), 106
Johnson, Douglas H., xiii, xv, xvi, 5, 7, 26, 55, 169
Joul, Bernedino Mou, 68, 69, 78
See also Mou, Capt. Bernedino
Juba (city), xiii, 12, 37, 38, 40, 41, 42, 43, 44, 46, 51, 52, 62, 67, 83–84, 85, 86, 87, 98, 99, 103, 136, 153, 167, 175, 181, 191
Juba (district), 37, 88
Juba Boys Intermediate School, 95
Juba Civil Hospital, 83

Juba Commercial Secondary School, 70, 97, 98
Juba Conference of 1947, 4, 5
Juba Girls Intermediate School, 95
Juba Massacre, 5, 83, 84, 85
Juba Technical School, 98
Juba-Nimule Road, 136
Juba-Torit Road, 88, 136
Jur (Lwo), 11
  people, 67
Jur Battalion, 138

KAR. *See* King's African Rifle
Kababish, 17
Kabashi, Samuel, 129
Kajo-Kaji, xi, xvi, 14, 49, 50, 60, 61, 66, 75, 76, 135, 146, 147, 149, 162
Kakwa, Kakwaland, 14, 49, 61, 135
Kali, 77
Kaliko, 13
KANU. *See* Kenya African National Union
Kapoeta incident, 57
Kapoeta, 57
Kapoeta District, 77, 88
Kassala Region, 55
Katire, 76, 155
Kator, 83
Kator Intermediate School, 98
Kau, Gabriel, 12
Kawac, Reg. Sgt.-Major Daniel Deng (Kawac, Daniel Deng), 68, 142
Kayango, 86
Kelei, Parmona, 78
Kenya African National Union (KANU), 114
Kenyan government, 161
Kenyatta, Jomo (president), 161
Kerbetta, Claud, 77, 78
Keriwa, 155
Khalid, Mansour, 187, 192
Khalifa, Sirr al-Khatim al-. *See* Khattim, Sirr al- (al-Khattim)
Khalil, Abdalla, 57, 58, 94, 154

khalwa (Koranic school), 87, 94, 95
Khartoum, 9, 10, 15, 19, 21–22, 25, 32, 34, 40–41, 62
Khartoum regime, 88, 166, 173, 174
   See also Sudanese governments
Khatmiyya Sect (Sufi religious order), 55
Khattim, Sirr al-; al-Khattim, 4, 118, 120
Khoi-san, 13
Khor Ghana (river), 146
Kifle, Nabiyelul, 187
Kikilai, 77
Kingdom of Kush, 15
Kings African Rifle (KAR), 42, 43, 47
Kinshasa, 63, 68, 114, 116, 127, 128, 132, 156, 158, 163, 182, 184, 185, 186
Kinubi, xii
Kisangani, 152
Kitgum, 74
Koak, David, 127
Kobar Prison (Khartoum), 51
Koc, Richard, 78
Koc Roor, 65
Kongor, 80
Kordofan, 10, 15, 16, 17, 20, 35, 193
Koro'be Hill, 61
Korokore (mountain), 60
Koryang, Cypriano, 57
Kozi, Daniel, 138
Kpaile, 52, 79
Kreish, 11, 67
Kuku, Kukuland, xi, xii, 4, 5, 14, 24, 31, 41, 49, 50, 61, 97, 135, 147, 149
Kuol, Matthew, 78
Kuze, Elia, 36
Kwajok, 98
Kwanai, Donato Deng, 69
Kwanai, George, 123
Kwanai, Akumbek, 62

Labana, Obebe, 74
Lacalili, Patrisyo Lochocyolli (rainmaker), 74
Lado, Loteka, 76
Lafon, 31
Lagos, 114
Lagu, Gen. Joseph (Joseph Yakobo; Lagu), 3, 63–64, 65–66, 114, 116, 118, 121, 125, 131–32, 134, 139, 142, 144, 156, 157
   Anya-Nya, 129, 133, 135–39, 141–44, 148, 154, 155, 156–59, 161, 163, 167, 175, 177, 179–80
   on causes of Torit Mutiny, 45
   NPG overthrow, 127–29, 164
   in peace process, 181, 184–86, 189, 190
   on treatment of Southerners, 36
Lajok, Lance Corp. Vincensio Heworu; Lajok, 60
landed proprietors, 55
Lango, 31
Lapon, 60
Latuko, xi, 14, 23, 30, 31, 49, 60, 61, 62, 63, 64, 65, 74, 116, 122, 131, 132, 133, 136, 137, 139, 142, 149
Latuko/Arab problem, 49
Lau, 13, 70
Lek, 13
Lenyakwo, 74
Leopoldville, 154
   See also Kinshasa
Lerango, 66
Lerwe, Rubong, 78
Liangari, 88
Liberal Party, 32, 33, 34, 35, 36, 37, 39, 57, 58
Libyan government, 166
Likitaung, 43
Lira, 121
Lirya, 88
Lobele, 77
Lobira, 74

Locatelli, Father Santino; Father
    Santino, 79
Lodongi, Amadeo Taffeng (Taffang,
    Amadeo; Taffang), 61, 77, 127,
    129, 137, 138, 139, 142, 143,
    157, 162, 163
Lodyongo, Angelo (chief), 74
Logali, Hillary Paul, 86, 119, 183
Logo, 13
Lohide, Lomiluk. *See* Lomiluk
    (Chief), 74
Lohure, Father Saturnino (Father
    Saturnino), 113, 114, 117, 135,
    136
    ALF/SALF relations, 120, 121
    Anya-Nya: bringing people to, 65;
        establishment of military of in
        Aru, Congo, 132, 133; founding
        leader of, 131; naming of, 64;
        relocation of headquarters, 132
    fundraiser, 149,154
    guerrilla and resistance movement,
        63, 119, 122, 131; discord in
        leadership of, 116, 117, 118,
        119, 121, 131
    Parliamentarian, 57; explaining
        Southern walkout from, June
        1958, 57, 58
    patron of SACDNU, 63, 114;
        Lagu joins with in, 66
    in SANU, 108, 115, 116, 119;
        patron of, 115, 118
Lohuri, Erodiene Guzer, 61
Lojuru, Modi, 149
Loka Intermediate School, 98
Lokiata, Bina, 61
Lokita, Corp. Martirio, 42
Lokoya, 65, 131
Lokuyiro, 61
Lolik, Pacifico Lado (Lolik), xvi, 4, 7,
    30, 177, 180, 186, 190
Lomilingwa, 135, 136
Lomiluk, Lohide (chief), 74
Longuta, Layahu, 74
Lopi, 60

Lopit-Iboni, 77
Lord Cromer, 22
Lorema, 77
loring ayela (meaning refugees), xi
Loruwe, Michael, 127, 141
Lotidak, Attilio, 77
Lotose-Imotong, 74
Loudo, 77
Lubega, 42
Luce, T. W. H., 44
Lueth, Brig-Gen. John Ukech (Lueth,
    Ukech; Lueth), xiii, xvi, 4, 84,
    140, 148, 159, 161, 166,
    176–77, 180
    arrest of Muortat and overthrow of
        NPG, 142
    joins Anya-Nya, 69
    lieutenant at time of NPG,
        involved in NPG coup, 129
    mediator between officers of
        Gogrial and Aweil, 69
    sent to Israel by Anya-Nya, 159
    student at Rumbek during strike,
        98
    view on timing of Addis Ababa
        peace agreement, 190
Luigi, Musa, 78
Lugbara, 13, 14
Lulubo, 13
Lupe, Elia, 24, 120, 122
Luwate, Micah, 76
Lwo, 4, 11, 13, 65, 69
Lwoki, Benjamin, 42

ma'ahad, 94, 95, 96, 107, 108
Maahad Intermediate Schools, 107
Mabior, John Garang de (Garang,
    John; Garang), 15, 19
Madi, xi, xii, 3, 13, 14, 61, 64, 65,
    116, 121, 131, 132, 144, 150,
    154
Madok, 74
Madok (mountain), 60

Madut, Col. Steven Baak, Madut, xvi, xiii, 3, 6, 7, 68, 98, 164, 184, 188, 190
Maggot, Frederick Brian (Maggot, Col. Frederick; Magot, Frederick Bryian), 137, 141, 142, 143, 187, 63
Magwi, 75
Mahas, 16
Mahdi, 21, 22, 54
Mahdi, Abdel Rahman el, 58
Mahdi, Mandour El, 12
Mahdi, Sadiq Al-, 154
Mahdi, Sayyid Abdel Rahman el-, 33
Mahdists, 25, 66, 28
   movement, 22, 33
   state, 22, 26
Mahgoub, Mohammed Ahmed (Prime Minister), 5, 83, 121, 150
Makaraka, 4, 117
Makerere University, 183
Malakal Secondary School, 95
Malakal (capital of Upper Nile Province), 11, 31, 49, 80, 82, 191
   El-Azarhi assassination attempt in, 38
   fundraising for undergrnd mvt in, 62
   Northern paratroopers attack on, 53
   related to Torit Mutiny, 49, 50, 51
   Southern garrisons in, 43, 46, 70
Malakia, 83
Malual, 13
Malwal, Bona (Malual), 39, 45, 56, 91, 119
Mama, Lawrence, 62
mamur, *ma'mur*, 24, 36
Manyanya. *See* Anya-Nya
Mar, 80
Marcello (chief), 74
Maridi, Maridi District, 88
   See also Meridi

Mariik, Col. Phillip Nanga (Mariik, Philip Nanga; Mariik), 68, 124, 138
Masiri, Wojia, xvi, 61, 147
Massacres
   Juba, 5, 84–85
   Koro'be, 61
   Wau, 84–85
Massalit, 15, 16
Matiang, Corp., 42
Mawien, Toby, 78
Mayar, Francis. *See* Akol, Francis Mayar
Mayardit, Salva Kiir (president), 5
Mayen, Akout Atem de. *See* Atem, Akout
Mazzoldi, Msgr. S. (vicar apostolic), 101
Mboki, 75
Mboro, Clement, xv, 4, 6, 7, 24, 33, 46, 86, 92
   in Addis Ababa talks, 186, 188, 190
   arrest and jailing of, 50–51
   on British treatment of Southerners, 24
   on exclusion from Cairo talks, 1953, 33
   investigation of massacres by, 85
   lack of Southerners rising in Sudan government,37
   Mading de Garang requests release of, 180
   orders people to "go into forest," 85
   in Southern Front, 84,119
Mboro Elementary School, 98
Meidab Arabs, 10, 15
Meir, Golda, 139, 156, 158
Meri, Korneli, 76
Meridi, 40, 42, 43, 175
Mestri, Guido del (archbishop), 106
Middle East, xiv, 6, 18, 19, 20, 43, 156, 166, 180
Middle East Air Force, 43

migrations, intra- and interregional, 12, 15
Military College (Khartoum), 144, 170
military takeover, 10, 54, 58, 59, 176
Mill Hill Fathers Mission, 106, 107
Mirghani, Sayed Ali el- (el Mirghani), 92
Missen, George, 63
missionaries. *See under* Protestant Church; Roman Catholic Church
Missionari Comboniani, xvii, 2, 6
Missionary Societies Act, 104, 105
Misriyya, 67
mobilization committee, 38
Mohammed, Dominic Akec (Mohammed, Dominic), xvi, 4, 6, 7, 85, 178, 180, 182, 188
Momoi, 78
Mongalla (town), 29, 43
Mongalla Province, 29, 45, 199
Monywir, Lt. Henry Deng, 68
Moroga, Julius, 64
Moru, Moruland, xi, 31, 64, 65, 88, 123, 133, 136
Moru-Madi, 13
Mou, Capt. Bernedino (Mou, Bernedino), 68, 69, 78
  See also Joul, Bernedino Mou
Moyo (town), xi, xvi, 50
Mukhtar, Al-Baqir Al-Afif, 18
Mundri, 98
Mundu, 31, 65, 135
Munich, 175
Munita, 77
Muortat-Mayen, Gordon (Mayen), 3, 62, 119, 101, 103
Mupoi, 103
Mura Hatiha, 77
Murle, 70, 146, 147
Murta, 61
Mut, Michael, 128
Mutek, Lazarus (chief); Mutek (Lance Corp.), 42, 61, 122, 143
mutineers, 37, 42–45, 47, 51, 52, 53, 64, 74, 76
Myers, Father A., 106

nadafa junub (meaning cleansing of the South), 92
Nasir, 70, 81, 82, 155
National Assembly (Khartoum), 4, 171
National Convention, 118
  of 1967, 127
  second, 125
National Liberation Council, 126
National Mobile Force, 138, 143
National Unionist Party (N.U.P./NUP), 31–35, 38, 39, 54–7, 120
Native Administration, 22, 23, 28
Navogo, 66
Nazi-type (extermination policy), 86
Nazi. *See* Hitler, 159
  "helpful Nazi," reference to Rossi, 146
NBC (National Broadcasting Company), 141, 153, 155
  reference to Steiner, 163
NCOs. *See* Non-Commissioned Officers
Ndogo, 67
Negro provinces, 29
Negroid, 12, 28
Neguib, Gen. Muhammed, 34
Neo-Colonialism, 45
Ngangala, NgaNgala, 43, 88
Ngijak, Paulino (chief), 76
NGOs (non-governmental organizations), 181, 191
Nhial, Col. Emmanuel Abur, 127, 128, 137, 142, 143
Niangara, 68
Niger, 15, 18
Nigeria, 15, 86
Niilus, Leopoldo J., 187
Nile
  Blue Nile, 10

drowning in, 84, 86
Gezira Scheme location, 10
Omdurman location, 10
Sudd location, 11
White and Blue Niles, 9, 10
White Nile, 10, 12
waters of, 164, 165
Nileans, 126
Nile Provisional Government (NPG), 3, 125–29, 140–42, 157, 162–64, 181
Nile Republic. *See* Nileans
Nile Valley, 19, 34
Nile Valley Unity, 32–35, 38, 45
Nilotes, 17
  Bari hostility towards, 140
  Eastern Nilotes, 12, 14
  fighting within Anya-Nya, 141
  influx into Cen. Eq., 140
  military prowess of, 70
  Western Nilotes, 11, 12, 13
Nilotic, 13, 23, 62, 70
Nimule, 43, 63, 64
Njagulgule, 67
non-commissioned officers, 4, 5, 37, 42, 47, 68
Northern Provinces, 29, 55
Northern Sudanese delegation to Addis Ababa Agreement of 1972, 186
Nuba (people), 10, 15, 16, 147
Nuba Mountains, 10, 15
Nubians, 16, 17
Nuer, 11, 13, 14, 23, 25, 31, 62, 70, 80, 81, 146, 147, 155
Nuer prophet, 70
Numayri administration, 172, 173, 179, 183
Numayri, Gen. Jaafar Mohammed; Numayri, 2, 167, 175–76, 190
  abrogation of Addis Ababa agreement, 192
  appoints Alier, 178, 179
  granting of Southern regional autonomy, 172, 173, 174

Egypt and, 166
explores peaceful resolution, 160, 176, 177, 178, 179, 180, 181, 182, 184,185, 186
rise to power, RCC and coup; 170, 171, 172
Soviets and: cooperation with and armament of, 167, 168, 175
Nyanya. *See* Anya-Nya
Nyago, Mahaliele. *See* Nyajo, Mahaliele
Nyajo, Mahaliele, 74, 76
Nyang, Daniel, 70
Nyang, Dhiew, 67
Nyang, Philip, 71
Nyangara, 146
Nyangiya, 100
Nyangwara, 100
Nyanya, 64
Nyidong, Sgt. Lonyakw, 60
Nyingori, Paul, 71
Nzara, 26, 36, 40, 67
Nzara Industrial Complex, 36, 65

O'Ballance, Edgar, 5, 12
Obbo, 77
Obiya Catholic Church, xii
Obo, 68, 75
Obote, Milton (Prime Minister); (Obote, Milton Apollo; Obote), xii, 64, 122, 150, 151, 157, 159, 160, 163, 180
Ocheng, Pangarasio, 97
October Revolution, 171
Oduho, Joseph, 126, 136
  ALF/SALF merger, 121
  flight to Uganda and arrest in, 116, 150–51
  founding SACDNU, 63, 64
  leadership struggle, 116, 117, 119, 121
  publishing of The Problem of Southern Sudan, 113, 114
  role in guer mvt & raising support, 114

in SANU, 115, 132, 150; call for
   1st Conv. of, 118, 135
   at Round Tab Conference, 120
Ofiriha Isaloro, 77, 88
Ohoriok (Lakoya), 31
Okaru, 97
OLIKA, 60
Olwak, Natale, 62
Omdurman, 9, 10, 32
Onama, Felix, 120, 150
Organization of African Unity
   (OAU), 86, 102, 177, 181
Otto, George, 62
Owiny-ki-Bul, 142, 143, 144, 159,
   160, 163

Pachalla, 71, 75, 81, 82
Pajok, 77
Panom De Gop, 155
Pan-African Freedom Fighters, 64
pan-Arabism, 176
pangas (machetes), 145
pan-Zande movement, 142
Parjok, 75
Paul, Beda, 61
peace villages, camps, 87–88, 173
Pedak, Phillip, 65, 70, 118, 119
People's Democratic Party (PDP), 57,
   58
People's Progressive Party, 4
Peter (Southern priest), 108
Pibor, 81, 82
plebiscite, 76, 116
Pojulu, 4, 14, 31
political elections, 35
political mobilization, 46
political parties, 31–35, 56, 58, 120,
   126, 171, 176, 177
   in Uganda, 122
Port Sudan, 55, 166
Protestant Church, 65, 122, 151
   Anglican Community, 121
   missionary activity, 27, 28, 109,
      106
   Missionary Societies Act, 104–5

priests, 101, 102, 108, 151
   See also Roman Catholic Church
Protestant Missionary Society, 107,
   108
   See also Church Missionary Society
public administration school, 24
Public Record Office (PRO), 2
Pwoni (Lafon), 31

Qantani (Southerners), 17

Radio Omdurman, 91, 93
RAF. See Royal Air Force
Raga, 79
Rahman, Ali Abdel, 57
Railway Battalion, 138
Ramba, Alfred Lumbari, 119, 183
Red Sea, 9, 17, 55, 166
Red Sea Hills, 10, 16, 17, 20
Reed, Allen, 141, 153, 155, 166
Reformed Church, 105
regional autonomy, 172, 178, 183,
   184, 191
Regional Government of Southern
   Sudan
   Ministry of Education, 7
   People's Regional Assembly, 188
Reign of Terror, 7, 53, 75, 89, 98
repression, vii, 2, 49, 81, 83, 91, 93,
   96, 100, 110
Republic of Sudan, 9, 13, 16
   See also Sudanese governments
resistance movement, vii, xi, 49, 62,
   63, 64, 65, 98, 110, 111, 173,
   174, 175, 177, 194
revolution, 50, 133, 171
Revolutionary Command Council,
   171
Rindemia, 68
Ring, Bona Malwal M. See Malwal
Roman Catholic Church, xii, 78,
   101, 103, 106, 110, 117, 119,
   121, 122, 131, 149, 150, 151,
   154

German Catholic Organizations, 110
Mill Hill Fathers Mission, 106, 107
Missionari Comboniani, xvii, 2, 6
Missionary Societies Act, 104–5
Vatican, 106, 114, 119, 122, 131
See also Protestant Church
Rossi, Henerick, 133, 134, 146, 161
"helpful Nazi," 146
Roton Camp, 52
Round Table Conference, 120
international observers, 73
Royal Air Force (RAF), 43, 44, 165
Ruay, Deng D. Akol (Ruay, Deng; Deng), 5, 12, 17, 18
Rumbek, 3, 41, 70, 98, 99, 124, 136
Rumbek Commercial (school), 97
Rumbek Elementary School, 98
Rumbek Secondary School, 24, 29, 39, 66, 67, 68, 70, 96, 97, 98, 99
Rume, Marko; Marko (Chief Propagandist), 5, 41, 42, 46, 51, 52, 70, 97, 98, 115, 127, 133
Ruot, Paul, 71
Rural Administrative Units, 37
Russian MiGs, 89, 166, 167

Salah, 82
SALF. *See* Sudan African Liberation Front
Salih, S. A. M., 105, 106
Sanderson, Lillian Passmore, 6
Sanderson, Neville, 6
SANU. *See* Sudan African National Union
Saoncella, Father Valentino, 79
Saturlino (Lt.), 40
Saturnino, Father. *See* Lohure, Father Saturnino
Saudi Arabia, 155, 165, 166
Savannah grassland, 13
Savannah woodland, 10, 11, 12
SCA. *See* Sudan Christian Association
SCC. *See* Sudan Council of Churches

Schools and schooling, 28, 63, 94–100
Arabic language in, 95–96
Islamization: Islamic institutes/ma'ahad, 94–96, 107–8
Koranic; *khalwa*, 87, 94–95, 100, 113
mission, 27, 92, 94, 95, 100, 106
Vocational and Technical, 26, 28, 84, 98, 108
School of Public Administration (Khartoum), 24
Second Civil War (1983–2005), xiii, xvi, 194
Second World War, 26
Seko, Mobutu Sese (President of Zaire), 157
Selassie, Haile (Emperor), 159, 187, 188
self-determination, 31, 33, 34, 35, 40, 41, 47, 49, 97, 116
self-government, 32, 33, 34, 35, 45, 188
self-rule, 31, 33
Seligman, C. G., 12
Seminary at Tore, 79
Sheriff, Ahmed el-, 171
Shilluk, 11, 12, 13, 14, 31, 62, 70, 71, 85, 138, 147
Simba (insurgent movement in Congo), 148, 149, 151–53, 161, 168
Sinai, 139
Six-Day War, 2, 139, 156, 161
slave traders, 27, 61, 65, 66, 67
Sloane, Father E., 106
Sobat River, 11, 13
Socotra (Djibouti), 166
Somalia, 18, 80
Soro, Col. Habakuk Kefu (Soro, Habakuk; Kefu, Habakuk), 66, 143, 148
South African mercenaries, 152

South Sudan Land Freedom Army (SSLFA), 116, 117
Southern Bloc, 39, 57
Southern Blue Nile, 10, 20, 193
Southern Corps, 40, 41, 46, 47, 67
Southern freedom fighters, 61, 108, 132, 146
Southern Front, 84, 85, 86, 119–20, 121, 178, 181, 182, 183, 184
Southern intellectuals, 26, 63, 84, 88, 99, 109, 110, 113, 114, 134, 182, 189, 190
Southern Kordofan, 15–16
Southern policy, 29
Southern priests, 101, 102
Southern Problem, 36, 63, 83, 114, 115, 118, 139, 154, 163, 166, 171, 172, 174, 176, 179, 194
Southern Provinces, 23, 25, 30, 39, 92
   forged telegram on, 40
   mutiny, onset of disturbances in, 42, 46
   post-Mutiny Sudanese troop occupation of, 53
   SACDNU political failure in, 115
   traditional courts in, 92
Southern rebels, xiii, 6, 38, 45, 61, 63, 73, 74, 75, 76, 77, 81, 83, 85, 88, 92, 113, 150, 177, 178
Southern refugees, xi, xii, 7, 28, 61, 63, 66, 67, 68, 76, 78, 81, 82, 89, 113, 114, 115, 121, 122, 149, 150, 151, 168, 174, 179, 177, 181, 182, 183, 184, 187, 192
Southern Regional Assembly, 4, 188, 190, 191, 192
Southern Resistance Movement
   See Resistance Movement
Southern strike force, 63
   Southern Students, 3, 28, 63 (USSY), 66, 95, 96, 97, 98, 107, 108, 110, 148, 181, 183
Southern Sudan Association, 88

Southern Sudan Information Service (SSIS), 165
Southern Sudan Liberation Movement (SSLM), 3, 7, 64, 89, 117, 128–30, 142–44, 169, 176, 179, 180–88, 190, 191
Southern Sudan Provisional Government (SSPG), 122–25, 136–37, 139, 140, 141, 156–57, 163, 186
Southern Sudan Students' Union (SSSU), 121
Southern Sudanese Resistance Movement
   See Resistance Movement
Southern withdrawal from Parliament, 57–58
Soviet Union, Soviet, Soviets, USSR, xiii, xiv, 1, 2, 6, 89, 118, 153, 155, 165, 166–68, 175–76
Soviet-U.S. Rivalry, 166
SSIS. *See* Southern Sudan Information Service
SSLFA. *See* South Sudan Land Freedom Army
SSLM. *See* Southern Sudan Liberation Movement
SSPG. *See* Southern Sudan Provisional Government
SSSU. *See* Southern Sudan Students Union
SSU. *See* Sudan Socialist Union
Stanford University, xiii, xvi, 2
Steiner, Rolf, 127, 159, 161–63
Stevenson, Sir Ralph, 34
Stigand, C. H., 29
student strikes, 63, 66, 67, 96–99, 101, 108, 110
Sub-*mamurs* (district officials), 24
Sudan African Closed Districts National Union (SACDNU), 63, 64, 68, 70, 114, 115, 131
Sudan African Liberation Front (SALF), 120–21, 137, 154

Sudan African National Union
(SANU), 108
114–19, 120, 121, 131–34, 181,
184
Sudan Airways, 41, 43, 134
Sudan Armed Forces, 4, 41–42,
59–60, 63, 145, 147, 156, 167
Sudan Council of Churches (SCC),
181, 187
Sudan Defense Force, 51, 170
Sudan Self-Government Statute of
1953, 34
Sudan's Independence Day, *1 January
1956*; 19, 41, 48, 53, 69, 193
Sudan-Congo Border, 138, 141, 149,
152
Sudan-Ethiopian Border, 16, 81, 81
Uganda-Sudan Border, 45, 67; S
Army posts established on, 91;
weapons supply on, 161
Sudanese Air Force, 75, 133
Sudanese Army. *See* Sudan Armed
Forces
Sudanese Governments (non-
Southern), xi, 2, 6, 8, 23, 32, 33,
40, 41, 43, 44, 47, 49, 50, 51,
58, 75, 80, 81, 87, 89, 96, 98,
101, 105, 107, 108, 109, 110,
113, 116, 118, 122, 134, 154,
155, 164, 165, 166, 168, 171,
177, 178, 180, 181, 184, 186,
187, 190, 195
Department of Education, 97, 107
Department of Religious Affairs,
94, 100, 104, 107, 108, 110
director of, 100
Director of Passports, Immigration
and Nationality, 107
Employment and Selection Boards,
54
Sudanese priests. *See* Southern priests
Sudanese Security Forces, xiii, 7, 50,
51, 52, 53, 60, 71, 73, 74, 89,
134, 145

Sudanese Socialist Union (SSU), 7,
176, 186, 190, 191
Sudanic, 12, 13, 23
Sudanization, 34–37, 39, 45, 47, 54,
65, 170, 194
Sudanization Committee, 35, 36
Sudd, 11, 12, 21
Suddeutsche Zeitung (Munich
newspaper), 175
Sue River Republic, 123, 129, 142,
157
Suez Canal, 34, 44, 139
Sugouro, 77
Sukkut, 16
Sule, Abdel-Rahman, 32, 35
Sultan Ring Lual, 87
Sunday Strikes. *See* student strikes
Supreme Commission, 58
Supreme Council, 59
Surur, Benaiah (doctor), 85
Surur, Eliaba James (Surer), xv, 4, 5,
7, 83, 182, 186
Swahili, xii
Swaka, Sarafino Wani, 157
swamplands. *See Sudd*
Symes, Sir Stewart (Governor
General), 25

Taffeng, Amadeo, 61, 77, 127, 129,
137, 138, 139, 142, 143, 157,
162, 163
Taffeng, M. T. (Lieutenant), 41
Tambura District, 88
Tambura-Wau Road, 67
Tanganyika, 115
TANU (Tanganyika African National
Union), 114, 115
Taposa, 14, 77, 100
Tawili, Michael. *See* Towili, Michael
Taylor, John V., 110
Technical Intermediate School, 84
Ted-Adhol, 138
Tel Aviv, 158, 167
Tembura, 108
tenth parallel, 11, 14, 15

Ten-Year Plan, 169
Terekeka, 37
Thiep, Albino Mathiang, 62
Thou, Col. Makur, 142
Thung, Buth Dui, 32, 35, 42
Times (London newspaper), 110
Tirangole, 77
Todesco, Rev. Anthony, 106
Tombe, Lawrence Modi (Tombe, Lawrence; Tombe), xiii, xvi, xvii, 3, 7, 97, 98, 183
Tonga, 82
Tongun, Daniel Jumi (Tongun, Daniel; Tongun), xv, 5, 6, 7, 38, 41, 42, 46, 51, 52, 83, 120, 185, 186, 187
Tongun, Lt. Albino, 43
Tonj, 46, 69, 98, 136, 138
Toposa. *See* Taposa
Torcce, Father Andria, 108
Tore, 79, 100
Torit District, 74, 76, 77, 88
Torit Mutiny, 5–6, 21–65, 67, 74, 91, 132, 194
Torit (town), 30, 31, 40, 42, 74, 76, 77, 85, 87
　missionaries in, 103
　student strikes in, 98
　See also. Torit Mutiny
Totwan, Ali Mulukwat (chief) (Totwin, Ali Mulukwat), 75
Towili, Michael, 123, 141, 142
Travella, Father John, 108
tribalism, 69, 116, 117, 123, 132, 191
Tripoli, 89
Tshombe, Moise, 152, 153, 154, 158
Tul, 135
Turco-Egyptian, 1, 21, 25, 66, 67
　displacement of people to, 2, 52, 53, 75, 89, 92, 110–11
　education system as model for Sudan, 28
　geographic relationship to Sudan, 9, 30

Obote crackdown on SS refugees in, xii
　students' flight to at time of strike, 98–99
　Sudan border with, 45, 67, 161; Sudanese Army posts on, 91
Uganda, xi-xii, 13, 50, 74–76, 122, 134, 136, 149, 150, 160
Tombe and students at Makerere University, 183
　discussion with Israeli officials in, 124, 128
　fund raising in northern, 149–50
　Israelis and, 159, 180
　Israelis depart from, 160, 180
　killing of Father Saturnino, 122, 136, 150
　Lagu goes to, 121; directing from, 132
　loyalty to Saturnino among Catholics in, 131, 157
　1963 arrest of Southern politicians in, 116
　political parties' Christian affiliation, 122
　route for Israeli military aid, 141, 157–58, 159–60
　SANU in, 116, 120
　Southern politicians' flight to under Abboud, 113
　Sudan Christian Assoc in, 113
　Uganda-Sudan joint efforts against Anya-Nya, 150
Uganda Argus (Kampala newspaper), 127
Uganda General Service Unit (GSU), xii
Uganda People's Congress (UPC), 151
Umdurman. *See* Omdurman
Umma Party, 31, 32, 33, 35, 54–55, 57, 58, 120, 169, 177
　See also Ansar

underground resistance movement. *See* resistance movement
Union of Southern Students and Youth (USSY), 66
unitary state, 26
United Nations, UN, 44, 102, 114, 134, 177, 181
United Presbyterian Church, 105
United States, xiii, xiv, xvi, 3, 4, 6, 27, 105, 106, 118, 152, 164, 165, 166, 167, 168, 170, 182
United States Army Command College
Ft. Leavenworth, Kansas, 170
unity of the Nile Valley, 32, 33, 34, 35, 38, 45
University of Bergen (Norway), 2
University of California, Santa Barbara (USA), xiii, xv, 2
University of Juba, xii, xvii, 191
University of Khartoum, xii
See also Gordon Memorial College
University of Memphis (USA), 13
Upper Nile, 11, 13, 14, 21, 46, 53, 70, 74, 75, 80, 81, 82, 94, 95, 106, 135, 136, 141, 142, 185
destruction in, 53
naming of Anya-Nya in, 64, 65
peoples of, 13, 14
security in, 74, 75, 80, 81, 82
soldiers of, 37, 41, 46, 67, 70, 71, 117, 135, 136, 138, 141, 142, 143, 146, 159
Upper Nile Province, 11, 23, 25, 28, 29, 31
Upper Nile Regional Government, 4
USSR. *See* Soviet Union
USSY. *See* Union of Southern Students and Youth

Vatican, 106, 114, 119, 122, 131
Velente, Giuseppi, 80
Verona, xiii, xvii, 2, 6
Verona Fathers, 106
Veronica, 77

veto powers (British), 34
Vicar Apostolic of the Bahr Al-Gebel, 101
Vigilant (Khartoum newspaper), 84, 86
Voice of Southern Sudan (London newspaper), 102
Vuga, Angelo, 149

Waat, 70
Wai, Dustan, 5, 6, 7, 12, 96, 169, 178, 183
Wani, Barnaba Dumo, xv, 5, 7, 24, 31, 36, 39, 41, 129, 177, 180, 181
Wani-Buluk, Anna Poni, xi, xvi, xvii, 4, 149
Wanji, Arkanjelo, 119, 127, 128
Wanto, Oteno (chief), 75
Waran-Wunyang, Daniel Poggo, xi, xvi, xvii
Wau, 11, 31, 43, 46, 49, 50, 51, 52, 55, 62, 67, 69, 75, 78, 79, 80, 83, 86, 87, 106, 108, 138, 147, 173, 191
massacre in, 84–85
Muo's attack on, 69
Wau Technical School, 98, 108
Wau-Raga Road, 146
West Germany, 110, 165, 168
Foreign Office in Bonn, 110
Foreign Office in Cairo, 23, 43
West Nile, xi, 14
Western Bahr al-Ghazal, 4, 79, 146
Western Equatoria, 12, 13, 26, 31, 36, 43, 65, 67, 88, 122, 132, 133, 135, 136, 137, 138, 140, 141, 142, 143, 146, 148
Western Nilotes, 12, 13
Western Nilotic, 11, 13
Wira, 65, 135
Wol, Lawrence Wol, 89, 182, 184, 185, 187, 188
Woodland, V. R., 29
World Bank, 55

World Council of Churches (WCC), 177, 179, 181, 182, 184, 185, 187, 188, 190
World Health Organization (WHO), 88
World War II, 31, 33, 40
Wunbarkou Camp, 75

Ya Dom, 65
Yambio, 36, 39, 40, 42, 43, 66
Yambio District, 39, 88
Year of Refugees, 181
Yei, 40, 42, 43, 49, 50, 53, 60, 61, 74, 77, 135, 147, 153
Yei District, 5, 61, 73, 77, 100, 117
Yei-Kaya road, 77
Yeinio, Manasseh, 146
Yosia, Paul, 60, 61, 66, 147
Yugoslavia, 1, 155, 168

Zaghawa, 10, 15, 16
Zaire, Zairean. *See* Congo
Zamir, General, 160
Zande Scheme, 26
Zandeland, 36, 65, 66, 101, 137, 141, 143